Foundations
of American
Education

Foundations of American Education

WILLIAM B. RAGAN
David Ross Boyd Professor
of Education, Emeritus
University of Oklahoma

GEORGE HENDERSON
Goldman Professor
of Human Relations
University of Oklahoma

HARPER & ROW, PUBLISHERS
New York, Evanston. and London

Illustrations by Ann Scrimgeour

FOUNDATIONS
OF AMERICAN
EDUCATION

Library of Congress Catalog Card Number: 74-99606

To Faye and Barbara

Contents

PART V   THE PROMISE OF AMERICAN EDUCATION

Preface

This book was written for the student who is taking his first course in education. Such an introductory course, listed under one of various titles, is generally required for all students who plan to teach; it is frequently open to other students who want to gain a better understanding of the American school as a social institution.

The primary emphasis is on the social forces affecting American education, but attention is also given to newer insights into human growth and learning, to contrasting views relating to the central purpose of education, to innovations in school programs designed to keep pace with the fast-moving events in our society, and to changes that seem likely to occur in school and society in the near future.

The following features of the book should be particularly noted:

Emphasis on current problems. We are living in a unique period in history. Educational models that once served us well must be altered to fit the revolutionary age in which we are living. This book, therefore, examines current conditions and trends as a basis for developing new models for the future.

An interdisciplinary approach. The book draws materials from several areas in the field of education and the social sciences in an effort to give the beginning student a balanced view of the forces affecting

American education. Students who wish to specialize in a particular area will have an opportunity to do so as advanced undergraduate and graduate students.

A "spiral" arrangement of content. Topics discussed briefly in the first few chapters are treated again, but in greater detail, in later chapters. This plan should not be thought of as repetition; rather, it is a way of expanding on relevant issues and problems. This approach is in harmony with the psychological principle that growth and learning are continuous.

Emphasis on problems of the poor. The consequences of poverty in both rural and urban America, of our failure to provide adequate educational opportunities for large segments of the population, and of the prejudices that continue to divide and weaken our nation are treated throughout the book. One entire section is devoted to education in the inner cities.

.   .   .

We are grateful to all who assisted us: to authors and publishers who granted permission to quote from their publications and to colleagues who gave us valuable suggestions. We wish to express our gratitude particularly to Franklin Parker, who helped to plan the scope of the book.

WILLIAM B. RAGAN
GEORGE HENDERSON

Part I
EDUCATION IN
A CHANGING SOCIETY

Contemporary Society:
Challenges to Education
The Role of the Culture
in Human Development
Social Forces
Affecting Teaching

Chapter 1 discusses the revolutionary changes that have been taking place in our society in recent decades and the implications of our democratic aspirations for education. Chapter 2 examines the process of socialization, through which children learn to participate in the activities of ever-enlarging groups of people, and the process of acculturation, by means of which immigrants learn the "American way of life." Chapter 3 deals with the impact of social forces on teaching.

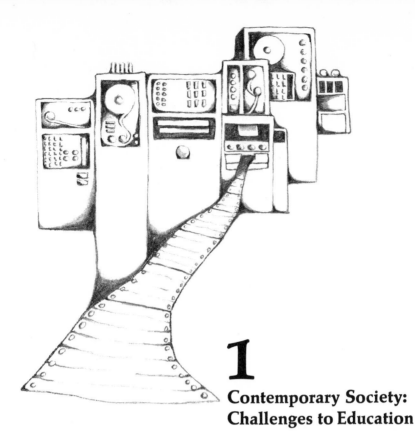

1

Contemporary Society: Challenges to Education

The task of bringing our old minds into accord with the facts of the new world is a gigantic and urgent educational undertaking.*

Altering educational programs to meet new conditions of living is a task that has confronted each new generation for centuries. Since 1945, however, changes have occurred with incredible speed. Thus the task of reforming education now presents a formidable challenge. In addition, more Americans than ever before realize that drastic reforms in education *are* necessary. They understand that children now in school will spend their adult years in a radically different society. Indeed, it is not an exaggeration to say that education will determine the outcome of the race between civilization and catastrophe. It is apparent that educational reforms must keep pace with changes in society.

Science and technology are, of course,

*George S. Counts, "Education and the Technological Revolution," Teachers College Record, March, 1958, p. 318.

two of the principal causes of the constantly accelerating rate of change. In an expanding process, each invention opens the way for several others; each research study leads to other related studies; each innovation lays the foundation for more elaborate innovations. Many of the resulting changes in the culture are so drastic that it is difficult for us to understand them and difficult, therefore, to sense fully their implications for educational programs. For instance, the release of the energy stored in the atom created, as one writer put it, "a blanket of obsolescence not only over the methods and the products of man but over man himself."[1] The launching of Sputnik I opened an era that has been aptly called the "post-modern world."[2]

SIGNIFICANT TRENDS
IN OUR SOCIETY
It is apparent that an understanding of the ever-changing American society is essential to an understanding of the changes that are taking place—and should take place—in education. Education always has been and always will be influenced by time, place, and circumstances. The social trends that affect the tasks the schools are expected to perform are too numerous and too complex to be treated in detail here. Thus only a few of the more significant trends are now analyzed.

Our Affluent Society
We live in a tremendously wealthy society. Here is an illustration: Imagine all the people in the world compressed into a village with a population of 1,000 persons. Only 60 inhabitants of the village would be Americans, but these fortunate few would enjoy fully half the total income of the village; the other 940 people would definitely have the short end of the stick—they would have to make do with the other half. Our wealth is great not only in relative terms but also in absolute ones —and it is increasing. The Gross National Product (GNP) of the United States was $157 billion in 1947, $370 billion in 1957, $730 billion in 1967, and $850 billion in 1968. (It is estimated that in 1975 our GNP will be up to $1.3 *trillion*.) Per capita income increased from $600 a year in 1900 to $2,000 in 1957 to $3,500 in 1968. Some comparative GNP figures make such statistics more meaningful. In 1966, our GNP was $690 billion, but France's was $116 billion, the United Kingdom's was $90 billion, Brazil's was $23 billion, and Nigeria's was under $5 billion. We have, in fact, moved from an economy of scarcity to an economy of abundance. Until recently, our main problem was to produce enough goods to go around. Now our problem is the proper distribution of the goods that are pouring from our farms and factories in ever increasing volume.

[1]Norman Cousins, *Modern Man Is Obsolete*, New York, Viking Press, 1946, p. 8.
[2]Peter F. Drucker, *Landmarks of Tomorrow*, New York, Harper & Row, 1959, p. ix.

This picture of prosperity and abundance is marred by the dark and threatening fact that all Americans do not share in it. The year 1960 was a prosperous one for the country, but in that year 38 million Americans—a fifth of the nation—lived in poverty. This was so even though the "poverty" line was drawn quite far down: multiperson families with an annual income of less than $4,000 and single persons with an annual income of less than $2,000. These poverty-stricken Americans constitute a subculture made up of people without the education or technical skills to admit them to the mainstream of American life and work. It is inconsistent with our democratic ideals of equality of opportunity and the worth of every human being to have allowed such a subculture to be formed and to allow it to continue. This is what Gunnar Myrdal, the eminent Swedish economist, had in mind when he said, "There is an ugly smell rising from the basement of the stately American mansion."[3] Can anyone deny that this waste of the talents of our disadvantaged minorities is the social problem that should lie heaviest on our consciences?

The Urban Crisis
Poverty and substandard educational opportunities in the United States are by no means confined to urban communities; discrimination and prejudice against those who are different from the majority are by no means directly only at Negroes and other minority ethnic groups. (Any American boy or girl who has completed grade school in a rural community and moved to an urban community to attend high school knows how difficult it is to become a member of the in-group.) Nevertheless, poverty in the cities presents a perhaps more difficult problem than rural poverty. Discrimination on ethnic grounds is more difficult to deal with than discrimination on social grounds, and it also has become a problem whose results are more acute in the cities.

There are many reasons for the urban crisis, most of them of quite recent origin. As a matter of fact, the big city itself is a relatively new development on the American scene. It was not until 1820 that any American city had a population of 100,000; we now have one city of 8 million (metropolitan area; including suburbs, 16 million) and four others of more than 3 million each. Two-thirds of the school children and school teachers of the United States are in metropolitan schools.[4] The Bureau of the Census now uses the term "Standard Metropolitan Statistical Area" (SMSA) to mean a city of 50,000 or more with its surrounding area that is economically and socially integrated with it. There were 219 SMSAs in the United States in 1968.

As technology has invaded the farms, the rural poor have moved to the central cities; at the same time, those who could afford to do so have

---

[3]Gunnar Myrdal, "It's Time To Face the Future," *Look*, November 19, 1963, p. 105.
[4]Robert J. Havighurst, *Education in Metropolitan Areas*, Boston, Allyn & Bacon, 1966, pp. 27–33.

moved from the cities to the suburbs. Chicago is a good example of the results of this trend. In 1940, 3,115,000 whites and only 282,000 non-whites lived in that city; by 1965, the whites had dropped to 2,579,000 and the nonwhites had increased to 980,000. In 1940, the suburbs of Chicago had 1,148,000 whites and 25,000 nonwhites; by 1965, the suburbs had 2,980,000 whites and 113,000 nonwhites. In Detroit, families living within six miles of the central business district gained 3 percent in median income between 1951 and 1959; families living in the suburbs gained 47 percent in median income during the same period. The trend has also produced proportions like these in the schools: In Washington, 93 percent of the elementary school pupils are Negroes; in Detroit, St. Louis, Baltimore, and Philadelphia, the figure is almost 70 percent.[5]

It is widely recognized that it will take the combined and coordinated efforts of *many* agencies to solve the urban crisis, but the schools are expected to play a major role. It is generally acknowledged that the schools cannot fulfill this role by trying to impose educational programs designed for middle-class children on children whose home environments have not prepared them for such programs. In an attempt to resolve this dilemma, expedients such as integration and compensatory programs specifically designed for disadvantaged children have been evolved and tried.

Nevertheless, the efforts to provide equality of educational opportunity for children in city slums have, for the most part, failed. Integration has not proceeded as rapidly as it was expected to, and it has been beset by many unforeseen problems. Compensatory education programs, such as Head Start, have to some extent made up for the absence of opportunities for learning in the home, but children who have been in such programs have generally fallen behind when they entered schools with no provisions for differentiated instruction. It can be said that education in the slums still presents a dismal picture, characterized by old buildings, poorly prepared teachers, and a high percentage of dropouts.

Although the federal government, states, and cities have spent billions on poverty, housing, health, employment, and education programs, urban problems continue to mount. Many think the solutions will come only through measures more drastic than any so far seriously considered. The National Education Association recently described one such proposal:

A consensus is developing among urban-oriented groups that massive financial outlays—by both private industry and government—are needed immediately to cope with the urban situation and the conditions in the ghettos. . . . Representative John Conyers, Jr. (D., Mich.) announced that he would propose a Full Opportunity bill designed to sweep away all racial discrimination and make employment and educational opportunities available for every citizen. Mr. Conyers said that 3 million jobs were needed, that 10 million new housing units should be built over the next decade and

[5]Ibid., p. 57.

that compensatory education and post-high school education should be a matter of right for all Americans. The Conyers plan would cost $30 billion annually.[6]

New International Responsibilities

For more than 150 years, our foreign policy was based on the principle of isolationism—staying out of international affairs. This policy of avoiding "entangling alliances," proclaimed by the first President, was reaffirmed at the close of World War I, when the United States Senate refused to allow this country to join President Woodrow Wilson's League of Nations.

There can be little doubt that this policy served us well when we were a young nation, separated from the rest of the world by two vast oceans and relatively free to develop a unique, self-sufficient society, unhampered by what went on in the rest of the world. We made a sharp break with our traditions, then, when we took active leadership in the establishment of the United Nations at the end of World War II. The harsh realities of the international scene, the increasing interdependence of nations, technological developments that had made the world much smaller in terms of travel time—all these had convinced Americans that it was no longer possible for a nation to live in isolation. President Franklin D. Roosevelt stated the situation clearly when he wrote, "We are faced with the preeminent fact that if civilization is to survive, we must cultivate the science of human relationships—the ability of people of all kinds to live together and work together in the same world, at peace."

Two significant developments since 1945 reflect the changes in international relations. The first is that Communism has expanded so rapidly that one-third of the world's population now lives under its political control. When we try to understand the appeal of Communism, we must take into account some basic economic facts: The development of a modern, industrialized economy depends, in the beginning stages, on saving—postponing consumption so as to accumulate capital. In the United States we have been able to leave saving and accumulating capital to individual choice, but it is a slow and difficult process in countries where the people are living at a bare subsistence level. Nevertheless, without capital, schools and universities cannot be maintained; without technical training, the skills needed for managing large industrial enterprises are not available. Communism offers a formula for overcoming these problems; the Communists claim that they alone know how to give poor societies a way to accumulate the capital without which no economy can hope to move forward (in essence, they compel people to postpone consumption).

The other significant development since 1945 is that forty-seven new

[6]Washington Outlook on Education, "The Crisis That Won't Go Away," Washington, National Education Association, September 15, 1967.

nations have come into existence. The people in these developing nations intensely desire independence and economic development. Should we in the United States allow men, women, and children in these new countries to continue to suffer not only poverty, but also ill health and hunger—even starvation—when we have the means to help them? That is one of the central issues that every American citizen must face when he considers our role in world affairs.

It is obvious that we need not and should not emulate the methods of the Communists. Indeed, we are perfectly well aware of methods we could readily use to help developing countries. The main problem is that we have had too little interest in such countries; we have not given enough thought to helping them make sound economic and political decisions. The problem of the future of these new nations illustrates the need for education for international understanding.

Education as an Investment
Another significant trend in American society during the last few decades has been the increasing recognition that education and technical training are important factors in economic growth. A few economists have advanced this theory over the years. As far back as 1776, for example, Adam Smith, in his *Wealth of Nations*, held that the acquired abilities of all the inhabitants of a country should be included as part of its capital. Irving Fisher, an American economist, said a half-century ago that both human resources and material possessions should be regarded as capital assets. Nevertheless, most economists, when formulating their concepts of capital, have included only tangible goods and possessions. In recent years, however, a number of economists have begun to take account of the human element. As one of them has put it:

It became clear to me that in the United States many people are investing heavily in themselves as human agents, that these investments in man are having a pervasive influence upon economic growth, and that the key investment in human capital is education.[7]

Many factors have accounted for the high standard of living in the United States; some of them are: an abundance of natural resources, a favorable climate, competent business managers, and technological developments that have supplied us with power-driven machinery and thus increased productivity. Another economist, after closely analyzing such factors, concluded:

The present writer has long been of the opinion that education—good education—has been a vital factor in this development. If the several factors discussed above are the proximate causes of productive gains, education may well be described as the cause behind the causes.[8]

[7]Theodore W. Schultz, *The Economic Value of Education*, New York, Columbia University Press, 1963, p. viii.
[8]John Philip Wernette, *Government and Business*, New York, Macmillan, 1964, p. 167.

Barbara Ward has expressed a belief that there is a "moral governance" in the universe—that when men or governments "work intelligently and far-sightedly for the good of others, they achieve their own prosperity as well."[9] The G.I. Bill of Rights (actually two acts of Congress) provides a very good example. Almost 10 million veterans have received financial assistance for education and training under this program. What was intended as a gratuity has proved to be a profitable investment—the money granted by the government has been repaid manyfold in increased earning power and thus in increased taxes returned to the government. If we invest more of our abundance to help Negroes, Puerto Ricans, Mexican nationals, poor farmers, and older citizens increase their earning power, if we invest in underdeveloped nations to help them build up their purchasing power, we may well find that we have furthered our own prosperity.

OUR DEMOCRATIC
ASPIRATIONS
The struggle for human freedom is as old as civilization itself. But this desire to have a share in shaping their own destiny has always been a particularly compelling motive for Americans. The right to do so, indeed, is one of the basic principles of our society. A system of education open to all American children and youth has helped to realize this American aspiration.

Education and the Achievement of Social Ideals
Schools have always been expected to assist other social agencies in furthering the social ideals of the people who support them. Napoleon recognized this when he said, "There cannot be a firmly established political state unless there is a teaching body with definitely recognized principles." Thomas Jefferson, James Madison, James Monroe, and many other leaders in early American political life urged the necessity of education as a basis for the success of a democracy.

A series of articles by 10 distinguished Americans appeared in 1959 in *Life* magazine and the *New York Times* dealing with the theme of *the national purpose*. They raised such questions as: What shall Americans do with the greatness of their nation? What *is* the national purpose of the United States? Have Americans lost, at least temporarily, their sense of national purpose? These articles, published in book form in the next year, created a great deal of national concern and debate.[10]

Goals for Americans, a report of the President's Commission on National Goals, also published in 1960, gave an explicit description of the nature of our basic aspirations and the steps that needed to be

---

[9]Barbara Ward, *The Rich Nations and the Poor Nations*, New York, Norton, 1962, p. 150.
[10]John K. Jessup, et al., *The National Purpose*, New York, Holt, 1960.

taken to achieve them.[11] The goals included concern for the individual, equality of educational opportunity, a democratic economy, and a peaceful world order. The program advocated included doubling expenditures for education during the 1960s, sharply reducing discrimination on the basis of color, and strengthening the United Nations.

There are, then, various purposes that are rather widely accepted in this country. Nevertheless, we often admit to confusion about them. Perhaps what this admission really means is that we are unwilling to face the difficult task of putting them into practice.

But we must face that task. We must realize that democracy is not merely a set of beliefs; it is a process that *can* be practiced in any group —nation, family, or classroom. In the classroom, we must strive to achieve the particular form of education that supports a democratic society. Such education promotes the continuous growth of the individual so that he can join fully and freely in the shared purposes of his society; so that he will never stop expanding his horizons; so that he can develop his innate capacity for becoming an adequate, self-actualizing person; in short, so that he can become fully human in the world in which he is growing up.

The Methods of Democracy

Democracy is a way to work out human relationships, a way to work together in group situations, a way to exercise control over group action. (Other methods of arranging relationships include force, domination, and laissez faire.) Although research has provided much evidence that democratic procedures in school situations work out better in the long run, many professional educators nevertheless object to the actual use of the term "democratic" in relation to teaching and administration. They contend that the term is frequently used as a rug under which inefficient or manipulative practices are swept; they deplore in general what they call "fuzzy, quasi-religious prating about democracy." (Interestingly, such educators usually admit that their opponents are able to "discuss" other topics but insist that they are only "prating" when democracy is the topic.)

Cavils about terminology are not important, however. The main point is that it is imperative, if the schools are indeed to serve as instruments for preserving and improving the democratic way of life, that teachers and administrators make greater efforts to discover and use the methods of democracy. Nor should we be deterred by the fact that some who talk about democracy are not practicing it.

The hallmarks of democratic procedures are not difficult to identify; indeed, capable teachers have been using many of them for decades. Recent curriculum projects have supplied new models for their application and recent research in the area of human growth and development

[11]President's Commission on National Goals, *Goals for Americans*, Englewood Cliffs, N.J., Prentice-Hall, 1960.

has provided new insights into their psychological foundations. These democratic methods fall into a number of categories. Some concern teacher-pupil relations; others concern pupil-pupil relations; still others involve administrative procedures, drawing up curricula, and the like. It is impossible here to discuss more than a few. Therefore we have selected four types of procedures that seem particularly important in their day-to-day effect on pupils. Two are of a rather specific nature: (1) learning by discovery; (2) growth through involvement in decision-making. The others are more broad in implications and practice: (3) the search for equality of opportunity; (4) respect for the individual.

1. Learning by discovery.   Authoritarian procedures, whether in government or in education, eventually dig their own graves by suppressing all ideas except those of individuals who are in authority. Authoritarian teaching is a one-way process—always from the teacher or the textbook to the pupils. The obvious—and almost insuperable— difficulty is that pupils simply are not interested in merely memorizing ready-made answers fed to them by the teacher and the textbook; thus teachers using such methods are compelled to spend much time and thought on inventing all sorts of devices intended to arouse interest.

In an attempt to solve this problem, the learning by discovery method was developed. Its advantages have been described thus:

If we help boys and girls learn the process of discovering knowledge and ways of working for themselves, we need not give our energies to finding fascinating ways to hold their attention or whip up their enthusiasm. The strong urge to pursue learning comes from within.[12]

Helping children learn to use the method of discovery—of finding their own solutions to problems—requires a concept of the role of facts in the educative process that is different from the one frequently held by teachers. Facts are important, of course, but they are *tools* used to solve problems rather than ends in themselves. John Dewey expressed this idea when he said that subject matter is anything that is used by a child in the solution of a problem.

Curriculum improvement projects are developing materials and techniques designed to produce something more lasting than the memorization of bits of information. Indeed, the goal is no less than a process of education that will help children and youth become self-propelling during a lifetime of learning in a rapidly changing world. Learning by discovery thus represents the kind of education that supports a democratic society, the kind of education that deserves the most heartfelt support of those who believe in democracy.

2. Growth through involvement in decision-making.   Plans developed by one person or a few people in authority and handed down to others

---

[12]Lucile Lindberg, "Learning Through Searching," *Childhood Education*, October, 1961, pp. 58–60.

as decrees seldom work out well in the long run. First, people who have had no part in formulating plans usually do not fully understand what is expected of them. Second, people work with more enthusiasm when they regard the plans as "our" plans rather than as "their" plans. Only through participating in decision-making can teachers grow professionally. Only through sharing in the planning of activities can pupils develop the qualities of initiative, cooperation, and concern for the welfare of the group that are essential to the success of a democratic society.

The teacher in a democratic classroom makes certain that every pupil takes a responsible part in the life and work of the classroom. Pupils are involved in formulating plans, in working them out, and in evaluating results; the teacher makes a careful appraisal of the readiness of each pupil for assuming certain responsibilities; the teacher encourages timid pupils to participate in classroom activities; pupils help in establishing rules for the orderly transaction of the work of the class. There is a free exchange of ideas, and members of the class take turns at serving as group leaders.

3. *The search for equality of opportunity.* The course of American history has been largely motivated by the search for a social system that would allow every individual to advance as far as his ability and effort permit—with no artificial barriers based on race, religion, sex, or socioeconomic status. The public school has been regarded as the principal instrument through which this democratic ideal would be achieved.

Most Americans believe in the democratic principles of respect for the worth of every human being and equality of opportunity. Nevertheless, these ideals have not been applied in reality to many poor whites, Negroes, Puerto Ricans, Mexican-Americans, and American Indians. The children of all these groups are described as *disadvantaged* because they are all denied the cultural, economic, and psychological advantages enjoyed by other American children. Disadvantaged subcultures have long presented a problem in America, but only recently has the problem received widespread attention. The Educational Policies Commission has put it this way:

For many years this problem was permitted to persist. It did not generate that unrest which in a democracy precedes the making of changes in major public policies. Today, conditions are different; unrest is widespread and critical.[13]

The increasing concentration of the poor and unskilled in urban areas and the increasing unwillingness of disadvantaged people to tolerate

[13]Educational Policies Commission, *American Education and the Search for Equal Opportunity*, Washington, National Education Association, 1965, p. 3.

the hopelessness of their efforts to get ahead—symbolized by protests and violence in the streets—have brought the disparity between ideals and practices to the attention of many Americans and caused them to look to the schools for help in eliminating what is now recognized to be an intolerable condition.

Many children whose potential for learning actually is high never have an opportunity to develop this potential through education because of the low income of their parents. Studies have been done that indicate that, when one considers only the group in the upper quarter of intellectual ability, 75 percent of upper-middle- and upper-class youth finish four years of college, whereas only 25 percent of working-class and lower-lower-class youth do so.[14]

If elementary schools and secondary schools are to provide equality of opportunity for culturally disadvantaged children and youth, they must be staffed by teachers who understand the handicaps these children labor under when they enter school: impoverished vocabulary, negative image of self, distrust of school as an institution for middle-class children, and little exposure to books or reading in the home. Yet, surveys conducted in 1966 revealed that, by and large, preparation for working with disadvantaged children was a neglected area in teacher education programs.

Children from impoverished homes are not the only ones who need curriculum adaptations in terms of their abilities and backgrounds. Minimum grade standards, rigid promotion policies, and narrow, book-centered curriculums stand in the way of helping each child develop whatever talents he has to the fullest extent possible. A school program that provides opportunities for only the intellectual elite is undemocratic; a program that does not challenge the more capable pupils is also undemocratic.

4. *Respect for the individual.* A democracy thrives on diversity; dictatorships therefore attempt to impose uniformity. Teaching procedures in a democracy are judged in terms of their effect on the children involved. Curriculum reforms, innovations in grouping for instruction, and trends in higher education are discussed in Part III. The democratic principle of respect for the worth of the individual is involved in all of these trends.

The right of the child to be different imposes many obligations on the teacher. Teachers who respect this right do not expect all children to learn at the same rate, they provide opportunities for slower pupils to experience success in terms of their ability, they challenge brighter pupils to achieve as much as their ability permits, and they permit individuals to spend some time working on individual projects in line with their interests and purposes.

[14]Harry L. Miller and Marjorie E. Smiley, *Education in the Metropolis*, New York, The Free Press, 1967, p. 12.

SUMMARY

1. Forces have been released during recent decades that have brought about drastic changes in American society; these changes demand drastic changes in educational programs.
2. Since 1957, we have been living in the postmodern era of history; much remains to be done in evolving a program of education that will match the hazards and potentials of the age in which we live. The specifications for such a program will be determined to a large extent by stern realities; these realities include an affluent society, an urban crisis, new responsibilities in the field of international relations, and an increasing recognition of the power of educatiton to raise standards of living.
3. American history has been largely shaped by the struggle to build a social order in which every individual would have an opportunity to achieve a measure of success, freedom, respect, and economic security; the public schools have had an important role in helping to achieve this American dream.
4. The most basic of American ideals are widely known and accepted; these values serve as guidelines for educational decisions and programs.
5. If the schools are to be effective instruments in preserving and improving the democratic way of life, teachers and administrators must discover and use the methods of democracy; these methods include learning by discovery, growth through involvement in decision-making, equality of opportunity, and respect for the individual.

SELECTED READINGS

Adams, James Truslow, *The Epic of America,* New York, Blue Ribbon Books, 1931. Chapter 12 explains how the schools in the early years of the twentieth century were no longer in step with changes in the society. The Epilogue (pp. 404–405) gives an excellent statement of the meaning of the American dream.

Brameld, Theodore, "World Civilization, the Galvanizing Purpose of Public Education," in Stanley Elam, *New Dimensions for Educational Progress,* Bloomington, Ind., Phi Delta Kappa, 1962, chapter 1. This author makes a strong appeal for education for a world civilization extending from the kindergarten through college.

Butts, R. Freeman, *American Education in International Development,* New York, Harper & Row, 1963. This book relates international studies to technical assistance, helping the rising nations, and self-education.

Chitwood, O. P., F. L. Owsley, and H. C. Nixon, *The United States: From Colony to World Power,* New York, Van Nostrand, 1954. Chapter 2 describes the hardships endured by the early settlers in order to establish a unique civilization on this continent.

Commager, Henry Steele, *Our Schools Have Kept Us Free,* Washington, National Education Association, 1962. This pamphlet explains the contributions of the schools to American ideals.

Counts, George S., *Education and the Promise of America,* New York, Macmillan, 1946. Explains our American heritage of freedom and sets forth the sources of a great educational program.

Cousins, Norman, *Modern Man Is Obsolete,* New York, Viking Press, 1946. Explains the impact of the atomic bomb on mankind.

Cremin, Lawrence A., *The Genius of American Education*, New York, Random House, 1966. Suggests a new, tough-minded progressivism that is at the same time consonant with the best in our tradition and appropriate to contemporary needs.

Drucker, Peter F., *Landmarks of Tomorrow*, New York, Harper & Row, 1959. Expresses the point of view that we have left the "modern" period in history and entered the "postmodern" period; that the old view of the world no longer makes sense.

Educational Policies Commission, *American Education and the Search for Equal Opportunity*, Washington, National Education Association, 1965. Explains the reasons for unrest among minority groups.

Havighurst, Robert J., *Education in Metropolitan Areas*, Boston, Allyn & Bacon, 1966. Provides data on the population shifts and the growth of slums.

Long, Harold M., and Robert N. King, *Improving the Teaching of World Affairs: The Glens Falls Story*, Washington, National Council for the Social Studies, 1964. A detailed account of a successful experiment in teaching world affairs.

Miller, Harry L., and Marjorie E. Smiley, *Education in the Metropolis*, New York, The Free Press, 1967. Cites research that shows that many youngsters with high potential for learning never have the opportunity to finish college.

President's Commission on National Goals, *Goals for Americans*, Englewood Cliffs, N.J., Prentice-Hall, 1960. Contains an excellent statement of basic American goals in education as well as in other areas.

Project on the Instructional Program of the Public Schools, *Education in a Changing Society*, Washington, National Education Association, 1963. Presents a discussion of eight characteristics of contemporary American society and explains the implications for education.

Schultz, Theodore W., *The Economic Value of Education*, New York, Columbia University Press, 1963. Chapter 3 discusses the major functions of the educational establishment, education as a source of economic growth, and capital formation by education, relating costs to benefits and rate of return from investment in education.

Ward, Barbara, *The Rich Nations and the Poor Nations*, New York, Norton, 1962. A brilliant account of what needs to happen in the underdeveloped nations before they can achieve higher standards of living and how important it is for peace and stability that they should do so.

Wernette, John Philip, *Government and Business*, New York, Macmillan, 1964. Presents an analysis of the factors that have contributed to the economic gains of the United States and concludes that education has been a major factor.

2

The Role of the Culture
in Human Development

We are now in possession of a much greater understanding of the ways that culture, social forces, values, social groups, the family, social class, and peer groups mingle with the individual's biological inheritance to affect his development.*

A study of the foundations of education serves two purposes: Broadly, it provides an understanding of how the culture influences human development; more specifically, it identifies the social problems that influence the tasks education must perform. This chapter is concerned with the first of these purposes; later chapters will explore the second purpose.

Since the time of Rousseau, educational theorists and practitioners have never ceased debating the principal function of education—should it be planned primarily to benefit the child or the society? Rousseau initiated a revolution in educational thought with *Émile* (1762), in which he said: "God makes all things good; man meddles with

*Glen Haas and Kimball Wiles, Readings in Curriculum, Boston, Allyn & Bacon, 1965, p. 133.

them and they become evil."[1] One of the main theories he advanced in this novel about the bringing up of a boy is that education should change with the various stages in a child's development. Profoundly influenced by Rousseau, educational reformers began developing educational programs based primarily on the interests, purposes, and normal activities of children. For instance, Pestalozzi's school at Yverdon, Switzerland (1805), John Dewey's at the University of Chicago (1896), Junius L. Meriam's at the University of Missouri (1904), and Ellsworth Collings' in McDonald County, Missouri (1917), were all "child-centered" schools.[2] The importance of using information about how children develop, grow, and learn as a basis for planning educational programs continues to be recognized. An almost staggering amount of such information is available. For example, in one publication, about 2000 studies in child psychology—most of them done between 1953 and 1963—are reviewed.[3]

It is really almost a truism now, as a matter of fact, to say that the nature and needs of children must be taken into consideration in planning school programs. But there are broader ramifications that are not so self-evident. Child development does not take place in a vacuum; the ideas, habits, attitudes, and behavior patterns of the individual are acquired from interacting with the culture in which the child lives. It is now generally acknowledged, in other words, that it is oversimplifying to say that the school program should be based entirely on a single factor, such as the interests and purposes of children, the major functions of social life, or the development of the rational powers of the individual. The more balanced approach that now seems desirable has been described by many experts, one of whom puts it this way: "No one area is sufficient for curriculum planning today. A combination of the three basic areas—organized knowledge, society, and the individual—seems to offer the best hope for curriculum improvement."[4] Teacher education programs today usually do include a study of these three basic areas.

THE SOCIALIZATION
PROCESS
The *culture* is the environment that man himself has made. It includes the distinctive ways of carrying on life processes, the artifacts, ideas, values, language, attitudes, and customs of a particular time and place. The culture is influenced to some extent by geography, resources, climate, and the history of a particular society; it is influenced to an

---

[1]Jean Jacques Rousseau, *Émile* (Barbara Foxley, trans.), London, Dent, 1955, p. 5.
[2]See William B. Ragan, *Modern Elementary Curriculum* (3rd ed.), New York, Holt, 1966, p. 166.
[3]National Society for the Study of Education, *Child Psychology*, Chicago, The University of Chicago Press, 1963.
[4]Donald F. Cay, *Curriculum: Design for Learning*, Indianapolis, Bobbs-Merrill, 1966, p. 15.

even greater extent by knowledge, which is the source of technological progress. As knowledge and skills increase, the culture changes; new ways of carrying on life processes are incorporated into it. Young people, therefore, do not simply repeat the life processes of their parents; they learn to live according to the demands of the latest developmental stage of the culture. The strain that inevitably develops between youth and their elders as a result of cultural conflicts is commonly called the "generation gap."[5]

The child is born into a culture, but he must learn the behavior patterns needed to live effectively with others in the culture. The changes that take place in children and young people as they acquire the knowledge and skills necessary for living harmoniously and effectively with other individuals and groups are called *social development*; the help they receive from parents, siblings, peer groups, schools, churches, and other educative agencies is called *social education*.

Diversity of Cultures Within American Society

Ours is a society of great cultural diversity. Although there are certain common elements in the life patterns and basic beliefs of all segments of our population, there are significant differences in the attitudes, interests, goals, even dialects that children internalize by interacting with their families and subcultures. Respect for individual differences and the desire to provide opportunities for every individual to learn, to realize his potential, and to find a place in society according to his ability and efforts have long been recognized as the essence of our democratic aspirations. Diversity is both permitted and prized in an open society, at least up to a certain limit; in a closed society, behavior patterns are not matters of personal choice—they are dictated by the "state." As early as 1835, Alexis de Tocqueville noted: "The American relies on personal interest to accomplish his ends and gives free scope to the unguided strength and common sense of the people; the Russian centers all the authority of society in a single arm."

The process of socialization, however, is complicated by the diversity of cultures in our society. (One glaring example is our failure to provide adequate educational opportunities for the children of the lower socioeconomic classes; this result of our public policy—or lack of policy—has finally begun to lie heavily on our consciences.) John Dewey's remarks in this connection are as pertinent today as when he made them in 1916:

A democracy is more than a form of government; it is primarily a mode of associated living, of conjoint communicated experience. The extension in space of the number of individuals who participate in an interest so that each has to refer his own action to that of others, and to consider the action of others to give point and direction to his own, is equivalent to the breaking

[5]For a more detailed analysis of this phenomenon, see Margaret Mead, "The Generation Gap," *Science*, April 11, 1969.

down of those barriers of class, race, and national territory which keep men from perceiving the full import of their activities.[6]

Among the "barriers"—the cultural differences—which children bring to school with them are those arising from differences between masculine and feminine roles, rural and urban backgrounds, ethnic groups, and social classes.

Masculine and feminine roles.   In our culture, as in almost all cultures, men are expected to play different roles from women. One of the first lessons a child learns from those about him is that his behavior must accord with that generally considered appropriate to his sex. A boy is frowned on if he takes on too many feminine characteristics; a girl is handicapped if she is not feminine in dress, speech, and behavior. The terms "sissy" and "tomboy" vividly reflect the common attitude toward a boy or girl who does not seem to possess enough of the proper sex-role attributes. One of the basic aspects of the socialization process for a child is the necessity to internalize sex-appropriate patterns of behavior.

Rural and urban backgrounds.   Though they are not so striking as they used to be, there still are differences in language, attitudes, and interests between rural and urban children. Some school systems, therefore, run a type of "orientation" program designed to acquaint rural children moving to cities with urban cultural resources and patterns of living. As we have mentioned, acquiring urban patterns of behavior is generally a painful process for rural children.

Ethnic groups.   This term refers to groups of different national or racial origins. The population of the United States is composed of people with a great variety of ethnic backgrounds; nearly everyone can trace his ancestry back to some country across the seas. These ethnic groups have enriched our culture with their own particular types of music, food, customs, and dress. Americans are proud of the fact that our nation has been a "melting pot," assimilating people who came here from many different nations. There is evidence that the schools have played a leading role in this accomplishment.[7]

However, it usually takes two or more generations for the members of a new group to be sufficiently absorbed into the life of the community so that they lose their separate identity; some groups never do achieve assimilation. The assimilation of the more recent immigrant groups seems to be problematical; most of them are of the lower socioeconomic class in our large cities, and they tend to maintain their own patterns of beliefs, attitudes, and behavior.

Social classes.   Many studies of the influence of social class on educational opportunities have been done. These studies justify the con-

[6]John Dewey, *Democracy and Education*, New York, Macmillan, 1916, p. 101.
[7]Henry Steele Commager, *Our Schools Have Kept Us Free*, Washington, National Education Association, 1962.

clusions that there are rather clearly defined social classes in the United States; that the social class to which his parents belong determines to a great extent a child's educational attainments; and that there are circumstances that make it difficult for an individual to advance from one social class to another on the basis of his own capabilities and efforts.

Our system is not, of course, a caste system. The difference between caste and class has been described thus:

The rules of caste demand that an individual be born, live, and die in one caste. Social mobility in a class system permits an individual during his lifetime to move up or down through the several social strata. A man may be born lower-class but in time climb into the upper ranges of society, although, ordinarily, a person stays in the class into which he was born.[8]

Nevertheless, for some in our society, the effects of the system are disturbingly similar to those of a true caste system. For example, education is generally regarded as the principal means of promoting social mobility, but our society has erected serious barriers to the acquiring of a good education and thus to the improvement of life chances for many of our youth. Indeed, the lowering of these and other barriers has become one of the major goals of our domestic policy. As the President's Commission on National Goals said in 1960:

Vestiges of religious prejudices, handicaps to women, and, most important, discrimination on the basis of race must be recognized as morally wrong, economically wasteful, and in many cases dangerous. In this decade we must sharply lower these last stubborn barriers.[9]

Family income is closely associated with class structure in this country. Education is generally regarded as the means to the better-paying jobs; nevertheless, there is evidence that, in 1960, although 50 percent of the white high school graduates had clerical jobs, only 20 percent of the Negro graduates held such jobs. Furthermore, 25 percent of the Negro graduates were employed in service occupations, but only 10 percent of the whites were. The results are apparent in statistics like these: In 1960, 15 percent of the Negroes and Puerto Ricans in New York had incomes under $2,000 a year; only 8 percent of the whites had incomes that low. In 1962, the average income of Negroes in the United States was only 63 percent of the average income of whites.[10]

The schools cannot, of course, be expected to provide all the levers for social mobility; the social and economic structures that surround

[8]W. Lloyd Warner, Robert J. Havighurst, and Martin B. Loeb, *Who Shall Be Educated?* New York, Harper & Row, 1944, p. 19.

[9]President's Commission on National Goals, *Goals for Americans*, Englewood Cliffs, N. J., Prentice-Hall, 1960, p. 3.

[10]Harry L. Miller and Marjorie B. Smiley, *Education in the Metropolis*, New York, The Free Press, 1967, pp. 9–12.

the children, particularly families and community agencies, must also contribute. But it is the business of the school to help children make the most of their individual capacities so that their life chances will be enhanced. Two informed observers have said that "even the most staunchly loyal professional educator with a knowledge of the urban situation would hesitate to claim that big-city schools are adequately performing the task that is squarely and particularly theirs to do."[11]

There are many factors that contribute to effective teaching, but it is generally recognized that truly effective teachers are those who seek to understand their pupils. A very important aspect of understanding children is understanding the life styles of the social classes from which they come. Pupils from different social classes have different manners, beliefs, and language and behavior patterns, acquired through the social pressures of home and community. To be specific, teachers must understand that children from impoverished homes come to school with many handicaps and that they need a school program designed to compensate for the lack of educational opportunities in the home and community.

THE SOCIAL DEVELOPMENT
OF CHILDREN

Information about child development has accumulated so rapidly that intellectual development, physical development, emotional development, and social development are now separate areas of research. The studies that treat each of these areas in greater depth than is feasible in one course or one book on child development are invaluable; nevertheless, it is important to realize that no one phase takes place independently of the other phases. Physical defects and poor health frequently interfere with academic achievement; the effective use of language is closely related to social relationships; the emotionally disturbed child is not likely to do well in school; and, as every parent knows, acceptance by the peer group is an important factor in a child's success in school.

Although there has been a trend in recent years to emphasize the importance of intellectual development—the development of the rational powers—many specialists in the psychology of cognition recognize that education involves more than this. Gagné, whose book is restricted in scope to what may be termed "intellectual" development, states:

The reader must be made aware, also, that there are some problems of great importance to education which cannot be solved by applying a knowledge of the principles of learning as they are here described. For example, there are many aspects of the personal interaction between a teacher and his students that do not pertain, in a strict sense, to the acquisition of skills and knowledges that typically form the content of the curriculum. These

[11]Ibid., p. 13.

varieties of interaction include those of motivating, persuading, and the establishment of attitudes and values. The development of such human dispositions as these is of tremendous importance to education as a system of modern society.[12]

Social development is an important phase of growing into the culture—of becoming fully human. The child must learn to live in a veritable sea of human relationships as he engages in the activities of ever enlarging groups of people. His life outside the school provides many opportunities for social development, but the school can be his most effective social laboratory; at least it can be when the school environment is structured to meet his social needs and release his social potential. In addition, there is the sheer number of other pupils involved.

The Measurement of Children's Social Development

The measurement of children's *intellectual* development, particularly as it applies to learning school subjects, has been developed to a high level of proficiency. For instance, a score of 4.3 on a standardized achievement test in reading can be interpreted to mean that a pupil is reading at the level of the third month of the fourth year in school in terms of national norms in reading. Moreover, these measurement instruments are well known and widely used in most schools. A great deal of progress has also been made in the identification of the stages through which a child progresses in other aspects of mental development, such as concept development.[13]

There has not been comparable progress in the measurement of *social* development, although there have been many attempts. For example, Edgar Doll has developed the Vineland Social Maturity Scale, which consists of a series of rating scales arranged in a developmental sequence, grouped according to the ages at which certain behavior traits generally appear in children. The sociogram is a device that can serve as an effective starting point for the study of a pupil's progress in gaining acceptance by his peers, but it must be used in connection with other methods of evaluating social development.[14] These instruments are by no means as well known or as commonly used as those used for evaluating intellectual development.

Benjamin S. Bloom, whose research reveals the tremendous importance of the first few years of the child's life, concludes that (1) many of the changes in human characteristics that take place with increasing age can be explained in terms of environmental variations, (2) because there is a lack of direct measures of the influence of

---

[12]Robert M. Gagné, *The Conditions of Learning*, New York, Holt, 1965, p. 23.
[13]See William B. Ragan, op. cit., pp. 50–57.
[14]Ibid., pp. 58, 467–470.

variations in the environment on changes in human characteristics, we must be content with considering only the influence of extreme differences in the environment, and (3) there is a need for the development of more precise measures of the influence of the environment.[15]

Factors in Children's Social Development
The social behavior of children can be observed and recorded, and these records can be used as indications of growth in such important characteristics as the recognition of the rights of self and others, the ability to make friends, the ability to cooperate with others, and the ability to exercise leadership in a group situation. The summary that follows is not inclusive, but it can be useful in recognizing the social characteristics of children at various stages of development.

1. The quantity and quality of relationships in the home influence the child's patterns of social behavior that tend to persist when he enters school.

2. The child's principal source of social experience during his first few years is free play. Until the age of 2, the child's play is solitary; even when other children are in the same room, no interaction takes place.

3. Between the ages of 3 and 5, there is likely to be an increase in social play. The first playmates are provided by the immediate neighborhood; the child's desire for playmates is so strong that he may resort to imaginary playmates if there are none in the neighborhood.

4. If circumstances in his home and neighborhood have been favorable, the child will be experienced in cooperative play by the time he enters school; he will have lost some of his self-centeredness; he will be able to share and take turns; he will be able to serve as a leader part of the time.

5. Young children are generally more concerned with the approval of parents and teachers than they are with the approval of other children. After they have been in school a few years, their interest in the approval of their classmates increases and their interest in the approval of adults decreases.

6. The social climate in the classroom has an important influence on the social behavior of children. The autocratic climate tends to produce expressions of hostility, demands for attention, and sharp criticisms of the work of other pupils. The laissez faire climate is the least effective type found in classrooms in experimental studies; the children tend to get in each others' way, and very little is accomplished. The democratic climate produces the most favorable results; pupils are more inclined to stay with tasks whether the teacher is present or not, form more

[15]Benjamin S. Bloom, *Stability and Change in Human Characteristics*, New York, Wiley, 1964, pp. 9–10.

favorable attitudes toward other pupils, and develop valuable social skills.

A Larger Task for the Schools

The schools, if they are to be effective in producing citizens who have the insights and skills needed in the preservation of a free society, must be concerned not only with what the pupil knows, but also with what kind of person he is becoming in his interaction with others. The free society puts more responsibility on the individual—on his inner controls of his behavior and his ability to participate in decision-making—than any other kind of society does. The school in a free society must, therefore, accept as one of its important functions the continuation of the socialization process that began in the family and the neighborhood.

This function of the school in a free society is by no means fully understood or universally accepted in this country. Those who want to limit the schools to the teaching of the basic subjects assert that the school is not a social club—that the process of socialization should be left to the home and other agencies. An increasing number of Americans, however, including most parents, are looking to the school for contributions in the areas of human relations, citizenship, and personal-social adjustment. They are not likely to demand a return to the elementary school of the "three Rs" or to the strictly academic high school. Neither are informed educational leaders likely to favor a retreat to lesser goals.

ACCULTURATION AND CULTURAL CONFLICT

Thus far, our examination of the relationship between the culture and education has been concerned primarily with the *socialization* process —with the problems involved in helping the child internalize the culture into which he was born. *Acculturation* is a somewhat different process; it involves a change-over from one culture to another. This is generally a difficult process even for the parent who has already achieved the organization of his behavior patterns in the culture in which he grew up; for his child, who is still trying to internalize one culture when he is expected to take on the ways of a brand-new culture, the transition is even more difficult. *Cultural conflict* is the term that is frequently used to denote the frustrations an individual experiences in such circumstances.

Problems Encountered in the Acculturation Process

It has become increasingly difficult during recent decades for metropolitan areas in the United States to provide adequate educational opportunities and life chances for children from immigrant families. Factors that complicate the problems include the following:

1. *Mass migrations to the cities.*   There were 500 persons of Puerto Rican birth in New York City in 1910, 7,000 in 1920, 45,000 in 1930, and 613,000 persons of Puerto Rican birth or parentage in 1961. Glazer has characterized the situation of the Puerto Ricans in New York as follows:

Something new, then, has been added to the New York scene—an ethnic group that will not assimilate to the same degree as others have, but will resemble the strangers who lived in ancient Greek cities, or the ancient Greeks who set up colonies around the Mediterranean.[16]

2. *Conflicts in social roles of parents.*   Parents play an important role in helping children internalize the culture in which they live. However, the social behavior the in-migrant child learns from his parents is usually not in tune with his new social environment. The typical Puerto Rican mother, for example, keeps her daughters under strict control, does not allow them to go out on the streets, and forbids them to talk with other people. The girls, therefore, grow up without developing the ability to relate to others. As one expert points out, "It is important in working with Puerto Rican parents to help them find ways to protect their children without completely depriving them of social interchange."[17]

3. *The language barrier.*   Language is an important tool used in interacting with others. The in-migrant child often lacks this tool for adjustment to new people, a new area, and a new culture. He brings to school a nonstandard form of English learned from parents, relatives, and friends. His acculturation depends to a great extent on learning to speak the standard dialect of the school and the larger community fluently. There are difficulties involved in this process, of course, but some teachers tend to magnify them. After all, it has been demonstrated that children can learn to speak a second language, such as Spanish or French, at an early age; thus they can surely learn to speak a second dialect. (As a matter of fact, most adults in our society find that they use different dialects when speaking to different people— a university professor, a service station attendant, or a young child.) Cheyney, who has provided many practical suggestions for teaching language to culturally disadvantaged children, has said: "I believe the idea that home conditions are an insurmountable barrier to effective language instruction is a myth we have comfortably hidden behind all too long."[18]

[16]Nathan Glazer, "The Puerto Ricans," in Harry L. Miller and Marjorie B. Smiley, op. cit., p. 105.

[17]Sophie L. Elam, "Acculturation and Learning Problems of Puerto Rican Children," in E. T. Keach, R. Fulton, and W. E. Gardner, *Education and Social Crisis,* New York, Wiley, 1967, p. 232.

[18]Arnold B. Cheyney, *Teaching Culturally Disadvantaged in the Elementary School,* Columbus, Ohio, Merrill, 1967, p. 58.

Oral communication is the most important phase of the curriculum for the culturally disadvantaged child; thus he should be encouraged to speak as often as possible. Quiet rooms are not always the best rooms in our schools; it is better for the child to be allowed to use his own dialect than to be discouraged from speaking at all; and the initial content of the language program should be relevant to the child's own experiences.

4. *Teacher education that is oriented to middle-class living.* Teacher education programs in the United States have generally consisted of preparing middle-class students to become teachers of middle-class children. The child whose native language is not English and the child from a lower socioeconomic level are rarely given the consideration they need and deserve. Teacher education programs do offer suggestions for dealing with individual problems of discipline and learning. They do not, however, provide sufficient opportunities for studying the differences between the cultures of minority groups and the culture of the larger society. How can children acquire new habits of speech and behavior without losing their sense of security? How can teachers help parents see that acquiring the basic elements of a new culture does not mean giving up all that is highly valued in the old culture? The insights of anthropologists, social psychologists, and sociologists can be incorporated into teacher education programs that will help teachers find better methods of teaching children who need to learn the ways of the majority society so that they will have a better chance of entering it. In fact, it is essential to give prospective teachers the insights and procedures needed to work with culturally different children.

5. *Reading textbooks and the development of ethnocentric attitudes.* Recent research indicates that the early years of the child's life are the critical ones not only for setting the pattern of academic achievement but also for the development of favorable attitudes toward self and others. The very young child is egocentric; his interests center primarily in himself and peer group membership means little to him. He has not been in school long, however, before he becomes very much interested in his peer group. It is during the years he spends in elementary school that he develops most of his ethnocentric tendencies. What happens to him during these years determines to a large extent whether he will think that only groups composed of those who are most like himself are "good" groups or whether he will realize that those who differ in some respects from the majority are desirable members of his group.

Although reading is by no means the only way to promote favorable attitudes toward minority groups, there is a considerable amount of evidence that it is an important factor in developing an appreciation of wholesome human relations. With these facts in mind, we should consider what children read in school during their early school years.

In cities of 100,000 or more, the school systems use one or more series of basal readers as the principal tool for teaching reading. A comprehensive survey of the systems in cities of that size revealed that 64 percent of their schools relied "predominantly" or "exclusively" on a single basal reader series in Grades 1–3; in 31.4 percent of the schools, multiple series were used. Basal readers were almost as heavily used in the intermediate grades.[19]

What are these readers like? There is disturbing evidence that a number of the most frequently adopted series of basal readers present a one-sided picture of the ethnic groups that compose American society. This aspect of basal readers must, therefore, be considered to contribute a significant difficulty to the acculturation process. Klineberg is one of those who has provided the evidence. He examined fifteen widely used basal readers and reported: (1) They give the impression that the American people are almost exclusively white or Caucasian, primarily North European in origin, and primarily blonds; (2) people with other origins are generally portrayed as peddlers, organ-grinders, or fruit and vegetable vendors; (3) people in the stories and illustrations are generally prosperous, well-dressed, friendly, and smiling. There is little evidence of poverty, and jobs appear to be readily available to everyone.[20]

The school cannot be held responsible for all the prejudices children develop, but some of the responsibility must be assigned to readers that portray certain ethnic groups in an unfavorable light. If the school is to play a major role in the acculturation process, readers that give a more realistic picture of American life must be devised.[21]

SUMMARY

1. Organized fields of knowledge, the nature and trends of society, and human growth and development must all be considered in planning the school program.
2. The changes that occur in the culture are influenced to some extent by geography, resources, climate, and social traditions; they are influenced to a greater extent by education, which is the source of technological progress.
3. The changes that take place in children and youth as they learn to live harmoniously with others are called *social development*; the assistance they get from parents, peer groups, schools, churches, and other educative agencies is called *social education*.
4. The essence of our democratic aspirations is respect for individual differences and the opportunity for every person to achieve self-realization and to find a place in society according to his ability and efforts.

[19]Mary C. Austin and C. Morrison, *The First R: The Harvard Report on Reading in Elementary Schools*, New York, Macmillan, 1963, p. 54.

[20]Otto Klineberg, "Life Is Fun in a Smiling, Fair-Skinned World," in E. T. Keach, R. Fulton and W. E. Gardner, op. cit., p. 269.

[21]A beginning has been made, as a matter of fact. The "Bank Street Readers" and a few other newer materials take a multiethnic approach in both illustrations and story line.

5. Cultural diversity in our society includes masculine and feminine cultures, rural and urban cultures, ethnic groups, and social class differences.

6. Life outside the school provides many opportunities for socialization, but the school is the most important agency because it is possible to structure the school environment for this purpose and because of the numbers involved.

7. There is a need for the development of more precise instruments for measuring the influence of the environment on human development and variability.

8. Factors that influence the social development of children include the quantity and quality of relationships in the home, opportunities for cooperative play, and the social climate of the classroom.

9. The free society puts more responsibility on individuals for decision-making; the schools in a free society must, therefore, accept responsibility for continuing the socialization process that began in the home and the neighborhood.

10. *Socialization* is the process by which the child internalizes the culture into which he was born; *acculturation* refers to the process by which the individual makes a changeover from one culture to another.

11. Difficulties encountered in the process of acculturation arise from mass migrations to the cities, conflicts in the social roles of parents, the language barrier, limitations of teacher education programs, and weaknesses in textbooks used in reading programs.

SELECTED READINGS

Association for Supervision and Curriculum Development, *Perceiving–Behaving–Becoming*, Washington, D.C., The Association, 1962. Chapter 11 emphasizes the importance of the capacity for identification with others and explains how the schools can help children gain a realistic feeling of belonging.

Baller, Warren R., and Don C. Charles, *The Psychology of Human Growth and Development*, New York, Holt, 1961. Chapter 8 explains the sociocultural basis of behavior. Chapters 12 and 13 deal with the influence of peer relationships and family relationships on behavior.

Bloom, Benjamin S., *Stability and Change in Human Characteristics*, New York, Wiley, 1964. Chapter 1 emphasizes the need for more precise measures of the environment. Chapter 4 presents data that document the importance of the early years of the child's life. Chapter 6 deals with the effects of the environment on behavior and growth.

Brookover, Wilbur B., *A Sociology of Education*, New York, American Book, 1955. Chapters 12 and 13 explain the function of the school in the socialization process.

Haan, Aubrey, *Education for the Open Society*, Boston, Allyn & Bacon, 1962. Chapter 1 explains the difference between an open and a closed society and points out that the schools in an open society must deal with more than facts to be learned.

Haas, Glen and Kimball Wiles, *Readings in Curriculum*, Boston, Allyn & Bacon, 1965. Section 1 presents an analysis of the impact of economic, social, and cultural factors on children.

Karier, Clarence J., *Man, Society, and Education*, Glenview, Ill., Scott, Foresman, 1967. Chapter 9 explains the philosophical foundations of the "child-

centered" and the "society-centered" schools along with an explanation of
the contributions of many prominent educators to each point of view.

Keach, E. T., R. Fulton, and W. E. Gardner, *Education and Social Crisis: Perspectives on Teaching Disadvantaged Youth*, New York, Wiley, 1967. An
excellent collection of forty-nine articles dealing with the social world of
the slum child, acculturation, value conflicts, language of lower-class children, and many other problems.

Lane, Howard, and Mary Beauchamp, *Human Relations in Teaching*, Englewood Cliffs, N.J., Prentice-Hall, 1955. Chapters 2 and 3 explain how children become fully human through association with others.

Miller, Harry L., and Marjorie B. Smiley, *Education in the Metropolis*, New
York, The Free Press, 1967. An excellent collection of readings dealing with
the conditions under which slum children grow up and suggesting teaching
strategy to be used with slum children.

Otto, Henry J., *Social Education in Elementary Schools*, New York, Holt, 1956.
Chapter 1 presents a picture of the social characteristics of children at different ages.

Prescott, Daniel A., *The Child in the Educative Process*, New York, McGraw-
Hill, 1957. Chapter 10 explains how the culture is internalized by the child
and how cultural diversity complicates the socialization process.

Ragan, William B., *Modern Elementary Curriculum* (3rd ed.), New York, Holt,
1966. Chapter 6 provides examples of "child-centered" and "social functions" types of curriculum organizations. Chapter 2 presents research findings relating to stages in concept formation and Chapter 15 explains and
illustrates the use of sociograms for evaluating the extent to which a child
has gained acceptance by his peer group.

Stanley, W. O., B. O. Smith, K. D. Benne, and A. W. Anderson, *Social Foundations of Education*, New York, Holt, 1956. Chapters 4–7 deal with the impact
of social classes and ethnic groups on the school.

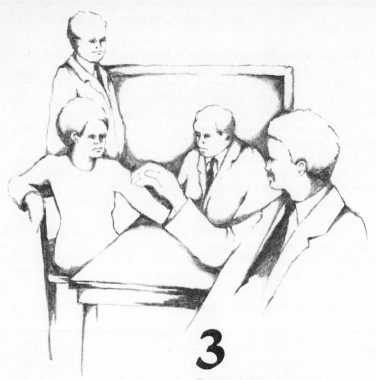

3

Social Forces
Affecting Teaching

In some parts of an urban community, the teacher image is a constructive one; he is seen by the adult community as a man of education, of helpful intent, of a somewhat better status than others. In other parts of the same community, he may be seen as being essentially in a serving role. . . . The serving status of the teacher is felt by children, and makes the teacher less usable as a figure of identification.*

Other chapters in this book deal with the impact of rapid changes in the culture on the program of the school and with the processes of socialization and acculturation through which children and youth learn to achieve self-realization through participation in ever enlarging groups of people. This chapter is focused on the influence of social and cultural forces on the teaching-learning process—on the effect of social and cultural forces on the teacher who must balance these forces, on the one hand, against the professional tasks to be performed, on the other.

There is increasing agreement that teaching is a task for professionals. A professional person is one whose preparation has been so extensive and so rigorous that he has knowledge and

*Aubrey Haan, *Education for the Open Society*, Boston, Allyn & Bacon, 1962, p. 180.

skills not possessed by others; a person whose work is so technical and important that society requires him to have legal authorization; and a person whose behavior is controlled by a code of ethics determined by members of his profession.

EFFORTS TO IMPROVE TEACHING

There is increasing recognition that the work of the teacher is intimately related to the release of human potentials and a better future for all. Current efforts to improve the quality of teaching in our schools have emerged from this better understanding of the important tasks performed by teachers. These tasks are exacting; indeed, they require high-level competence comparable to that of the surgeon or the engineer. Some of the more important of them are: (1) engendering interest in the world of ideas; (2) developing problem-solving abilities; (3) maintaining discipline; (4) creating an intellectually stimulating classroom atmosphere; (5) keeping several different groups working productively in the classroom; (6) recognizing and making provision for individual differences; and (7) using evaluation procedures that measure more than mere recall of information.

Recent Emphasis on Improving Instruction

The history of American education is replete with examples of efforts to improve instruction. The period since 1960 has been particularly fruitful in the development of new approaches. Thus the student who wants to understand the meaning of the "revolution in instruction" must examine many publications, including articles in educational journals that each deal with a single phase of teaching and books like the *Handbook of Research on Teaching*, which contains thirty-one articles relating to the problem.[1]

Efforts to develop a theory of instruction. There has been an interesting trend during the last two decades toward developing theories in educational administration, curriculum, and instruction. The development of a theory of instruction can be taken to mean the development of a set of principles that seem to predict or account for events much more accurately than mere chance; it implies that instead of following hit-or-miss methods, the teacher can operate in accordance with carefully developed procedures. Bruner has stated that a valid theory of instruction must be concerned with the factors that predispose a child to learn effectively, the optimal structuring of knowledge, the optimal sequence required for learning, and the nature and pacing of rewards and punishments. "You take the child where you find him and give

[1]N. L. Gage (ed.), *Handbook of Research on Teaching*, Chicago, Rand McNally, 1963.

him the structure that is economical, productive and powerful for him and that allows him to grow."[2]

Efforts to define the professional role of the teacher.   The term "role" can be taken to mean the set of expectations applied to a person who occupies a particular position in a social system or in an organization. Techniques of role analysis have been developed by social psychologists; they are proving to be useful in the effort to improve instruction in classrooms. It is becoming apparent that the teacher cannot be expected to achieve maximum proficiency in the performance of his truly professional tasks—the ones that cannot be done by others— unless there is a more precise definition of these tasks than has generally existed in the past. The advantages of role analysis have been stated as follows:

The concept of role provides a natural basis upon which to view teaching behavior. It is task-oriented; it is function-oriented. It is behavior-oriented not in a general sense but in terms of the job to be done. It is concerned with behavior relevant to the effects desired. Thus it is a useful tool in the hands of teachers and students of teaching.[3]

The need for giving more attention to role analysis and role expectations is evident when we examine teacher education programs, the role expectations of some school systems, and procedures for evaluating teacher effectiveness. As a matter of fact, the development of teacher education programs in terms of the actual professional tasks teachers are expected to perform in school systems has been called "An Unstudied Problem in Education."[4] (Surveys of teacher education programs have revealed, for example, that preparation for working with culturally disadvantaged youngsters is a neglected area in teacher education. Another problem that needs study is the time that must be spent on nonteaching chores, estimated to be 26 percent of the teacher's working day in many school systems. Policing playgrounds and hallways, supervising lunchrooms, collecting money for a variety of purposes, and making out complicated attendance reports take valuable time from the professional tasks for which the teacher was employed and which he alone can perform.)

Until recently, efforts to evaluate teacher effectiveness were based on the "traits" theory; it was assumed that all effective teachers possessed certain traits in common. As late as 1961, an extensive study of the measurement and prediction of teacher effectiveness listed fifteen traits as essential to successful teaching: buoyancy, considerateness, cooperativeness, dependability, emotional stability, ethicalness, expressiveness, flexibility, forcefulness, judgment, mental alertness,

[2]Jerome S. Bruner, "Needed: A Theory of Instruction," *Educational Leadership*, May, 1963, 523–527.

[3]Gale W. Rose, "Performance Evaluation and Growth in Teaching," *Phi Delta Kappan*, October, 1963, 51.

[4]Seymour B. Sarason, et al., *The Preparation of Teachers: An Unstudied Problem in Education*, New York, Wiley, 1962.

objectivity, personal magnetism, physical energy and drive, and scholar-liness.[5] Aside from the difficulty of obtaining objective evidence of the presence or absence of these traits, it is evident that they are desirable attributes for any person in *any* type of occupation; they are not traits unique to successful teachers.

More recent efforts to evaluate teacher effectiveness have emphasized the identification of the professional roles of teachers and the effective performance of these roles—performance evaluation instead of traits evaluation. Efforts are also being made to determine the effects certain styles or patterns of teaching have on pupil performance. The ultimate criterion of teacher effectiveness is, of course, the effect that the teacher has on the behavior of pupils. It is no longer accepted that this effect cannot be evaluated until the pupils have lived their entire lives.

THE SOCIAL CONTEXT
OF TEACHING

Effective teaching, then, presents challenges that are difficult and technical enough even when they are viewed only in terms of current information about the kinds of classroom behavior that produce desired changes in the behavior of students. But teaching does not take place in a neat classroom vacuum; it is always influenced by the social rela-tionships in which the teachers are involved. (It is also influenced, of course, by the social relationships in which the pupils are involved; they are considered elsewhere in this book.)

Changes in the culture have been so rapid in recent decades that it has become difficult for teachers to understand the full implications of the social context in which their work is embedded. This chapter analyzes four of the most important social relationships in which teachers participate and which affect their work: (1) their relationship to American society, (2) their relationship to the teaching profession, (3) their relationship to the community in which they work, and (4) their relationship to the local school system.

The Teacher in American Society

Teaching is inevitably influenced by time, place, and circumstances. Teaching in the second half of the twentieth century, in the United States of America, in an interdependent, urban society differs in im-portant ways from teaching at different times, in different cultures, under different circumstances. The thesis that teaching is expected to help shape the future of American life is presented elsewhere in this book; this chapter is concerned with the ways in which American society in turn shapes the teaching-learning process.

[5] A. S. Barr, et al., *Wisconsin Studies of the Measurement and Prediction of Teacher Effectiveness*, Madison, Dembar Publications, 1961.

AMERICAN SOCIETY

Realities

Dynamic
Interdependent
Urban
Industrialized
Affluent
Unsolved problems

Ideals

Basic values
Divergent value systems
Changing values

THE TEACHING PROFESSION

Magnitude — Organizations — Prestige — Income

LOCAL STRUCTURE OF THE SCHOOL

The Community
⇩
The Board of Education
⇩
The Superintendent
⇩
The Principal
⇩
Teachers
⇩
Pupils

Figure 1. The Social Context of Teaching.

Social realities affecting teachers. The most potent social reality affecting the work of the teacher is the fact that we live in a dynamic rather than a static society. The role of the teacher in our society used to be defined in terms of the teacher's responsibility for transmitting the culture as a social heritage from the past. Today, however, the impact on individuals of new forces in the culture is so dramatic that education for social change is a necessity. Helping students make satisfactory adjustments to a dynamic society is much more difficult than helping them make adjustments to a relatively static society.

The major social realities of contemporary American society are discussed in detail elsewhere in this text. Thus only a brief statement of their effect on the work of the teacher is necessary now. The threat of a world war, the armaments race, the plight of the underdeveloped nations, the population explosion, and the intense desire for a peaceful world mean that today's teachers must educate for international understanding. The prejudices that exist and the discriminations that are practiced against minority groups in our society produce disunity and friction at home and distrust of the sincerity of our professed beliefs abroad. These stern realities in our culture mean that intercultural education is a responsibility that must be met by teachers. The rapidly increasing rural-urban migration of recent decades has confronted American cities with problems of education—to say nothing of problems involving housing, jobs, sanitation, and safety—that they were not prepared to handle. Providing the kind of learning situations from which children who live in the city slums can profit is another obligation placed on teachers by the realities of the society in which we live.

Value systems affecting the work of the teacher.   As we have said, it is possible to identify certain ideals to which a vast majority of Americans subscribe and it is possible to develop teaching procedures that harmonize with these basic ideals. These ideals for the most part cut across the various subcultures in our society. Nevertheless, in attempting to implement them, we must take into account our diverse value systems, for example, lower class, middle class, upper class; native American and immigrant; traditional and emergent. This diversity is, of course, one of the sources of the strength of our nation. As a noted historian has put it:

Freedom implies humility, not absolutism; it implies not the tyranny of the one but the tolerance of the many. Against the monolithic world, free men affirm the pluralistic world. Against the world of coercion, let us affirm the world of choice.[6]

Diverse value systems also, however, present problems for the teacher. Here is a specific example, the case of an intelligent but unruly Korean-American boy:

Unaware of the veneration accorded by Koreans to the head of the household, school representatives tried persistently to reach the mother. Finally, when the father was approached in the manner to which he was accustomed, he cooperated with the school in controlling the child.[7]

The vast majority of American teachers are imbued with middle-class values: politeness, respect for the property of others, industry, sportsmanship, and ambition. But lower-class children have a different set of values; the result is that they feel alienated from the school, and many intellectually capable ones drop out. This represents a tremendous waste of human talent that is needed in our society. The teacher, therefore, is challenged to acquire a better understanding of the values of lower-class children and to help culturally disadvantaged children win acceptance in the social system of the classroom and make academic gains in line with their mental capacities.

There is another dichotomy of cultural values with which the teacher must deal: traditional versus emergent values. As our society has moved from an economy of scarcity to an economy of abundance and from an agrarian society to an industrialized society, some traditional values growing out of the Puritan ethic have changed or at least been reinterpreted. For example,

[6]Arthur Schlesinger, Jr., "The One Against the Many," *Saturday Review*, July 14, 1962, 55.

[7]E. T. Keach, Jr., et al. (eds.), *Education and Social Crisis*, New York, Wiley, 1967, p. 17.

In order to provide for its own growth, business must constantly persuade people to consume ever larger quantities of nonessentials. As a result, abstinence is retreating before consumption, thrift before installment buying. . . . Self-reliance is giving way to group-mindedness.[8]

There seems to be some evidence that educators tend to be less traditional in their value systems than the general public: Teachers are generally less traditional than administrators, but administrators are generally less traditional than school board members, who lean strongly toward traditional values. These value conflicts affect teachers when they engage in curriculum development; when they decide what instructional methods to use; when they participate in the selection of textbooks and teaching aids; and when they decide how much emphasis, relatively, to place on group enterprises and individual efforts.

What the teacher can do about cultural values. The teacher cannot be completely neutral about the basic values of democracy as opposed to those of authoritarianism. He lives by and fosters democratic values —respect for individual personality, cooperation toward the common welfare, faith in the method of intelligence. He does not attempt to compel pupils to accept his own opinions on authority; he rejects all efforts to create mental strait jackets; and he does not try to impose any "party line," either right or left, on his pupils.

The teacher consciously tries to synthesize the best elements from conflicting value systems so that he can reach more children in more ways. His job is to stimulate young and growing minds—to prod them to think and to formulate and live by their own value systems. His responsibility is to guide pupils in the use of the method of intelligence so that their values will not be determined by pressure groups or by the fluency in expression of those around them. Young people are entitled to build their own beliefs on the basis of facts, theories, and experiences. Teachers must help young people to locate, use, and evaluate information about contemporary problems and to form judgments about them; they must not compel any particular judgments.

The Teacher as a Member of a Profession
The teacher is a part of an enterprise of tremendous magnitude. During the school year 1968–1969, more than 60,400,000 Americans were engaged as full-time students, teachers, or administrators in the nation's public and private schools at all levels; another 136,000 were serving as school board members or college or university trustees. This constituted about 30 percent of the population of the United States. When we add to these groups those who are engaged in the production and distribution of textbooks and other supplies and equipment, in school building and school transportation enterprises, and in other school-

[8]Ibid., p. 12.

related occupations, the nation's educational enterprise involves perhaps 40 percent of the people.

Professional organizations.   Countless people have labored for many years to develop professional educational organizations. These organizations have been responsible for much that has been accomplished in improving both the general performance of teachers and the conditions under which they work. The organizations provide services that include: (1) disseminating information throughout the profession, (2) conducting and promoting research, (3) sponsoring improvements in teacher education, (4) seeking adequate salaries and reasonable teaching loads, (5) defending the basic freedoms of teachers, (6) informing the public about the achievements and needs of the schools, (7) influencing public policy relating to education, and (8) developing a code of ethics for the teaching profession.

The National Education Association (NEA) had its beginnings in 1857 in Philadelphia, when the National Teachers Association was established. The National Education Association of the United States was chartered by an act of Congress in 1906; the present name was adopted in 1907. It has more than a million members and 59 state and territory and 8,264 locally affiliated associations. The organization has 33 departments, representing almost every professional group interested in education. The annual membership fee of $10 (life membership is $225) includes a subscription to the *National Education Association Journal.* The NEA sponsors Future Teachers of America for high school students interested in teaching as a career and Student NEA for college students preparing to teach.

The American Federation of Teachers was founded in 1916; it now has more than 135,000 members in more than 460 local organizations. It has experienced appreciable increases in membership in recent years, especially in the large cities. It vigorously promotes integration within the schools, supports equality of educational opportunities, and opposes merit-rating salary plans. Although it is affiliated with AFL-CIO, it is a legal entity in its own right. Unlike the NEA, the membership of the AFT is restricted to classroom teachers.

The occupational prestige of teaching.   Teacher morale is generally recognized as an important factor in effective teaching. When morale is high, the teacher works with enthusiasm, obtains satisfaction from his job, and achieves satisfactory results; when morale is low, teaching becomes drudgery, the teacher receives little satisfaction from his job, and his achievement is far below his potential. Even though the teacher is convinced, as he should be, that the long-term effects of his work are vital, he may become discouraged if he sees no tangible evidence that his work is so regarded by others. Capable young men and women are reluctant to enter a profession that ranks low in social prestige and financial rewards when compared with other professions. The importance of occupational status has been described as follows:

The influence of occupational status on the practitioners is both pervasive and fundamental. It affects who will enter the occupation and what specializations within it they will seek. It affects the quantity and quality of the work that is done, the job satisfactions of the practitioners, and the dress, manners, outlook, and moral ideas of the practitioners.[9]

Much has been written about *teacher stereotypes*. Charters presented the most extreme model of such a stereotype under the title, "The Teacher in the Sacred Community."[10] He pointed out that educational sociologists writing during the 1930s had in mind a special type of community—a small town or village relatively untouched by industrialization, where the cultural values were homogeneous or dominated by a single controlling group. The teacher was pictured as the victim of strict controls imposed by the community. The only status he had in the community was his occupational status; contractual provisions precluded courtship or marriage, at least by female teachers. The male teacher was highly visible in the small town, but always as "the teacher"; the only escape he had from this identity was to leave town, and this was prohibited except during summer vacations.

There are, perhaps, a few small towns and villages in which teachers are still subjected to strict controls, but considering that two-thirds of them now work in metropolitan areas and that most of them—both men and women—are or have been married, the picture is far from an accurate portrayal of the position of the teacher in American society today. Unfortunately, the idea that entering the teaching profession means being subjected to petty regulations and the scrutiny of prying eyes still persists.

There is some evidence that the occupational prestige of teachers has been increasing. For instance, the Gallup organization made identical nationwide surveys in 1953 and 1962. A representative sample of adults was asked to rank a number of major occupations in terms of the one they would recommend first to a young man. The results relating to nine of these occupations revealed some interesting trends.[11]

	1953	1962
1. Doctor	29%	23%
2. Engineer-builder	20	18
3. Professor-teacher	5	12
4. Clergyman	7	8
5. Government career	3	7
6. Lawyer	6	6
7. Business executive	7	5
8. Dentist	6	4
9. Banker	2	2

[9]Myron Lieberman, *Education as a Profession*, Englewood Cliffs, N.J., Prentice-Hall, 1956, p. 455.

[10]W. W. Charters, Jr., "The Social Background of Teaching," in N. L. Gage, op. cit., pp. 764–765.

[11]Robert W. Richey, *Planning for Teaching* (3rd ed.), New York, McGraw-Hill, 1963, p. 19. Used by permission of the publisher.

Six of the occupations received a higher percentage of the responses than the "professor-teacher" category in 1953, but only two received a higher percentage in 1962. Also, the "professor-teacher" category increased from 5 percent of the responses in 1953 to 12 percent in 1962.

Teachers' salaries. It has been difficult to convince our people that teaching is one of the major professions; that it requires rigorous preparation, technical skills, and professional competence comparable to the requirements for a successful practitioner in any of the major professions; and that teachers need higher salaries if our schools are to compete successfully with other occupations for the services of capable young men and women. Although teachers' salaries have been increasing, beginning salaries are still far below those of other occupations that require four years of college preparation.

Teachers' salaries did increase during the 1960s. The average annual salary of classroom teachers in 1958–1959 was $4,797; the figure for 1968–1969 was $7,908. However, the percentage of the Gross National Product (GNP) that was spent for teachers' salaries did *not* increase significantly during the 1960s. The amount spent for this purpose in 1960–1961 was $8.2 billion—about 1.6 percent of the GNP. The NEA estimated at that time that it would take 3.8 percent of the GNP to

Table 1
Average Starting Salaries: Teachers vs. Private Industry

	1965–1966	1968–1969
Beginning men and women teachers with bachelor's degree (school systems with enrollments of 6,000 or more)	$4,925	$5,941
Men with bachelor's degree		
Engineering	$7,984	$9,312
Physics	7,164	8,916
Chemistry	7,032	8,520
Accounting	6,732	8,424
Mathematics-statistics	6,672	8,412
Economics-finance	6,600	7,800
Sales-marketing	6,276	7,620
Business administration	6,240	7,560
Women with bachelor's degree		
Engineering-technical research	$7,260	$9,672
Chemistry	7,056	8,532
Mathematics-statistics	6,324	8,484
Accounting	6,768	8,304
Economics-finance	6,000	7,224
General business	5,520	7,104
Home economics	5,664	7,056
Secretary	4,620	5,820

Source: Research Bulletin, National Education Association, March, 1969, pp. 17, 22.

provide reasonable class size and adequate salaries for teachers. Nevertheless, by the school year 1968–1969, although we then spent a little over $15 billion for teachers' salaries, this was still only 1.8 percent of the GNP.[12]

The Teacher as a Member of the Community

Teachers are generally active participants in the life of the community. Nationwide surveys have indicated that about 90 percent of them are church members, compared with about 60 percent of the total population, and that 9 out of every 10 of them voted in the last presidential election.

It is generally recognized that classroom teachers are the most effective public relations agents connected with the school system. But, aside from the public relations service, there are many personal and professional rewards that come to teachers who understand the communities in which they work and participate in community activities. Contacts with the great variety of personalities found in the local community enrich the life of the teacher, and participation in the on-going activities of the community provides a means of self-realization. Most important of all, however, is the professional advantage that comes from understanding the community forces affecting the development, achievement, and behavior of pupils in school.

From the standpoint of community expectations, however, the "serving" status of the teacher has been overemphasized. The frequently reiterated theme that teaching is a public service, paid for at public expense, can become the rationale for loading teachers down with so many community responsibilities that little time and energy are left for the truly professional tasks that have been identified in the first part of this chapter. Furthermore (see the quotation at the beginning of this chapter), when pupils feel that the teacher is in a "serving" status, he is less useful as a person with whom they want to identify.

Yauch, Bartels, and Morris, writing for the beginning teacher, suggest that a new teacher guard against the expectation that his services to the community also include guiding children in Sunday School classes, Boy or Girl Scout groups, and community playgrounds.

After spending an exhausting week of intensive devotion to children, it is only reasonable to propose that teachers be permitted to vary their efforts in out-of-school hours. If they are to maintain a desirable, balanced outlook on life, part of their time should be spent in activities unrelated to teaching. It is strongly urged that you seek to make your contribution to community living in adult activities.[13]

---

[12]Based on the latest available issues of the *Research Report* and the *Research Bulletin* of the National Education Association. The student should consult the latest issues of these bulletins for information about recent trends in teachers' salaries.

[13]Wilbur A. Yauch, et al., *The Beginning Teacher*, New York, Holt, 1955, p. 247.

The Teacher and the Local School System

President Garfield, describing a "true teacher," said, "Give me a log hut, with only a simple bench, Mark Hopkins on one end and I on the other, and you may have all the buildings, apparatus and libraries without him." Garfield meant, of course, that excellent teachers are all that is needed for a good education. This point of view, appealing as it is and partially true as it also is, nevertheless overlooks the importance of instructional materials, school organization, and educational leadership, especially in our complex modern society.

Of all the social forces affecting the teaching-learning process, the quality of human relations existing in the school system is by far the most important. Teaching, particularly in an urban school system, is carried on in a veritable sea of human relationships. In addition to the pupils, other teachers, administrators, supervisors, librarians, and custodians with whom teachers have been accustomed to working in the past, many new branches have grown on the educational tree in recent years. Some of these are school psychologists, counselors, school social workers, speech and hearing therapists, directors of research, public relations specialists, teacher aides, systems analysts, and still others. The effectiveness of the services of the new auxiliary personnel depends on how well teachers understand their functions and make use of their services in improving the teaching-learning process.

Organization and administration. Education in the United States is a responsibility of the various state governments. The states, however, generally delegate much of their authority over schools to local school districts. The people in the school districts in most states elect members of a board of education to employ personnel, establish policies, and keep the public informed about the school program. The quality of instruction in classrooms, the morale of the teaching staff, and the progress that the school system is able to make in keeping its program in line with current demands on the schools depend to a large extent on the types of persons who serve as members of boards of education and particularly on how well they understand the functions of a board of education.

State and national associations of school board members have provided useful services during the last decade or more, particularly in developing manuals or guides for policies and procedures. There is little objective evidence, however, on how well boards of education throughout the country actually perform their functions. One study, confined to the schools of Massachusetts, provides some grounds for believing that most of them do a good job. Of the superintendents contacted, 49 percent thought their boards of education were doing an "excellent" job and 33 percent thought that they were doing a "good" job.[14]

The regulations established by state and local boards of education leave a great deal of freedom for the superintendent of schools, the

[14]Neal Gross, *Who Runs Our Schools?* New York, Wiley, 1958, pp. 90–91.

central office staff, and building principals to initiate innovations in organization and instruction. The work of the teacher is, therefore, affected to a great extent by the quality of leadership provided by the administrative and supervisory staff of the school system.

Teacher militancy and negotiations.   Evidence of increasing teacher militancy in recent years has been seen in three principal activities: strikes, sanctions, and negotiations. A jurisdictional dispute closed the San Francisco schools for one day; the teachers in New Mexico staged a one-week strike; 25,000 Florida teachers left their classrooms for three weeks; and 55,000 teachers in New York City taught only 11 days between the opening of school in September and late in November. Many other school systems, particularly in the large cities, have seen their teachers go out on strikes. Many state educational associations have invoked sanctions, notifying colleges and universities nationwide that unsatisfactory educational conditions existed in that state and that students in their institutions should be discouraged from seeking positions in the state.

Teachers, particularly in the large cities, have banded together and sent representatives to negotiate with the boards of education concerning salaries and working conditions. This labor-management type of arrangement bypasses the superintendent in his traditional role as a representative of the teachers in dealing with the board and thus requires many adjustments; some undoubtedly will cause further controversy.

Increasing teacher militancy cannot be attributed to any single cause. Teachers in many states have become concerned when they learned that salaries are lower in their states than they are in other states, causing an exodus of competent young teachers. Yet, 9 of the 10 states that were lowest in average salaries had no strikes. When teachers in one large school system were asked to list needed improvements, "better salaries" was far down in eleventh place, with only 5.8 percent of the teachers listing it. Smaller classes (45.1 percent), more planning time (35.1 percent), relief from nonteaching chores (24.3 percent), and other items far outranked better salaries.

The presence of more men teachers on school faculties, the desire to have more to say about school policies, greater recognition in educational associations, and time to teach seem to be important factors causing unrest among teachers. Strikes and sanctions have usually brought about slight improvements, but it is generally agreed that militant teachers must find better ways of getting their message across to the voting public before greater gains can be made.

SUMMARY
1. The teacher must intervene between the social and cultural forces in the environment and the professional tasks that must be performed.

2. The truly professional tasks that teachers must perform include: engendering interest in the world of ideas, creating an intellectually stimulating classroom atmosphere, making discipline educative, providing for individual differences, keeping several different groups working productively in the classroom, and using evaluation procedures that measure more than mere recall of information.

3. Significant facets of the revolution in instruction include: efforts to develop a theory of instruction, efforts to define the professional role of the teacher, and efforts to evaluate teacher effectiveness in terms of performance.

4. Changes in the culture have been so rapid in recent decades that it has been difficult for teachers to understand the full implications of the social context in which their work is embedded.

5. Four of the most important social relationships in which teachers participate and which affect their work are: their relationship to American society, their relationship to the teaching profession, their relationship to the community in which they work, and their relationship to the local school system.

SELECTED READINGS

Barr, A. S., et al., *Wisconsin Studies of the Measurement and Prediction of Teacher Effectiveness*, Madison, Wis., Dembar Publications, 1961. Explores ways and means of evaluating teacher effectiveness; includes a list of personal qualities needed by teachers.

Bruner, Jerome S., "Needed: A Theory of Instruction," *Educational Leadership*, May, 1963, pp. 523–532. Explains the essential elements in a theory of instruction.

Gage, N. L. (ed.), *Handbook of Research on Teaching*, Skokie, Ill., Rand McNally, 1963. The section by W. W. Charters, Jr., "The Social Background of Teaching," is particularly useful.

Gross, Neal, *Who Runs Our Schools?* New York, Wiley, 1958. Reports the results of an evaluation of school board members in Massachusetts.

Haan, Aubrey, *Education for the Open Society*, Boston, Allyn & Bacon, 1962. Explains the differences among communities in relation to prestige accorded teachers.

Keach, E. T., Jr., R. Fulton, and W. E. Gardner, *Education and Social Crisis*, New York, Wiley, 1967. Gives examples of problems arising from divergent sets of values.

Lieberman, Myron, *Education as A Profession*, Englewood Cliffs, N.J., Prentice-Hall, 1956. Explains the influence of occupational status on practitioners in education.

Richel, Robert W., *Planning for Teaching: An Introduction to Education* (3rd ed.), New York, McGraw-Hill, 1963. Provides useful information about national educational organizations.

Yauch, W. A., M. H. Bartels, and E. Morris, *The Beginning Teacher*, New York, Holt, 1955. Advises beginning teachers to make their contributions to community living by engaging in adult activities rather than work with children.

Part II
FORCES AFFECTING AMERICAN EDUCATION

The Changing American School

Contrasting Views of the Purpose of Education

Newer Insights into Human Behavior

Socioeconomic Forces Affecting Education

Chapter 4 documents the thesis that schools generally reflect the needs and aspirations of the people whom they serve at a given time. Chapter 5 reviews four current proposals relating to the central purpose of education in American society. Chapter 6 explains how human behavior develops in the social context. Chapter 7 identifies some socioeconomic forces that influence education in the United States.

4

The Changing American School

*The story of the American public school is a story of dreams and ideas, of battles and struggles, of setbacks and losses, but of achievements and victories as well. Horace Mann viewed the common school as the greatest discovery that man has ever made.**

This chapter is not intended as a substitute for a systematic course in the history of American education. It is designed merely to document the thesis that schools have generally tended to reflect the needs, circumstances, and aspirations of the people during various periods of history.

A brief summary of the forces that have influenced the development of American schools does not imply that history repeats itself. The circumstances that demand changes in school programs today are not comparable to those that brought about educational innovations in earlier years. (For instance, the modern elementary school building providing one instructional area for several hundred pupils is a far cry from the one-room school of the

*Ellis F. Hartford, *Education in These United States*, New York, Macmillan, 1964, p. 80.

past.) Although traces of the ideas of Pestalozzi, Francis W. Parker, John Dewey, and other educational reformers can be found in modern schools, these ideas have been modified by more recent research and experimentation.

A study of the forces that have brought about changes in the American school over the years will, however, help the student to understand the reasons why a changing society calls for continuous educational reforms, the relationship of the school to the society, and the changing responsibilities of the school as a social institution that result. It will also give the prospective teacher an appreciation of the fact that the American school of today is a product of more than 300 years of effort by intelligent, courageous Americans.

EDUCATION IN
THE AMERICAN COLONIES

The "Old Deluder Satan" Act, passed by the General Court (legislature) of the Massachusetts Bay Colony in 1647, was the first legislation in America requiring the establishment of schools. This law was designed to make the education of the young a public rather than a private enterprise. As a matter of fact, the same legislative body had already taken an important step, five years earlier, when it had established the new principle that the education of children is a proper subject for legal control. (The 1642 act empowered local officers to find out whether parents and schoolmasters were teaching the children to read and to levy fines on those who failed to report to them.) The idea of *public*, organized education, however, was something new in American thinking about education. More than 200 years passed, moreover, before the idea had been effectively implemented by the establishment of public school systems in all the states.

The idea that local governments should be responsible for providing schools was not entirely original when our Puritan forefathers enunciated it. Like many American ideas and practices in the field of education, it had its origin in Europe. Martin Luther, in his famous document addressed to the mayors and aldermen of German cities, had urged in 1524 that the task of educating the young should immediately be taken hold of by the city officials lest they ". . . be obliged to feel in vain the pangs of remorse forever."[1] It seems likely that the Puritans in the Massachusetts Bay Colony were familiar with Luther's ideas.

The Religious Motive

The "Old Deluder Satan" Act required each town with 50 or more families to provide a teacher to instruct in reading and writing and each town with 100 or more families to establish a grammar school; the

[1]John Dale Russell and Charles H. Judd, *The American Educational System*, Boston, Houghton Mifflin, 1940, pp. 19–21.

religious motive for education that prevailed in New England and the middle colonies is clearly revealed in this act, the preamble to which began with the main reason for requiring towns to establish schools: "It being one chief project of the old deluder Satan to keep men from the knowledge of the Scriptures. . . ."

Discipline.   The discipline in colonial schools was in harmony with the Puritan theology that children were conceived in iniquity and born in sin; that they were possessed by the Devil and that only by the most severe beating could the Devil be persuaded to depart from them. Thus, it was a moral obligation of parents and teachers to "beat the Devil out of children." The whipping post was a familiar item of furniture in colonial classrooms and anyone passing a school house could hear constant wails of anguish from children. Indeed, college students were not exempt from brutal discipline:

Thomas Sargent, a Harvard student, convicted in 1674 of speaking blasphemous words, was publicly beaten in the library before all the scholars; but the solemn punishment was preceded and followed by prayer by the president, under whose supervision it was inflicted.[2]

Yet, we are told that children were often as rebellious in those days as they are now; there were "sit-down strikes" and "lock-outs" of teachers.

Discipline in colonial schools can be understood only when one considers the climate of opinion of the time. Government was regarded as ruling over rather than as serving people; there was no confidence in the ability of common people to participate in government; the rights of the individual depended on the class into which he was born. Harsh and cruel punishments were inflicted on adults and children alike in the world outside the school. There was no concern for the need of children for play; they were to become virtuous by performing unpleasant tasks; and fear was the only method known for maintaining order in school. Unmindful of the changes in the climate of public opinion that have taken place since colonial days, some people today express the opinion that all the problems relating to rebellious youth would suddenly disappear if parents would just use this harsh type of discipline with their children. Fortunately, numerous competent authorities in the field of child development have evolved more humane and more effective methods of dealing with children.

Textbooks and teachers.   *The New England Primer*, which was the most used book in colonial schools for more than a hundred years, was a religious book in the strict, narrow sense of Calvinistic theology. It contained a list of the books in the Old and the New Testaments, the Lord's Prayer, the Apostles' Creed, the Ten Commandments, and the Shorter Catechism. Pupils started reading by learning the alphabet by means of rhymes beginning with "In Adam's fall we sinned all" and

[2]Edgar W. Knight, *Education in the United States* (rev. ed.), Boston, Ginn, 1951, p. 127.

ending with "Zacheas he did climb a tree his Lord to see." The principal qualifications required of the colonial teacher were that he be sound in the doctrines of the church and that he be a good disciplinarian. The teacher generally "boarded around" in the homes of his pupils; frequently he was paid in Indian corn, rye, barley, or tobacco. He led the singing at church, read the sermon in the absence of the minister, dug the graves, and did odd jobs in the community to supplement his income.

The New England colonies (with the exception of Rhode Island) adopted the Massachusetts type of school. The population of the middle colonies, on the other hand, was made up of people of many different religious denominations; there was little chance to establish a church-state system like that in Massachusetts. Each church provided its own educational program; whatever education was available to people as a whole was limited, narrow, and inadequate. Legislatures in these colonies showed little interest in education. Some schools were established in the southern colonies by grants from interested individuals, but generally the plantation-owners and government officials feared that education would bring disobedience and heresy to indentured servants and slaves. Governor Berkeley wrote in 1671 that he thanked God that there were no free schools in Virginia and hoped there would be none for a hundred years.

Changing Circumstances in Colonial America
According to one authority, "The passage of the Massachusetts act of 1647 was followed by a period of educational decline in that colony."[3] The reasons for this decline are not difficult to understand when one examines the changing circumstances of colonial life. When towns established schools in Massachusetts, the people lived in compact villages; when the danger of attack by the Indians was diminished as a consequence of King Philip's War, the colonists spread out and set up more schools. The first town schools in Massachusetts were under the strict domination of the Calvinists; when other Protestant groups began to establish places of worship, they founded their own sectarian schools. Thus the educational program was weakened by a multiplicity of competing schools. Sectarian schools became obstacles to the establishment of free, public, secular programs of education and remained so for more than 200 years.

The rise of the school district system also weakened education during colonial times and for many years to follow. By the middle of the eighteenth century, the practice of dividing townships into school districts had become common throughout New England. The people who lived in outlying parts of townships demanded that the control of the schools be left in their hands; the small school districts were not able

[3]Ibid., p. 108.

to maintain good schools; and local disputes arose over the selection of school committeemen, teachers, and school sites. The school district system was to spread throughout the United States; indeed, it remains an obstacle to educational progress in rural areas even today.

THE PUBLIC
SCHOOL REVIVAL

The desire of many early national leaders to establish public school systems in all the states met with opposition from religious sects, private schools, and taxpayers. The public school revival succeeded, during the middle years of the nineteenth century, in overcoming these obstacles. Actually a series of movements, the revival involved persuading voters to cast their ballots for increased school appropriations, establishing state departments of education, providing programs of teacher education, and expanding and enriching the curriculum. It represented an awakening of the American conscience concerning the importance of educating children and youth, and its contribution to the strength of the nation in the years that have followed can hardly be overestimated.[4]

Credit for the success of the public school revival cannot be assigned to any one section of the country. Massachusetts, as we have noted, was first to establish many important agencies for public education. Developments on the frontier also were influential. When new states were formed in the territory west of the Appalachians, property qualifications for voting and holding offices were omitted from state constitutions; the number of offices to be filled by popular elections was increased; and the basis for representation in state legislatures was changed from wealth to population. These reforms represented increasing confidence in the ability of people to participate in government. When the right to vote was extended, the agitation for free public schools increased.

The ideas of Pestalozzi; the example of the systems of public education in Prussia and other German states; and the infant school, the Sunday School, and the monitorial system imported from England were important factors in the success of the public school revival. Perhaps the most important factor in its success was the prodigious labor of intelligent leaders in the various states. These leaders were not all educators. One of the most influential was Samuel Gompers, who was thirty-seven times elected president of the American Federation of Labor. He saw in the public school a means by which every child, regardless of the circumstances into which he was born, could develop his talents to the fullest degree possible and bring into the life of the nation a force that would make for a larger degree of freedom. Without

[4]William B. Ragan, *Modern Elementary Curriculum* (3rd ed.), New York, Holt, 1966, p. 10.

the support of organized labor, it is doubtful that the battle for free public schools could have been won at the time.

Horace Mann, who left a promising career as an attorney and a statesman, became the most effective leader in the battle for public education. He had a definite plan for state systems of public education; he also had the eloquence and logic to awaken an apathetic public to an appreciation of public education as the foundation of democracy. When the first permanent state board of education was established in Massachusetts in 1837, Horace Mann became its first secretary—a position now generally known as state superintendent of public instruction. He was instrumental in the establishment of the first public institution for the education of teachers at Lexington, Massachusetts, in 1839. Selling his law library and donating the money to this institution, he explained, "The bar is no longer my forum. I have abandoned jurisprudence and betaken myself to the larger sphere of mind and morals. . . . I have faith in the improvability of the race—in their accelerating improvability."

Other leaders in the battle for public schools included James G. Carter of Massachusetts, Henry Barnard of Connecticut, Calvin H. Wiley of North Carolina, and Caleb Mills of Indiana.

The battle for tax-supported high schools began during the first quarter of the nineteenth century. The first public high school for boys was established in Boston in 1821, followed in 1826 by a public high school for girls. High schools grew rapidly after 1874, when the famous Kalamazoo case in Michigan established the legality of taxing people for their support. Thus, at long last the American people had established a system of public education extending from the first grade through the college and university.

EXPANSION
AND REFORM
The early history of American public education falls rather readily into two definite periods. The colonial period began in 1647 and, of course, ended in 1776, when the 13 colonies declared themselves independent. The dominant motive for education during this period was religious. The national period then followed for a century, until the end of Reconstruction in 1876. This period of expansion, during which the country survived the supreme test of the Civil War, proved that we were a nation. The dominant motive for education was political, and, impelled largely by this motive, political and educational leaders established public school systems in all the states.

After 1876, the boundaries between periods became less distinct and the motives for education became more complicated. Political and educational movements tended to become links in an endless chain rather than entirely new phenomena belonging to specific periods in history. The United States entered a period of rapid expansion in area, population, industrial and agricultural production, and influence in world affairs. The expansion was halted during the Great Depression of the 1930s, but it was resumed during World War II and has been increasing in tempo ever since.

Since 1876, 13 states have been admitted to the Union. The first official census taken in 1790 placed the population of the United States at 3,929,214. We had 100 million people by 1917, 131 million by 1940, 175 million in 1959, and 200 million in 1968. The GNP increased from $197 billion in 1947 to $343 billion in 1957, $700 billion in 1967, and $850 billion in 1968. Since science and technology have made the world smaller in terms of travel time, our national needs have become more closely mingled with the needs of all mankind. The individual American could at one time be concerned primarily with circumstances in only one of the 13 independent states; later, he had to become concerned with circumstances in a nation of many states; he must now be concerned with the problems of a global society.

The rapid expansion of the United States brought prosperity, but it also brought conditions that spurred reform movements:

Social and economic forces and the energy and initiative of individuals were building a powerful nation, but progress was not always measured in terms of human welfare. The exploitation of human and natural resources, the slums and sweatshops, child labor, and the unwholesome influence of money in politics brought with them the demand for reform.[5]

Reform as a goal has dominated American political history, particularly since 1876. It was the theme of the famous "Cross of Gold" address delivered at the 1896 Democratic Convention by William Jennings Bryan; it was reflected in the efforts of Grover Cleveland to bring about tariff reform; it motivated the energetic efforts of Theodore Roosevelt to reduce the power of "malefactors of great wealth"; it was the mainspring of Franklin D. Roosevelt's "New Deal"; and it reached new heights in Lyndon B. Johnson's "Great Society." When Frederick Lewis Allen wrote a book that described the reforms of the first half of the twentieth century, he called it *The Big Change*; he emphasized that we have tried to make our economic system provide a maximum of security for all by using the method of evolution rather than that of revolution. He suggested:

... when the ship of state was not behaving as it should, one did not need to scrap it and build another, but by a series of adjustments and improvements, repair it while keeping it running—provided the ship's crew were forever alert, forever inspecting it and tinkering with it.[6]

"Expansion" and "reform" are also appropriate terms to describe developments in public education during the years since public schools were established in all the states. Enrollments in public and private

[5]Ibid., p. 14.
[6]Frederick Lewis Allen, *The Big Change*, New York, Harper & Row, 1952, p. 105.

elementary and secondary schools increased from 9.8 million in 1880 to 32.3 million in 1934 to 51.5 million in 1970. Enrollments in secondary schools alone increased from 700,000 in 1900 to 7 million in 1950 to 14.6 million in 1970. The total cost of public and private elementary and secondary schools increased from $214 million in 1900 to $5.8 billion in 1950 to $42 billion in 1970.

Other significant developments have included the establishment of land-grant colleges, the addition of kindergartens and junior colleges to many public school systems, the addition of many new subjects to the curriculum, changing the two-year normal school to a four-year college for the preparation of teachers, the consolidation of schools, the establishment of schools or colleges of education at universities, the development of a profession of school administration, and the increased participation of the federal government in financing public education at all levels. (The results of increased federal participation are many and far-reaching; a number of them, including Project Head Start, are discussed or referred to at appropriate places elsewhere in this book.)

Although public schools expanded rapidly in number and type, they were slow to respond to demands for reform in the education they were providing. Many factors operated to entrench the formal, regimented type of school program. One of these was the mechanistic, stimulus-response psychology that regarded repetition as the means of learning and the reproduction of the words of the textbook or the teacher as the proof of learning. Another factor was the influence of the example of the factory on school practice. This rather strange trend had been vividly described as follows:

The subject matter was analyzed for the teacher into minute parts, each of which was different from every other part. . . . A pupil was put through many machines. At the end of each operation he was inspected by someone other than the teacher. This person with a series of educational calipers determined whether the pupil was properly machined to standard form.[7]

Educational reforms have, of course, gained momentum during the 1960s. The public has been made more aware than ever before both of innovations in education and of the need for them. More people than ever before are concerned with what is happening in the schools; an increasing amount of time and space is being devoted to "the revolution in the schools" in newspapers and magazines, in books and pamphlets, and in radio and television programs. But educational reform has actually been going on for many centuries—at least since the time of Plato (428–348 B.C.). Many principles that are firmly established in educational theory today were enunciated by educational reformers of previous centuries. For example, the extensive use of material objects to help children gain an understanding of concepts in the "new" mathe-

[7]L. Thomas Hopkins, *Interaction: The Democratic Process*, Boston, Heath, 1941, pp. 403–405.

matics and the "new" science programs of today was anticipated by John Amos Comenius (1592–1670) when he insisted that the proper order of learning must be things, ideas, then words. The student can and should gain perspective on current educational reforms by examining the ideas of Erasmus, Rousseau, Pestalozzi, Herbart, Froebel, and other European pioneers who helped to lay the foundations for modern educational reforms. Here, however, we must limit our discussion to a few of the reforms undertaken in *this* country since public school systems have been established in all the states.

Two Influential Educators
Francis W. Parker was principal of the Cook County Normal School in Chicago from 1883 to 1890. He conceived it to be the function of the normal school to help teachers learn to use the methods of democracy, so that they could "set the souls of children free." He reorganized the teacher education program so that the child became the center of interest; introduced the practice of cooperative planning of the school program by parents, teachers, pupils, and administrators; made the use of textbooks supplementary to a variety of learning activities closely related to the life of the community; encouraged spontaneous expression on the part of pupils; regarded effective living in the present as the best preparation for future living; and demonstrated that competence in the use of basic skills could be achieved by a program that emphasized their use in meaningful situations. Parker's work undoubtedly was influenced by the ideas of Froebel, who said: "To learn a thing in life and through doing is much more developing, cultivating, and strengthening, than to learn it merely through the verbal communication of ideas."[8]

John Dewey (1859–1952) regarded education as a social process— helping the child to share in the inherited resources of the race and to use his powers for social ends. He regarded education as a continuous process, beginning almost at birth and proceeding gradually as the individual participates in the life about him. He believed that education must begin with insight into the child's capacities, interests, and habits, but he also emphasized the social side of education. He taught that the only true education was that which stimulated the child's powers by the demands of the social situation in which the child found himself. In other words, Dewey regarded the school as a form of community life; he said that it should be as real and vital a part of a child's life as the home, the neighborhood, and the playground and that the influence of the school should flow into the life of the community. He defined subject matter as anything that helped a student solve a problem; thus he was more interested in the social contributions of science than he was in the search for truth for its own sake.

[8]Edgar W. Knight, op. cit., p. 520.

Four Theories
Four theories of education that have influenced the development of the American school are perennialism, essentialism, reconstructionism, and progressivism.

Perennialism. According to this theory, education should teach the eternal verities. Human nature never changes; therefore, good education should not change, either. Adjustment to the world as it actually exists is not a proper goal of education; real-life situations have no place in the school program; the school exists to discipline the rational powers and develop the intellect of the child; and this can best be done by confronting him with the "Great Ideas" developed in Western civilization.

Essentialism. Adherents of this theory maintain that an educated person is one who has mastered the fundamental fields of knowledge; that education should be made up of the timeless basic academic disciplines. The Council for Basic Education is currently the leading advocate of essentialism. (This theory is explained in more detail in Chapter 5.)

Reconstructionism. This theory holds that education should be the principal means for building a better social order; that the schools should take the lead in building the widest possible consensus relating to the values that should motivate mankind in the reconstruction of the social order; and that the overarching purpose of American education should be to help in the development of a world civilization. (This theory also is explained in more detail in Chapter 5.)

Progressivism. This theory can perhaps be best understood by paraphrasing its essentials as stated by the Progressive Education Association itself. They include: (1) the dominant ideals of our democratic society provide the basic direction for American education; (2) these ideals should be continuously reinterpreted and refined; (3) every child should have adequate opportunity for achieving his fullest potential through education; (4) education should make students aware that social changes demand reforms in education; (5) it is only through living and working together that optimal development of personality can be achieved; (6) the physical and mental health of children should be a major concern of the school; (7) children should be provided with opportunities for self-expression at all stages of development and in many diverse areas of experience; and (8) the child should have increasing freedom to direct his own behavior as his knowledge and experience increase.[9]

The Progressive Education Association was founded in 1919 by a group of leading citizens, most of them not professionally connected with education. During the 1920s, a number of professional educators, including John Dewey and William Heard Kilpatrick, joined and became

[9]The Progressive Education Association, "Progressive Education: Its Philosophy and Challenge," *Progressive Education*, May, 1941.

active in it. The total membership never was large, but it included many people of great knowledge and vigor. Although the association did not even approach gaining control of American schools, the many activities it engaged in gave it a considerable influence on educational theory and practice in this country. For instance, it initiated and stimulated the workshop technique now widely used in teacher education. During the 1930s it sponsored what is perhaps the most widely known of its activities. This was an experiment, known as the Eight-Year Study, involving 30 selected secondary schools and 250 accredited colleges and universities. In order to free the schools (half of them public high schools) for creative experimentation, the colleges and universities were persuaded to waive their technical admission requirements for graduates of the 30 schools and accept them on the basis of their achievement in broad fields and on their scholastic aptitude and intelligence rating.

A thorough study of how well these students actually did at college was conducted later (by a commission headed by Wilford M. Aikin). The study revealed that the grades of these progressive-school graduates were higher during the first three years of college than were those of a control group of graduates of traditional-curriculum high schools. The progressive-school graduates showed a slight lead in every subject except foreign languages. They also wrote more, talked more, took a livelier interest in politics and social problems, went to more dances, and had more dates.[10]

In the 1940s, progressive education was subjected to an increasing amount of criticism. The public tended to blame progressive theories for what seemed to be inadequacies in educating youth in the fundamentals. Defenders of progressive education retorted that any such inadequacies as did exist should be attributed to the widespread persistence of traditional education. In any case, the membership of the Progressive Education Association steadily declined, and the association was disbanded in 1955. Nevertheless, during the 36 years it existed, the association made many lasting contributions and raised many issues that are still very relevant.

The Tests and Measurement Movement

The development of standardized objective tests to explore individual differences began with the work of Francis Galton in Wundt's laboratory at the Sorbonne in Paris. With the publication of the Binet Scale in 1905, the movement was well underway. In this country Cattell published his study of mental tests and measurement in 1890 and Rice issued his study of spelling ability in 1897. After World War I, Otis, Terman, and Thorndike developed tests that had broader application to classroom practice. During the first decade of the twentieth century, courses in tests and measurement were set up at Columbia University,

[10]Edgar W. Knight, op. cit., pp. 651–655.

the University of Chicago, and Stanford University. During the next decade, centers for the distribution of tests and the interpretation of test scores were established at universities in Oklahoma, Indiana, and Minnesota.

The earlier tests were used primarily to measure individual differences in the rather general aspects of intelligence, achievement, and personality traits. But the number of types of tests has increased rapidly; as they have increased, they have also become more specific and more widely used. But as the use of tests has increased, charges that test results are being misused have also increased. As a matter of fact, the testing controversy has been building up for the past quarter of a century. Tests now stand accused by many of increasing the likelihood of a controlled curriculum and of unduly emphasizing simple recall at the expense of thinking and reasoning.

Newspapers and popular magazines have carried articles with sensational titles such as "The Evils of School Testing Techniques," "The Scandal of Educational Testing," and "Testing Versus Your Child." *The Tyranny of Testing* was the title a professor of mathematics at a leading university gave his book in which he severely criticized standardized achievement tests that tend to penalize the bright and imaginative child and to reward the child who conforms.[11] Five departments of the National Education Association cooperated in the production of a pamphlet that emphasized the child's right to be different and raised the question: "If the individual pupil counts, is good or evil to be found in a barrage of standardized tests, college board examinations, searches for talent, state-wide examinations, and national survey tests?"[12] Some writers have asserted that the malfunctioning of testing lies with the users of the tests rather than with the designers of the tests, some have suggested that teachers and school administrators need more adequate preparation in the nature and uses of tests, and others have attempted to answer the criticisms by evolving procedures for testing educational outcomes involving more than the simple recall of information.

The foregoing brief summary of educational reforms since 1876 necessarily has omitted many important ones; the student is encouraged to investigate other reforms by using other sources. In this book, curriculum reforms in public schools, innovations in grouping for instruction, expanding programs in higher education, and integration in the schools are treated in Chapters 8, 9, 10, and 11, respectively. Part IV is devoted to changing conditions in the inner cities.

Significant Dates in Educational Reform
1524   Martin Luther's letter to the mayors and aldermen of German cities.
1636   Harvard College established in Massachusetts.

[11] Banesh Hoffman, *The Tyranny of Testing*, New York, Crowell-Collier, 1962.
[12] American Association of School Administrators, *Labels and Fingerprints*, Washington, D.C.: National Education Association, 1961.

1647 "Old Deluder Satan" Act passed by General Court in Massachusetts.

1785 Northwest Ordinance required that land be set aside for education.

1805 Free School Society organized in New York City.

1813 Gideon Hawley became the first State Superintendent of Schools in New York.

1823 First private normal school established at Concord, Vermont.

1829 First pedagogical book published in the United States (Samuel Hall, *Lectures on School-Keeping*).

1834 Pennsylvania became the first state to establish a state system of public education.

1837 Horace Mann became the secretary of the Massachusetts State Board of Education.

1838 First state normal school established at Lexington, Massachusetts.

1848 First graded elementary school in the United States established at Quincy, Massachusetts.

1852 First state law making school attendance compulsory passed in Massachusetts.

1855 First college of agriculture in the United States established in Michigan.

1857 The association that later became the National Education Association was founded.

1862 Congress passed the Morrill Act, which granted land to the states, the income from it to be used to establish colleges of agricultural and mechanical arts; the act, with later amendments, led to the establishment of sixty-nine land-grant colleges.

1867 First United States Commissioner of Education—Henry Barnard.

1873 First public school system to establish a kindergarten—St. Louis.

1874 Decision in Kalamazoo, Michigan, case legalized taxation for support of high schools.

1876 Principle of tax-supported schools accepted in all states.

1879 First professional chair in education in a university—Michigan.

1890 First state law making full-time school attendance compulsory passed in Connecticut.

1896 John Dewey established an experimental school at The University of Chicago.

1916 The American Federation of Teachers was founded.

1917 Congress passed the Smith-Hughes Act, granting aid to vocational education in the public high schools.

1918 Compulsory attendance laws in effect in all states.

1919 The Progressive Education Association was founded.

1944 The Educational Policies Commission of NEA published *Education for All American Youth.*

1944 Congress passed the Servicemen's Readjustment Act, providing financial assistance for the education of veterans of World War II (known as the G.I. Bill of Rights).

1948 The Educational Policies Commission published *Education for All American Children.*

1952 Congress passed the Veterans' Readjustment Assistance Act, providing financial assistance for the education of veterans of the Korean War.

1954 The United States Supreme Court ruled that public school segregation on the basis of race is unconstitutional.

1958   Congress passed the National Defense Education Act chiefly to promote improvement in science, mathematics, and foreign language instruction.

1964   Congress passed the Economic Opportunity Act, to improve the education of the poor; Project Head Start and the Job Corps are among the programs made possible by the act.

1965   Congress passed the Elementary and Secondary Education Act, appropriating more than a billion dollars primarily to provide better educational opportunities for culturally disadvantaged children.

SUMMARY

1. A study of the history of American education helps the student understand the relation of the school to the social order, the changing responsibilities of the school as a social institution, and the fact that a changing society demands educational reforms.

2. The idea that education should be a public rather than a private enterprise was new in American thinking about education when the first legislation in America requiring that public schools be established was enacted in Massachusetts in 1647.

3. The religious motive for education during colonial times was revealed by the language used in the preamble to the "Old Deluder Satan" Act, by the type of discipline used in the schools, and by the nature of the most used textbook.

4. Outside the New England colonies, little interest was shown in education by colonial legislatures.

5. The public school revival was a series of movements that resulted in the establishment and improvement of public schools in all the states during the middle years of the nineteenth century.

6. Important factors in the success of the public school revival included (1) the influence of the frontier, (2) the support of labor leaders, (3) the influence of educational developments in Europe, and (4) the contributions of able and dedicated leaders.

7. Soon after 1876, the United States entered a period of rapid expansion in area, in population, in production of material goods, and in influence in world affairs.

8. Rapid expansion brought with it certain abuses that called for political reforms; reform became the central theme of American politics soon after 1876 and has remained so until the present.

9. Public schools also expanded rapidly after 1876, but the quality of education provided did not keep pace with the rapid quantitative expansion; the public school, like the factory, remained a thoroughly regimented organization.

10. Reforms in public education were sponsored by Francis W. Parker, John Dewey, the Progressive Education Association, and other individuals and groups.

11. The testing movement, which began in this country during the first two decades of the twentieth century, has grown rapidly in recent decades. Charges that tests are misused have been increasing for a quarter of a century.

SELECTED READINGS

Drake, William E., *The American School in Transition*, Englewood Cliffs, N.J., Prentice-Hall, 1955. Contains sections on colonial foundations, the struggle for independence in education, the era of transition, and modern tendencies in education.

Hartford, Ellis F., *Education in These United States*, New York, Macmillan, 1964. Chapter 3, "The Story of Common Schools," gives a synopsis of the story of public schools in this country.

Hoffman, Banesh, *The Tyranny of Testing*, New York, Crowell-Collier, 1962. Presents a penetrating criticism of the testing practices found in schools.

Keppel, Francis, *The Necessary Revolution in American Education*, New York, Harper & Row, 1966. Provides interesting arguments in favor of providing for more quality and equality in American education.

Knight, Edgar W., *Education in the United States* (3rd ed.), Boston, Ginn, 1951. An excellent source of information about the men and the movements that have influenced the development of American education.

Ragan, William B., *Modern Elementary Curriculum* (3rd ed.), New York, Holt, 1966. Chapter 1 provides a brief treatment of various periods in the historical development of public education.

Russell, John Dale, and Charles H. Judd, *The American Educational System*, Boston, Houghton Mifflin, 1940. Chapter 2 deals with European antecedents of American education.

Ulich, Robert, *History of Educational Thought*, New York, American Book, 1945. Characterizes the work and theories of educational reformers from Plato to John Dewey.

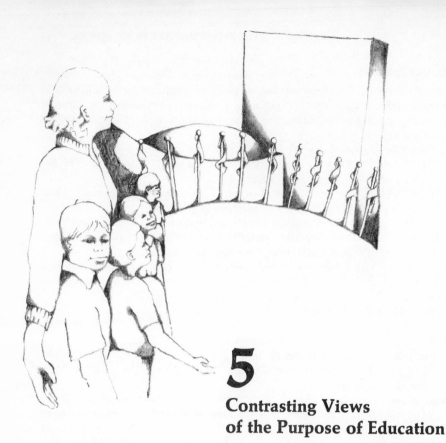

5

Contrasting Views of the Purpose of Education

*Each generation gives new form to the aspirations that shape education in its time.**

The last chapter discussed the American school as it has changed in response to changes in American life during the past three centuries. This chapter explains how, in an open society, individuals and groups may hold differing beliefs about the central purpose of education. A closed society attempts to govern all human activity in conformity to one body of principles existing at a given time; an open society permits individuals and groups to hold contrasting views. In an open society, the individual has a moral obligation to base the beliefs that guide his behavior on an intelligent evaluation of all relevant facts.

The scope of this book does not include a detailed discussion of spe-

*Jerome S. Bruner, *The Process of Education*, Cambridge, Harvard University Press, 1962, p. 1.

cific philosophies of education—realism, pragmatism, experimentalism, and so on. Most students, later in their college careers, will take a systematic course in the philosophy of education that will give a comprehensive treatment of this very broad topic. Nevertheless, because there are inextricable links between philosophy and purpose, as we now consider purpose, it will be apparent that philosophy cannot be ignored. Indeed, since philosophy is one of the *sources* of purpose, we turn now to a brief discussion of it in that role.

The rest of the chapter explores four current views of the central purpose of American education: learning the basic disciplines, becoming adequate persons, developing the rational powers, and creating a world civilization. These purposes are not mutually exclusive, of course, but they can be treated separately in terms of their principal emphases.

The Teacher's Philosophy of Education

Decisions made by the teacher emerge from his convictions about the worth of each individual, the quality of human nature, the nature of the good life, and the role that the school should play in a democratic society. These convictions constitute his philosophy of education—his educational objectives—at any given time. His philosophy of education, however, is a living, growing one; as he gains greater insight into the results of his work in terms of richer lives for individuals and a better society for tomorrow, his philosophy of education matures. A broader, less personal source of educational objectives is the realities and ideals of contemporary American society (discussed in an earlier chapter).

The purposes of education take into consideration what children *should* learn. Recent curriculum improvement projects have, therefore, drawn heavily on subject-matter specialists for suggestions concerning the contributions their disciplines can make to the achievement of the purposes of education. What children *can* learn is also an important consideration. Studies of children and of the learning process are, therefore, important sources of the purposes of education.

There are basic differences among Americans about the purposes of education and the roles that schools should play, just as there are differences about religion, politics, medicine, and styles of clothing. There also are, however, widespread agreements. For instance, according to one authority, the American people as a whole believe that ". . . the purposes of education are the development of critical thinking, effective communication, creative skills, and social, civic, and occupational competence."[1]

The disagreements center around the problem of what central, overall purpose should receive major emphasis. They also arise from differing interpretations of what an end is and what a means is. For example, those who argue that the "one overarching purpose" of edu-

---

[1]Myron Lieberman, *The Future of Public Education*, Chicago, The University of Chicago Press, 1960, p. 17.

cation must be the creation of a world civilization would, no doubt, admit that the teaching of world geography serves as a means to that end. Those who argue that the development of the rational powers is the central purpose of education recognize that this is not the exclusive purpose of education. Those who propose the development of adequate persons as the new focus in education include a rich and available perceptual field—that is, knowledge of various kinds—as one of the characteristics of the adequate person. One cannot be both adequate and stupid at the same time, but his knowledge must have a personal meaning for him if it is to affect his behavior and be available to help him understand the events that take place in his environment.

LEARNING THE BASIC
DISCIPLINES
The rationale of those who believe that learning the basic disciplines is the principal function of education (essentialism) has been outlined by Phenix. He maintains that educators should understand the kinds of meaning that have proved effective in the development of civilization; that these meanings may be found in the various scholarly disciplines; and that these realms of meaning indicate the kinds of understanding a person must have if he is to function well within the civilized community.[2]

Separate Subjects Versus the Unified Program
The case for organizing learning experiences around basic subjects has been presented by Hansen in a book about the Amidon School in Washington. He lists the basic academic subjects for elementary schools as reading, composition, grammar, spelling, speech, mathematics, science, geography, history, art, and music. His fundamental thesis is contained in the following:

It should be common practice for teachers to assign problems for study, to encourage independent research, to elicit creative work in the arts and sciences. But these should not overwhelm and push aside order and substance in basic subjects as does the unit-dominated curriculum.[3]

He says that the unit method of curriculum organization has become "the Frankenstein's monster of the classroom" and that the core program is "wide, undefined, shifting, and soft."[4]

Whether or not the Amidon School was actually "a successful demonstration in basic education," as Hansen described it in his subtitle, is not the point here. The broad educational issues are: (1) What are the basic academic disciplines that can make significant contributions to

[2]Philip Phenix, *Realms of Meaning*, New York, McGraw-Hill, 1964, pp. 28–29.
[3]Carl F. Hansen, *The Amidon Elementary School: A Successful Demonstration in Basic Education*, Englewood Cliffs, N. J., Prentice-Hall, 1962, p. 9.
[4]Ibid., pp. 11–12.

the achievements of the purposes of elementary and secondary schools? (2) How can learning experiences be organized so that these disciplines can make their maximum contributions? (3) Are these disciplines the means or the ends of education?

The basic academic disciplines.   If one accepts the premise that it is the central purpose of elementary and secondary schools to teach the basic academic disciplines, the list suggested by Hansen is too narrow. Social studies programs, for instance, now usually draw materials from history, geography, political science, economics, sociology, and anthropology. Indeed, it has been suggested that the broad framework of a coordinated social studies program should be developed by a team including specialists from each of these disciplines, plus a psychologist and a curriculum planner.[5]

The organization of learning experiences.   It is not feasible for an elementary or secondary school to offer separate courses in the six social sciences; there would be little time left for other subjects. Even if the school day, week, and year were lengthened, there would not be room for "twenty academic subjects in the kindergarten."[6] One alternative is the "ladder" system of grade placement, in which history is taught at one grade level, geography at another, and the other social sciences are left for senior high school or college. A second alternative is the "spiral" system of grade placement, in which the social studies curriculum is built around themes, drawing materials from all the social sciences at the primary level and "revisiting" these themes or concepts in increasingly more difficult and complex forms at higher grade levels.

Both research and prevailing practice support the "spiral" system. Studies of child development indicate that growth and learning are continuous—that new learnings are built on earlier learnings. Therefore, concepts are not fully developed at any one grade level; they are introduced early in the school program and take on new, expanded, and more complex meanings at later levels. Children do not wait until they are in senior high school to become interested in economics; after all, they have experienced many economic aspects of living from their earliest years. This is also true of mathematics, geometry, and physics. These views are now widely accepted; a survey of the states revealed several years ago that only two of the fifty were planning to return to the separate subjects organization in the social studies.[7] The same trend toward a unified program has been evident in other curriculum areas.

The means and the ends of education.   Whether or not the basic academic disciplines have important contributions to make at all levels

[5]Paul R. Hanna, et al., *Geography in the Teaching of Social Studies Concepts and Skills*, Boston, Houghton Mifflin, 1966, p. 50.

[6]John I. Goodlad, "Changing Curriculum in America's Schools," *Saturday Review*, November 16, 1963, 65.

[7]John D. McAulay, "What the States Are Doing: Elementary Social Studies," *Pennsylvania News and Views*, March, 1964, 3.

of the school program is not an educational issue. What is an issue is how the basic facts are regarded. Are they ends in themselves or means? The prevailing opinion now is that they are tools to be used in the solution of problems rather than ends in themselves. Van Til has described the real "basics" in education, the goals we set out to achieve using the study of basic subjects as one of the effective means.

Let us not be misled by the oversimplifiers who would restrict education to rote learning of the three R's without recognizing that skills must be taught meaningfully and applied to problems which grow out of social realities, needs, and values; who would have the child study a cultural heritage without relating it to his surrounding society and his life as a learner, without exercising critical thought and applying human values. . . . True intellectual development draws upon the cultural heritage in order to use it thoughtfully in dealing with issues real to the learner and important to society.[8]

BECOMING ADEQUATE PERSONS

The authors of the 1962 Yearbook of the Association for Supervision and Curriculum Development suggest as a new focus for education the production of adequate persons. The authors—Earl C. Kelley, Carl R. Rogers, Abraham H. Maslow, and Arthur W. Combs—believe that the production of such persons must be the primary goal of education. They raise this intriguing question: "Who can say what kind of world we might create if we could learn to increase our production of adequate persons?"[9] The book describes the adequate, self-actualizing person in terms of his characteristic ways of seeing himself and the world, listing and explaining the following characteristics: (1) a positive view of self, (2) openness to experience and acceptance, (3) identification with others, and (4) a rich and available perceptual field. The book also presents new school practices suggested by these concepts of the adequate, fully functioning person.

A Positive View of Self

A person with a positive view of self is not a person who never recognizes any of his faults or weaknesses; he generally regards himself as a person who is liked, wanted, accepted, and able. When he looks objectively at himself he decides that, although he is not perfect, he is able to face life with confidence. As Kelley says, he sees himself as "enough." The person with a positive view of self is less disturbed by criticism, more likely to remain calm in the midst of stress and strain,

[8]William Van Til, "What Are the Real 'Basics' in Education?" *Childhood Education*, November, 1962, 107–109.

[9]Association for Supervision and Curriculum Development, *Perceiving—Behaving—Becoming*, Washington, D.C., The Association, 1962, p. 62.

and less likely to carry around abnormal doubts and fears that would prevent him from living life to its fullest.

A positive image of self is gained from experience; a child comes to view himself as capable, wanted, and liked by being treated by others in a way that indicates they believe he is that kind of person. The school, therefore, has as much responsibility for helping children develop a positive view of self as it has for teaching school subjects. Indeed, there is a high correlation between school achievement and a positive view of self. The school can foster the development of such a positive view by giving attention to the classroom climate, respecting the uniqueness of each pupil, individualizing instruction, and pacing school tasks in harmony with the rates of learning of different children.

Openness to Experience

A person with a closed mind is wedded to a single dogma; he rejects all evidence from experience that conflicts with his rigid set of beliefs. "Mankind," wrote John Dewey, "likes to think in terms of extreme opposites. It is given to formulating its beliefs in terms of either-or's, between which it recognizes no intermediate possibilities."[10] Extremely ethnocentric individuals live within codes of behavior of their own groups and are unable to profit from the experience of other groups.

The person who is open to experience has a much wider source of data on which to base his decisions. Openness to experience, like the development of a positive image of self, is learned from experience. Teachers can help pupils learn to be more open to experience, to be willing to gain new ideas, and to learn to face new problems. Teaching for openness and creativity helps pupils to develop new goals for learning and to explore a great variety of materials.

Combs states the case for openness to experience as follows:

Truly adequate people possess perceptual fields maximally open to experience. That is to say, their perceptual fields are capable of change and adjustment in such fashion as to make fullest possible use of their experience.[11]

Identification with Others.

The adequate person is capable of expanding his concept of self to include others; he is unable to think of self apart from significant others with whom he has been associated or with whom he shares ideas and purposes. Identification with others is learned; it is a part of growing from immaturity to maturity. The very young child is egocentric: He is interested primarily in himself, and his desire to be first in everything makes it difficult for him to get along harmoniously in a group. He first learns to play harmoniously with one other child of

[10]John Dewey, *Experience and Education*, New York, Macmillan, 1938, p. 1.
[11]Association for Supervision and Curriculum Development, op. cit., p. 141.

approximately his own age; he then learns to identify with increasingly larger groups; the truly adequate person eventually learns to identify with all mankind, even with those who differ from himself in color, creed, and nationality. Combs points out that identification, like the self-concept, is learned. He states:

The more positive the individual's feelings about self, the easier it is to identify with an ever broader sample of mankind. The capacity for identification appears to be a product of an essentially positive view of self and of successful, satisfying experiences in interaction with other people. Here is a place where a child's experiences in school can be made to count.[12]

It is appropriate in this context to mention a new estimate of human nature that has been emphasized by some biologists and psychologists. It has been customary in the past to blame human nature for conflicts between men and nations: "Human nature being what it is, nothing else can be expected." There is evidence, however, that human nature contains no specific war instinct, that the aggressive tendency in man's make-up is not an unvarying instinct, and that it can be molded into the most varied forms. The best hope for mankind—indeed the only real hope—lies in developing the science of human relations. As long as environmental forces continue to mold man into a viciously competitive animal, as long as man continues to exalt change in everything but himself, human misery and war will remain distinct possibilities.[13]

A Rich and Available Perceptual Field

As we have noted in earlier chapters, the American system of universal, public education was established in this country because our forefathers realized that the success of popular government depended on enlightened citizens. Today, the minimum level of what one must know in order to understand the forces and events that affect his well-being increases year by year; the future belongs to the well-informed person. It should not be assumed, therefore, that emphasis on the production of adequate persons as the primary goal of education minimizes the importance of information.

A rich and available perceptual field, however, involves a great deal more than mere exposure to the contents of the basic disciplines. Perceptions are gained not only from formal schooling but also from informal sources and from first-hand involvement in human relations. Each individual selects from the myriad stimuli to which he is exposed the items he includes in his perceptual field; he selects them in terms of his previous experiences, his interests, and his purposes. "The deeper, more personally significant the perception, moreover, the more likely it is to affect behavior."[14]

There is a considerable amount of evidence also that the way a thing

---

[12]Ibid., p. 56.

[13]See William B. Ragan and John D. McAulay, *Social Studies for Today's Children,* New York, Appleton-Century-Crofts, 1964, pp. 50–51.

[14]Association for Supervision and Curriculum Development, op. cit., p. 61.

is learned determines its future usefulness to the learner. Combs explains this principle as follows:

Something more than confrontation with events is necessary to insure inclusion of perceptions in the field and their availability on later occasions. This availability seems dependent upon at least two factors: (a) the individual's discovery of personal meaning, and (b) the satisfaction of need.[15]

Gertrude Noar has raised this pertinent question: "What kinds of learning experiences do children need besides reading, writing, figuring, and reciting?" She includes in her answers (1) creating a self-concept that permits the pupil to like himself and others, (2) learning human relations skills, and (3) providing status-building experiences for minority group children.[16]

DEVELOPING THE RATIONAL POWERS

In 1961, the Educational Policies Commission (EPC) of the NEA published a pamphlet in which the development of the rational powers of the individual was presented as the central purpose of American education. The publication mentions the seven cardinal principles evolved by an NEA committee and published in 1918: health, command of the fundamental processes, worthy home membership, vocational competence, effective citizenship, worthy use of leisure, and ethical character. It calls attention to another classification published in 1938 by the Educational Policies Commission: self-realization, human relationship, economic efficiency, and civic responsibility.

The EPC admits that these are all desirable objectives, but maintains that ". . . neither the schools nor the pupils have the time or energy to engage in all the activities which will fully achieve all these goals. . . . The school seeks rather to equip the pupil to achieve them himself."[17] The Commission, therefore, suggests that the central purpose of American education is the development of the rational powers of the individual—helping students to learn to think clearly. The rational powers are listed as recalling and imagining, classifying and generalizing, comparing and evaluating, analyzing and synthesizing, and deducting and inferring.

The twenty-one-page pamphlet presents an excellent summary of the principles on which modern educational theory and practice are based: (1) Americans regard education as a means for improving themselves and their society; (2) the schools are charged with fostering the development of individual capacities that will enable each human being to

---

[15] Ibid., p. 60.

[16] Gertrude Noar, "Information Is Not Enough," in August Kerber and Wilfred Smith, *Educational Issues in a Changing Society* (rev. ed.), Detroit, Wayne State University Press, 1964, pp. 117–119.

[17] Educational Policies Commission, *The Central Purpose of American Education,* Washington, D.C.: National Education Association, 1961, p. 2.

become the best person he is capable of becoming; (3) a free society must create circumstances in which all individuals may have opportunity and encouragement to attain freedom of the mind; (4) the development and use of the rational powers are indispensable to a full and worthy life; (5) the pupil who feels inadequate, insecure, or unduly apprehensive is hampered in his learning; (6) good teaching can help students to learn to think clearly; (7) man has already transformed his world by using his mind.

The fascinating series of events through which new materials and new teaching procedures have been introduced into elementary and secondary school programs in recent years is too well known to require detailed treatment here. It can be said by way of summary that the current curriculum reform movement has been proceeding from the national level down to the local school system; that attention has been sharply focused on single subjects; that projects at the national level have been generously supported by funds from the federal government and from the foundations; that scholars from the various disciplines at the universities have been involved in planning the precollegiate curriculum as never before.

The emphasis in all of these programs has been on teaching the student to think. The search has been for something more lasting than the memorization of isolated bits of information; the purpose has been to provide a kind of education that would enable the student to become self-propelling during a lifetime of learning. For example, as Renner and Ragan have put it, "Recent curriculum developments in elementary-school science encourage the learner to develop his rational powers which are the essence of the ability to think."[18]

In the EPC statement, however, there is evidence of confused thinking about what are the purposes and what are the means of education. For instance, immediately after the list of rational powers is this statement: "These processes enable one to apply logic and the available evidence to his ideas, attitudes, and actions, and to pursue better whatever goals he may have."[19] Following this is an explanation of how the use of the rational powers helps in the achievement of the objectives of the seven cardinal principles already listed. The statement would have been more consistent if the title of the pamphlet had been: "The Importance of Developing the Rational Powers as a Means of Achieving the Purposes of American Education."

CREATING A WORLD
CIVILIZATION
The title of this section reflects a fourth view of the central purpose of American education, reconstructionism. Brameld has expressed this view as follows:

[18]John W. Renner and William B. Ragan, *Teaching Science in the Elementary School*, New York, Harper & Row, 1968, p. 299.
[19]Educational Policies Commission, op. cit., p. 5.

I hold with the strongest conviction of which I am capable that our schools and colleges, abroad as well as in America, require one overarching purpose, by comparison with which all others, bar none, are of subordinate importance. This purpose is to channel and release the full resources of education in behalf of the creation of world civilization—a world civilization capable both of preventing destruction and of providing the peace and abundance that men everywhere crave.[20]

The schools have always been charged with the responsibility of developing intelligent citizens of the United States; today they have the additional obligation of developing citizens of the world. This responsibility is not one that educators sought in order to broaden the scope of an already overcrowded curriculum; it is one that has been forced upon the schools by the realities of the world in which we live. Science and technology have reduced the size of the world in terms of travel time—each individual's community is in a real sense now a world community. Events that take place in China, Russia, or Africa are likely to have more impact on the lives of individuals living anywhere in the United States than events that took place at the state capitol had on the lives of our grandfathers. Technology has been dictating to the schools, and the schools have had to respond, regardless of the philosophies of their personnel.

One Overarching Purpose

The schools have, of course, traditionally provided opportunities for students to gain information about various countries in the world through instruction in history and geography. But information is not enough in terms of bringing the full resources of education to bear on the problem of creating a world civilization. This would involve placing greater emphasis on the forces that operate to cause conflict among nations and the agencies at work to promote peaceful settlement of disputes, providing more opportunities for pupils to engage in cooperative enterprises, helping pupils develop attitudes that permit them to identify with others who differ from themselves, and using much more effective methods and materials.

Teaching for World Understanding

Teaching for world understanding generally consists of (1) helping students to understand that conflict is a part of life that must be reckoned with, (2) helping them to understand its costs to individuals and nations, (3) helping them to realize how much cooperation there is at the community, national, and international levels, (4) providing opportunities to practice the skills of cooperative living, (5) helping them to understand that war is not inevitable, (6) providing them with informa-

[20]Theodore Brameld, "World Civilization, the Galvanizing Purpose of Public Education," in Stanley Elam (ed.), *New Dimensions for Educational Progress,* Bloomington, Ind., Phi Delta Kappa, 1962, pp. 11–12.

tion about man's long struggle for a peaceful world society, (7) helping them to understand the economic and social interdependence of nations, and (8) helping them to develop an appreciation of the worth of individuals of all races and nationalities.

Teaching world affairs, like teaching anything else, must take into consideration not only what children *should* learn, but also what they *can* learn. Kenworthy has suggested content and activities that are appropriate for the preschool and primary grades, the middle grades, and the upper grades. Stories about the Christ of the Andes statue (celebrating the end of hostilities between Chile and Argentina) or the Peace Arch and gardens between the United States and Canada are tangible evidences of international cooperation easily understood by children in the primary grades; the long history of collaboration between nations in health and other fields provides appropriate content for the middle grades; by the time children reach the upper grades they are generally ready for a detailed study of the organization and achievements of the United Nations.[21]

Jarolimek suggests the central role that teaching for international understanding must play in the school curriculum:

War, peace, and depression have all been strong influences in curriculum building; today it is international relations which is dominating the attention of the nation. Consequently, social studies programs are being planned to equip the young citizen to deal thoughtfully and intelligently with problems of international import.[22]

He points out that motivation for teaching world understanding emerges from (1) the fear of total destruction, (2) the desire to settle differences through peaceful means, (3) the economic interdependence of nations, and (4) the desire to help all peoples of the world obtain for themselves a full share of freedom and abundance. He lists objectives, activities, and criteria for selecting countries to be studied at the various grade levels and sources of materials relating to the teaching of world affairs.

The Project on the Instructional Program of the Public Schools suggests ten broad concepts or themes around which the program in international understanding might be built for Grades 1–12. These are: nationalism, the population increase, the desire for peace, the power conflict, similarities and differences among cultures, the balance among aspects of society, national characteristics and stereotypes, United States foreign policy, foreign assistance, and international organizations.[23]

There are many materials already available that attempt to help

[21]Leonard S. Kenworthy, *Introducing Children to the World*, New York, Harper & Row, 1956, chap. 13.

[22]John Jarolimek, *Social Studies in Elementary Education* (2nd ed.), New York, Macmillan, 1963, chap. 15.

[23]Project on the Instructional Program of the Public Schools, *Education in A Changing Society*, Washington, D.C., National Education Association, 1963, chap. 9.

teachers carry out recommendations like these. See the Selected Readings at the end of this chapter.

SUMMARY

1. Clearly defined educational purposes indicate the directions in which it is considered desirable for growth to take place, provide criteria for the selection of learning activities, and provide the framework within which the evaluation of pupil progress operates.

2. Educational purposes grow out of a philosophy of education, an understanding of the realities and ideals of contemporary American society, and information concerning what children are capable of learning at various stages of development.

3. There is substantial agreement concerning specific goals that the schools should be expected to achieve; the differences center around what purposes should receive major emphasis and different interpretations of what are the ends and what are the means of education.

4. One school of thought holds that teaching the basic academic disciplines should be the principal concern of the schools. This theory has been examined in terms of what the basic academic disciplines include and in terms of whether these disciplines constitute the ends or the means of education.

5. Another group presents as a new focus for education the production of adequate persons—persons who have a positive view of self, openness to experience, ability to relate to others, and a rich and available perceptual field. All of these depend on the quality of experiences children have in home, school, community, and other relationships.

6. The school can foster the development of a positive view of self by giving attention to the intellectual, social, and emotional climate of the classroom and by respecting the uniqueness of each pupil.

7. A person who is open to experience is capable of making changes and adjustments in his perceptions in such a fashion as to make the fullest possible use of his experience.

8. The adequate person is capable of expanding his concept of self to include others; this ability develops gradually as the individual learns to identify with increasingly larger groups until eventually he learns to identify with all mankind.

9. The minimum level of what one must know in order to understand the forces and events that influence his well-being increases year by year; the production of adequate persons, therefore, involves not only gaining information but gaining it in such a manner that it is available when needed.

10. The view that the central purpose of education in American society is the development of the rational powers of the individual has had a profound influence on educational planning in recent years. Recent curriculum improvement projects have emphasized helping students develop the ability to think, rather than merely memorizing isolated bits of information; the purpose has been to provide the kind of experience that would enable the student to become self-propelling throughout a lifetime of learning.

11. The question raised in this chapter is not concerned with the importance of developing the rational powers; it is concerned with whether this is the end sought or the means of achieving important goals of education.

12. Increasing attention has been given in recent decades to the problem of releasing the full resources of education in behalf of the creation of a world civilization. Indeed, it has been stated that this should be the one over-arching purpose of education by comparison with which all other purposes would be of subordinate importance.

13. The increaing amount of attention being given to teaching for world understanding has emerged from (1) the fear of total destruction by modern weapons of warfare, (2) the conviction that differences between and among nations can be settled by peaceful means, (3) the increasing economic interdependence of nations, and (4) the desire to help all peoples of the world obtain for themselves the fullest possible measure of freedom, security, and abundance.

14. Teaching for world understanding, like teaching anything else, requires an understanding not only of what children *should* learn but also of what children at various stages of development *can* learn.

15. Sources mentioned in this chapter provide an abundance of information concerning the objectives, content, and effective teaching procedures in the area of international understanding.

SELECTED READINGS

Association for Supervision and Curriculum Development, *Perceiving—Behaving—Becoming,* Washington, D.C., The Association, 1962. Chapter 5 presents a summary of the characteristics of an adequate person.

Educational Policies Commission, *The Central Purpose of American Education,* Washington, D.C., National Education Association, 1962. This pamphlet contains a statement of American ideals that have traditionally influenced the schools, reviews well-known statements of educational purposes formulated by educators, and suggests that the development of the rational powers of the individual should be the central purpose.

Elam, Stanley (ed.), *New Dimensions for Educational Progress,* Bloomington, Ind., Phi Delta Kappa, 1962. Chapter 1, written by Theodore Brameld, suggests that the development of world civilization should be the galvanizing purpose of public education.

Goodlad, John I., "Changing Curriculum in America's Schools," *Saturday Review,* November 16, 1963, p. 65. This article points out that scheduling each of the basic disciplines in the elementary schools is not practical.

Hanna, Paul R., Rose E. Sabaroff, Gordon F. Davies, and Charles R. Farrar, *Geography in the Teaching of Social Studies Concepts and Skills,* Boston, Houghton Mifflin, 1966. Suggests that the broad framework of a coordinated social studies program should be planned by a team including specialists from the various social sciences, a psychologist, and a curriculum specialist.

Hansen, Carl F., *The Amidon Elementary School: A Successful Demonstration in Basic Education,* Englewood Cliffs, N.J., Prentice-Hall, 1962. The author lists the basic academic subjects for elementary schools and presents criticism of the core curriculum and unit teaching.

Jarolimek, John, *Social Studies in Elementary Education* (2nd ed.), New York, Macmillan, 1963, chap. 15. This chapter presents practical suggestions for the teacher who is interested in including international understanding in the social studies program.

Kenworthy, Leonard S., *Introducing Children to the World,* New York, Harper

& Row, 1956. This volume suggests the objectives of a program in world understanding; suggests content and activities appropriate for the primary, intermediate and upper grades; and lists sources of materials.

Kerber, August, and Wilfred, Smith, *Educational Issues in A Changing Society*, Detroit, Wayne University Press, 1964. The article by Gertrude Noar, "Information Is Not Enough," is particularly pertinent to the problems discussed in this chapter.

Lieberman, Myron, *The Future of Public Education*, Chicago, The University of Chicago Press, 1960. Chapter 2 lists the purposes of education on which he says there is substantial agreement and points out how differences arise from confusion of ends with means.

Phenix, Philip, *Realms of Meaning*, New York, McGraw-Hill, 1964. States that the scholarly disciplines contain the kinds of meaning that have proved effective in the development of civilization. Offers a new classification of these disciplines.

Project on the Instructional Program of the Public Schools, *Education in A Changing Society*, Washington, D.C., National Education Association, 1963. Chapter 9 suggests ten broad concepts around which the program in international understanding should be built.

Ragan, William B., and John D. McAulay, *Social Studies for Today's Children*, New York, Appleton-Century-Crofts, 1964. Chapter 7 contains suggestions for teaching international understanding.

Van Til, William, "What Are the Real 'Basics' in Education?" *Childhood Education*, November, 1962. The author maintains that true intellectual development draws upon the cultural heritage in order to use it thoughtfully in dealing with issues real to the learner and important to society.

6

Newer Insights into Human Behavior

There are no tests of native intelligence. In fact, the concept of "native intelligence" is essentially meaningless. Every response to the stimulus material in intelligence tests is, of necessity, a learned response. The kind and amount of learning an individual acquires depends upon the experiences that come to him from the environment and upon his structural assets and liabilities. To some extent, they are environmentally determined.*

It is not merely a brain or an isolated set of nervous tissues, but a whole child that confronts the teacher. For this very good reason, student teachers are told that they must teach "the whole child." Each child comes to school with good and bad habits, with misinformation as well as accurate knowledge, with loosely formulated goals and, sometimes, obvious impediments. In addition, he may be ill-nourished or well-fed, energetic or listless, placid or tense. It is this extremely complex mass of characteristics that teachers must attempt to shape and mold into a productive adult.

Every individual's development is limited by both *heredity* and *environ-*

*Melvin M. Tumin (ed.), *Race and Intelligence: A Scientific Evaluation*, New York, Anti-Defamation League of B'nai B'rith, 1963, p. 24.

ment. Broadly speaking, his heredity determines *whether* he will learn and his environment determines *what* he will learn. The usual direction of intellectual development is, first, the expression of behaviors that evolve out of physical maturation and, later, the expression of behaviors that grow out of group acculturation experiences.[1]

PERCEPTUAL
DEVELOPMENT
As early as he is able to comprehend, the child is taught to perceive the world around him. This phenomenon has given rise to the expression that many people "look at" but few "see" the same things. "Seeing" cultural objects and giving them the same meanings is the result of learning within social (group) settings. This *perceptual development* takes place through the senses—vision, hearing, touch, taste, smell. Most psychological studies conclude that the major portion of an individual's development occurs within the first five years of his life. This development is, of course, especially related to the home.

Homes vary in their suitability for the development of *cognitive skills.* Home environments in depressed urban neighborhoods are noticeably deficient. Living quarters are overcrowded, the noise level is generally high, and the result is continual interpersonal strain. In addition, amenities such as games, toys, books, magazines, and furniture are scarce or even nonexistent, creating a very limited visual environment. Another condition of intellectual development is the amount of interaction between parents and child. Parent-child interaction is greatly reduced in most depressed-area homes. Frequently the mother must play two roles, serving both as the main wage-earner and also as the housekeeper. If the family is large, the interaction is further reduced between parents and children. Reduced interaction of this type results in less intellectual stimulation of the child.

The most important aspect of intellectual growth is *verbal communication.* School learning is heavily dependent on language skills. Adults in middle-class homes use words freely and teach them to the child constantly, both indirectly and directly. Middle-class parents encourage their children to say words aloud, correct them when they apply words to the wrong objects or events, and reward them when they learn correct usages. This type of feedback, which is essential to the learning of language, is more readily available to relatively affluent children.[2]

As a child develops complex language patterns, he becomes more able to perceive aspects of his environment, to abstract relevant portions, and to commit them to memory. Through language he can grasp such important concepts as "past," "present," and "future." Symbols and their implications allow him to compare and differentiate material and

[1]See Warren R. Baller (ed.), *Readings in the Psychology of Human Growth and Development,* New York, Holt, 1962, part III.
[2]Ibid.

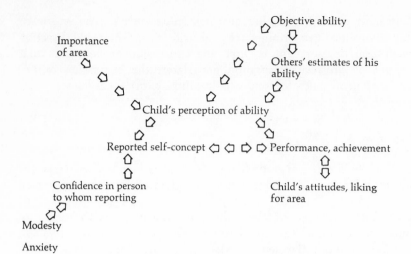

Figure 2. Factors Relating Children's Self-Concepts and School Achievements. (From *In Pursuit of Self-Esteem* by Pauline Sears and Vivian Sherman. Copyright 1964 by Wadsworth Publishing Company and reproduced with their permission.)

nonmaterial cultural items. The ability to order and reorder the physical environment also allows him to change his self-conceptions. In other words, the fundamental difference between human and animal behavior is that human beings can talk and animals cannot.

Self-Conception

Because he possesses language and high intelligence, man is able to think about his body, his behavior, and the impression he makes on other persons. Only the human being is able to become an object to himself. The notion of self grows out of interaction and communication with other persons. In short, *the self is a social product.* Three conditions are necessary for the formation of a self-concept. Charles Cooley explained this process in his concept of "the looking-glass self":[3] An individual gets a reflected view of himself from the actions of others toward him. First, the individual must imagine how he is judged by other persons around him. These judgments may be explicit, as when a teacher tells a student he is "a terrible scholar"; or they may be implicit, as when a student interprets his teacher's frown as a sign of disapproval.

The second condition for formation of a self-concept is the individual's ability to judge his reflection of self against a set of norms that he and others hold in reference to how he *should* behave and what characteristics he *should* have.

Finally, if he meets or exceeds these standards, he is likely to feel proud; if he does not, he is likely to feel ashamed. The social self,

[3]Charles H. Cooley, *Human Nature and the Social Order*, New York, Scribner's, 1902.

therefore, refers to the way a person views himself in relation to others and the way he perceives his role expectations and the roles of others. As might be expected, students in the classroom constantly seek to achieve positive feedback from their teachers.

Self-concept is the organization of qualities that the individual attributes to himself in varying situations.[4] An individual's behavior is largely determined by his pictures of himself. In reference to school, a student's behavior is largely determined by his academic self-conception. For example, students who believe that they are weak, bad, or stupid will behave accordingly. Arthur Jersild has described such a situation:

When a person resists learning that may be beneficial to him he is, in effect, trying to protect or to shield an unhealthy condition. But more broadly speaking, he is not actually protecting something unhealthy as such; he is trying to safeguard his picture of himself, his self-concept, the illusions concerning himself which he has built and which give him trouble.[5]

In the early days of experimentation in education, much time and energy were devoted to seeking the best "method" of teaching. Implicit in this approach was the belief that what was *learned* was a direct consequence of what was *taught*. Only lately have educators begun to realize that method as such is only one variable in a complex learning pattern that has *attitudinal* as well as *instructional* determinants. In short, learning appears to be related to the learner's membership in various subgroups, his readiness to learn, and the degree of significance he perceives in the materials being presented. Recently, another step has been taken in recognition of the relevance of the thoughts that students think about themselves—the self-concepts or self-images they have come to hold. The beginnings of this focus can be traced back to experiments in genetic, experimental, and clinical psychologies.

Internal dialogue that reflects the self-conception of students includes their questions:

What type of student am I?
How do I compare with other students?
What do other people think of me?

Answers to these questions affect both *continuity of mental functioning* and *progressive personal development*. Negative or positive responses tell students:

This is what I am.
This is how I compare with others.
This is what others think of me.

Specifically, for the child who wants to succeed in school, the school-task-related questions become:

---

[4]See Edon E. Snyder, "Self-Concept Theory: An Approach to Understanding the Behavior of Disadvantaged Pupils," *Clearing House*, 40 (December, 1965), 242–246.
[5]Arthur T. Jersild, *In Search of Self*, New York, Teachers College, 1952, p. 114.

Can I do it?
Am I adequate?
Do teachers like me?
What is school all about?

The thoughts of a once-reluctant student who managed to succeed might go as follows:

Can I do it?
The teachers think I can.
Perhaps I can.
I can!

How, one might ask, does the student develop a positive attitude toward school? In addition to receiving passing grades, he picks up verbal cues and physical gestures that, when decoded, mean "You can succeed." Consider the psychological impact of the following types of classroom prompting: "Well done." "Think this time." "Wrong again." "Let's look at this together." "You wouldn't understand." "Be careful." "Now isn't that a stupid question?" Test scores and the remarks of administrators and teachers cause children to think of themselves as being trustworthy, responsible, and competent, or unwanted, unattractive, and stupid. Eventually, their behavior falls into line with their thinking.

Maturation
There are certain *motor behavior* patterns that are common in all children. Experimental evidence indicates that physical maturation determines the rate and pattern of mental growth. Little skill development is possible until the child has matured sufficiently to engage in a particular activity. Each child's developmental pattern is unique. The internal growth process of body organs and functions is called *maturation*. Specific organs do not function until minimum growth has taken place. For example, a child does not walk until his legs and other parts that coordinate walking movements are able to function properly; a child does not learn to read until his nervous system has developed sufficiently for language capacity, eye control, ability to concentrate, and other related body functions.

Most of the tasks which we set for the child are complex activities combining many basic sensory-motor skills. If basic skills necessary to this complex of abilities are lacking, the total activity may break down. Consider the problem of laterality. If laterality is not established in the child and if the directionality resulting from laterality has not been developed, then certain relationships in space will be meaningless. . . . It is fruitless to attempt to teach the child the complex activities involved in reading as long as he continues to lack this basic skill.[6]

[6]Newell C. Kephart, *The Slow Learner in the Classroom*, Columbus, Ohio, Merrill, 1960, p. 32.

For many children, teachers may have to devise artificial means of providing additional practice in sensory-motor skills. This would include providing students with ladders to climb, fences to walk, or bicycles to ride. Improvements in these and related basic skills help children master the more complex activities of reading, writing, and arithmetic.

The age at which a child is "ready" to read and write is determined by his developmental level—neuromuscular, physical, and intellectual—and by his earlier experiences.[7] Children with physical and social handicaps tend to be slower in learning school assignments, but all children tend to move in their learning from the concrete to the abstract. Therefore, they should be actively involved with materials, substances, tools, and situations.

Piaget demonstrated that the very young child is easily and quickly confused by apparent changes in sizes of objects.[8] The preschool child has not yet learned some of the basic physical constants of his environment. That is, he does not know that the weight, volume, length, or quantity of objects remains constant despite changes in their shapes or the contexts in which they appear. Thus a 3-year-old will acknowledge that two identical jars contain the same number of cookies, but if the cookies in one jar are emptied into a taller jar, he is likely to decide that the taller jar contains more cookies. His understanding of the concept is not yet stable and abstract.

Bruner emphasized four factors related to maturation: linguistic skills are best taught at an early age; mental growth is not based on gradual increases of associations or stimulus-response connections, but on sudden sharp rises and stops as certain capacities develop; children are in a state of "readiness" at an earlier age than previously had been thought; the emphasis in education should be on skills and areas related to learning skills, with curriculum leading to self-reward sequences.[9] Bruner stressed the importance of children learning to learn in a nonlinear, or spiral, manner.

Skinner noted that grades, medals, diplomas, and other awards are reinforcers that facilitate learning.[10] Young children who succeed in playing games, solving puzzles, and building simple objects receive positive learning reinforcement. In short, an act of approval on the part of the teacher can, if repeated, lead to more complex forms of behavior. "Teaching machines" are based on this principle. For optimum learning to occur, furthermore, the process must eliminate the threat of punishment.

[7]Evelyn Goodenough Pitcher, et al., *Helping Young Children Learn*, Columbus, Ohio, Merrill, 1966, p. 100.

[8]Jean Piaget, *The Construction of Reality in the Child*, New York, Basic Books, 1954; *Judgment and Reasoning in the Child*, New York, Harcourt, Brace & World, 1928.

[9]Jerome S. Bruner, *Toward a Theory of Instruction*, New York, Belknap, 1966.

[10]B. F. Skinner, *Science and Human Behavior*, New York, Macmillan, 1953.

Achievement Motivation

Student desires for better grades and high test scores have very little relation to the types of tests administered or whether or not they are national tests. Personal achievement has multiple origins, including fear of failure, desire for social prestige, and anxiety created by parental pressures.[11] Social constraints or group definitions of acceptable behaviors, plus individual abilities, are the primary factors influencing a student's motivation for academic achievement. For some students, achievement in school is an avenue to high prestige and social status. For others, it is a sign of nonconformity.

There are at least four basic factors that determine the level of achievement a student will accept.[12] First, each student must have an appraisal of his *capacities* and *limitations*. A student is likely to seek to become a scholar if he believes that it is within his capacity. But if he imagines himself to have extremely limited intellectual ability, he will not expect to become a Phi Beta Kappa.

Second, each student must be aware of what *levels of achievement* are possible. It is not enough to tell a student that he can achieve great heights. The specific criteria of achievement must be defined, for example, an "A" average, the dean's list, the National Honor Society. To be meaningful, achievement must relate to concrete goals that allow the student to evaluate his performances.

Third, each student must be prepared to experience *success* and *failure*. A high-motivated successful student raises his goal expectations higher and higher until he perceives that he has reached his full potential. Conversely, a low-motivated failing student progressively reduces his goals in order to protect himself against further failure. Consistent failures will cause him to drop out of school.

Finally, each student must have an acceptable *position* or *status* within his group. If his peer group encourages academic achievement, then he will try to get minimum passing or higher grades. A nonacademically oriented peer group will have a dampening effect on academic achievement. *Motivation makes learning possible.* If a student does not have academic achievement needs, he is not likely to perform well in scholastic tasks.

The activities of the teacher are, of course, important in sustaining or curtailing achievement motivation. Praise and blame, rewards and punishment, and rivalry are the major techniques used. Studies indicate that praise tends to stimulate average and below-average students, but has less effect on superior students. Blame usually lowers the achievements of all students. Rewards and punishment, if not used properly, can be very ineffective. Punishment can breed antagonism, resentment, and avoidance of learning tasks to which it is attached, whereas rewards

[11] John W. McDavid and Herbert Harari, *Social Psychology: Individuals, Groups, Societies,* New York, Harper & Row, 1968, p. 60.

[12] David Krech, Richard S. Crutchfield, and Egerton L. Ballachey, *Individual in Society,* New York, McGraw-Hill, 1963, pp. 80–81.

are most effective when they are commensurate with the performance. Rivalry between individuals is the least desirable technique for building the achievement motivation of low-performing students. Self-rivalry—competition with one's own records—tends to be the most efficient way to secure optimum effort from *all* students.

Most students have intrinsic motives for learning, such as satisfaction in the successful termination of an activity. They are attracted by curiosity to things that are unclear or unfinished. Rewards come from satisfying that curiosity. Other intrinsic motives for learning are the needs to achieve competence, to cope with the environment, and to be good at something. These drives are related to the need for approval by others. The student must feel that his needs are shared by the teacher and that they have common objectives. Obviously, an understanding of childhood and adolescence gives valuable insight into motives for academic achievement.

DEVELOPMENT OF SOCIAL BEHAVIOR

Although social development begins slowly at birth, it is greatly accelerated during the preschool and elementary school years when a child's interaction with his peers becomes more frequent and intense. As preschool children grow older, demands for socialization cause them to spend less time in nonsocial, individualistic activities. They gradually learn to repress *egocentric* behaviors in favor of group-approved responses. The social-psychological processes of interaction through which the individual learns the habits, beliefs, values, and skills for effective group participation are known as *socialization.* As we shall see, the periods of socialization are overlapping. The major function of socialization is to transform an untrained human organism into an effective member of a society. The most important elements of socialization take place during childhood. In a complex modern society, the individual is subjected to many diverse socializing influences, many of which may not be consistent with one another.

Preschool Behaviors

Social conflicts tend to decrease and friendly interactions increase during *early childhood* (ages 2 through 5), when children form their first friendships. The patterns of friendship change markedly with age changes. For example, between the ages of 2 and 3 the *number* of friends increases; after this age the major change is in the *closeness* of attachment to a few peers.

A socially oriented and responsive preschool child seeks out companions and has a variety of contacts with them. In the course of learning the modes of social interaction, such a child has both satisfying and frustrating experiences, and, consequently, exhibits social responses that seem to be contradictory. For example, preschool friends tend to argue more frequently with each other than children who rarely associate with one another.[13]

The very young child cannot play hide-and-seek because he cannot understand the concept of being hidden but yet present. Nor can he play simple games that involve taking turns and making choices because he cannot understand these concepts. Similarly, he is unable to distinguish between reality and fantasy. Feeling extremely little in a world filled with big people, he is thrilled when he succeeds in controlling a situation or learning new concepts. His gradually emerging sense of self binds him to his parents and immediate family members.

During this period varying modes of popularity and leadership patterns emerge. By the time they reach kindergarten most children have a fairly definite idea of other children with whom they would like to play. Some children are constantly sought out by others for playmates; others are rejected and avoided by their peers. Some children quickly assume leadership roles; others are content to be followers. Obvious styles of leadership emerge: "statesmen" control others by using subtle, indirect techniques, whereas "bullies" use force to get others to obey them. The drift toward group activities is often threatened by what seems to be an endless number of minor conflicts. Boys frequently fight each other; girls tend to argue. On the whole, however, the interactions of preschool children are characterized by cooperation and friendship.

Elementary School Behaviors

Unlike preschool friendships, which are casual, unstable, and transient, elementary school relationships become more intense, stable, and lasting. With the exception of his parents and perhaps some of his teachers, the child's closest friends are his agemates. Indeed, his classmates are his most important socialization agents. Elementary school is the first group experience outside the home in which membership is mandatory for all children. This shift from rather informal home situations to formal group experiences may be the greatest shift in role expectation the child will ever encounter. Within a relatively short period of time he must learn to share the attention and supervision of one adult with unknown children and to respond to demands for conformity (e.g., "take your seat," "stay in line," "put your paper away").

The *middle childhood* period (ages 6 through 12) is dominated by "gang" activities. Gangs at this stage are usually informal groups with rapid turnover in membership. Middle-class children between the ages of 10 and 14 are likely to join highly structured, formal groups such as YMCA, YWCA, Boy Scouts, and Girls Scouts. The middle childhood period is the beginning of learning to play appropriate *sex-roles*. Dif-

[13]Paul H. Mussen, *The Psychological Development of the Child*, Englewood Cliffs, N. J., Prentice-Hall, 1963, p. 88.

ferences in the behavior of men and women have some biological basis, of course, but they are largely produced by teaching appropriate role-expectations to boys and girls. Boys are taught not to be "sissies" and girls are conditioned not to be "tomboys." This delineation of sexual identity also leads to different reading and vocational interests. The importance of middle childhood can be underscored by noting that the child's choice of extracurricular games, dress, speech, and food are heavily influenced by his peers' choices during this period.

Preadolescence (ages 10 through 12) is characterized by many conditions, including a growth spurt, awakening sexuality, and (as noted above) an increase in peer-group relationships. Except for infancy, the body undergoes the most rapid changes in size and shape during this period. Children aged 10, 11, and 12 begin to "look down on" little children. Along with these changes, the reproductive system starts to mature, causing sex-linked physical characteristics to begin to appear; girls develop obvious breasts and begin to produce feminine hormones; boys get more muscular and begin to produce masculine hormones. This is hardly the period of "latency" early psychologists imagined it to be.

During elementary school, friends tend to resemble each other in social class, chronological age, physical maturity, and race. Racial and religious attitudes are developed. Studies indicate that attitudes toward children of various religious faiths develop more slowly than racial attitudes, largely because perceptual differentiations are more difficult to make on religious grounds. Seeking to conform to group expectations, children tend to echo their dislike for children of other religious or racial backgrounds. The Protestant child, for example, ritualistically dislikes Jewish children; Caucasians dislike Negro children.

This is also the time, however, when positive contacts can alter prejudicial attitudes. Social values are transmitted both within and outside the classroom, but the classroom influence is extremely important. In a classroom where social class, racial, and religious intolerance are encouraged, intolerant children will result. The reverse, of course, is also true. Thus the behaviors of adolescents are conditioned by early childhood experiences.

Adolescent Behaviors

Adolescence has often been described as the "impossible" period between childhood and adulthood. And it is true that to a great extent adolescents are marginal people. Being denied many of the rights of either children or adults, they are nevertheless expected to fulfill many of the obligations of both groups—to remain obedient to their parents, to control their sex impulses, and still to select a vocation and otherwise begin to act as adults. This is a period in which young people need association with the opposite sex; they also need to evolve their own theory of life. Adolescents identify most strongly with their own peers, who form *cliques*. Members of cliques usually come from the same racial and socioeconomic backgrounds and, therefore, have much the same interests and social values. Cliques are dominant forces because they are based on personal compatibility, congeniality, and mutual admiration. College-bound youths, for example, tend to associate with other college-bound youths; high school dropouts tend to associate with others who are planning to drop out or who have dropped out.

The peer group gives rewards and punishments to its members on account of their moral behavior. Those who are honest, responsible, loyal, kind, and self-controlled tend to be rewarded. It is not moral qualities alone, however, that determine whether a child will be rewarded or punished by his peer group. Operating in addition to the moral qualities are such non-moral qualities as diffuse geniality, and skill in games, which sometimes overshadow the moral qualities in determining the status of a child in a peer group. In general, though, the forming of stable, positive relationships within the peer group is indicative of sound character development, while inability to make friends may indicate the opposite.[14]

Most adolescent groups reinforce and strengthen the values that members have acquired from their parents. In other words, peer groups are less originators than reinforcers of values and behaviors developed in the family. However, in some areas, such as dress and the use of slang, peer groups aid adolescents in achieving independence from adults. By sticking together and behaving alike, they are able to insulate themselves from outside pressures to abandon nonadult-conforming behaviors.

During the junior high school years, girls and boys are noticeably different in their levels of biological and social maturity. Girls usually are quite advanced biologically and show considerable interest in the opposite sex, but their male agemates are less developed in both areas. This is especially true of eighth- and ninth-graders, among whom the girls have more problems centering on social life and heterosexual behavior than the boys do. Around the tenth grade, boys begin catching up with girls in biological and social maturity. Dating then becomes a central concern for both sexes. Along with the problem of getting dates come issues involved in "making out," that is, issues raised by the necessity to define the outer limits of heterosexual relationships. In general, adolescent girls engage in much less premarital sexual intercourse than boys, but standards of acceptable sexual behavior vary with social class. For example, studies indicate that masturbation is quite widely tolerated and practiced among middle-class boys, whereas sexual intercourse is a much more frequent outlet among lower-class boys.

Contrary to some opinions, most adolescents do *not* generally view their parents as unnecessary authoritarians. Rather, they consider them as necessary teachers of moral and ethical values. Thus most adolescents grow up to behave like their parents in particular and like members of

[14]R. F. Peck and R. J. Havighurst, *The Psychology of Character Development*, New York, Wiley, 1960, p. 139.

the larger society in general. In a recent study, Muzafer and Carolyn Sherif clearly demonstrated the extent to which all adolescents are affected by the values of middle-class-oriented adults:

There is one clear and striking generalization about the high school youth which holds in all areas and despite their differing backgrounds: Their values and goals earmark them all as youth exposed to the American ideology of success and wanting the tangible symbols of that success. There were no differences between the youth in different areas with respect to desires for material goods. In addition to comfortable housing, the symbols of success for these adolescents include a car in every garage, a telephone, television set, transistor radio, fashionable clothing, time to enjoy them, and money to provide them. It is obvious, however, that the present accessibility of these items differed enormously for youth in the different areas. . . .

Youth in areas of low, middle, and high rank did have different scales for evaluating success in a variety of activities essential to acquiring the desired standard of living. Their latitudes of acceptance differed even for the financial achievement necessary to support it. Relative to these latitudes of acceptance, and especially relative to their parents' accomplishments, school youth in low rank areas appear as more ambitious than those in high rank areas.

The differences in absolute level of goals in different activities are significant, but more striking are the differential opportunities available in the different areas for achieving these goals. . . .[15]

The significance of peer groups in relation to an adolescent living in the slums, his activities within a school situation, and his feelings about society is their reinforcement of limited opportunity structures and growing frustration. For the lower-class student, school is a negative microcosm of the community; racial, academic, and social segregation are commonplace. In any case, the young adolescent tends to exhibit patterns of behavior that will be characteristic of him during his later adolescence and his adult life.

CHANGING VIEWS
OF INTELLIGENCE TESTS

The hypothetical consruct of *intelligence,* an important concept in education, can be modified by changing environmental conditions. Generally, intelligence is a term that covers a person's "capacities" and "potentialities" in a wide range of tasks involving vocabulary, numbers, problem-solving, concepts, and so on. It is measured by standardized tests, which usually involve several specific abilities, often with emphasis on verbal ability. A score on an intelligence test can be converted into an intelligence quotient, or IQ, which indicates the subject's relative standing in a population independently of his age. The intelligence quotient reflects several abilities, not just one, and each of these

[15]Muzafer Sherif and Carolyn W. Sherif, *Reference Groups,* New York, Harper & Row, 1964, pp. 199–221.

is fairly complex. Any intelligence test should be used with care. As Anastasi concluded:

Another area of psychology in which confusions regarding heredity and environment are likely to arise is that of interpretation of psychological tests. Persons unfamiliar with the way in which psychological tests are developed and used sometimes expect such tests to measure "native intelligence," "innate capacities," "hereditary predispositions of personality," and the like. By now it should be apparent that such expectations are sheer nonsense. . . .

Every psychological test measures a sample of the individual's behavior. No test provides any special devices or "tricks" for penetrating beyond behavior or for eliminating the subject's past experiences. All conditions influencing behavior will inevitably be reflected in test scores. In so far as performance on a given test correlates with performance in other situations the test can serve in diagnosing or predicting behavior. It is in this sense only that a psychological test can be said to measure "capacity" or "potentiality."[16]

In other words, tests and other types of psychological measuring devices are merely instruments for describing in quantitative terms a *sample* of an individual's behavior. In many school systems, unfortunately, it is still customary to administer an intelligence test and to conclude that poor performance is caused simply by low native intelligence.

As we discuss the changing views of intelligence tests, we shall look first at the extent to which test performance is influenced by cultural factors; next we shall assess the efforts aimed at eliminating cultural bias from tests.

Cultural Biases

Every intelligence test is a sample of behavior and as such reflects factors that influence behavior. It should also be apparent that every intelligence test is constructed within a specific cultural framework and that it is evaluated and standardized against practical criteria dictated by a given culture.[17] One of the faults of intelligence tests is that most such tests assume not only that the test-takers share a common cultural background, but also that they have all been equally prepared, either directly or indirectly, for the tasks imposed on them by the test.[18] This usually is not the case, however. Irving Lorge noted that differences are found among individuals and groups in terms of sex, age, education, geographic origin, and occupation of father.[19] Futhermore, most existing tests emphasize middle-class concepts and information.

[16]Anne Anastasi, *Differential Psychology* (3rd ed.), New York, Macmillan, 1958, p. 82.

[17]Anne Anastasi (ed.), *Testing Problems in Perspective*, Washington, D.C., American Council on Education, 1966, pp. 453–457.

[18]S. A. Kendrick, "College Board Scores and Cultural Bias," *College Board Review*, Winter, 1964, 7–9.

[19]Irving Lorge, "Difference or Bias in Tests of Intelligence," in Anastasi (ed.), op. cit., pp. 465–471.

Critics say that intelligence tests are unfair for the simple reasons that all test-takers are *not* of the same sex, age, and geographic origin; they do *not* all have equal levels of educational achievement; they do *not* have fathers in the same occupation; and they are *not* all members of the middle class, and, therefore, have *not* all been exposed to the commonalities assumed by test-makers. It is not surprising that we find the highest IQs among children in professional families and the lowest in children in semiskilled and unskilled families. In addition, the argument continues, extreme environmental deprivation or a depressing emotional climate can restrict the growth of even the most intellectually alert, whereas an optimal intellectual stimulation and climate can improve the measured development of those with little inherent capacity.

William Turnbull documented conspicuous depressions in test performance by students in Alabama and Georgia as compared to students in New York, Iowa, Nebraska, and California.[20] Even more strikingly apparent in his results was the fact that students from large communities in all geographic regions were much more facile verbally than those from small communities, although in mathematical ability their superiority was slight, and in terms of ability to answer common-sense science questions, the two groups were equal. In a similar study of social and cultural differences and mental abilities Fifer concluded that we have strong evidence of differential patterns of mental abilities and responses among different ethnic groups.[21] An anecdote from Kendrick succinctly illustrates this point:

Many years ago I administered an intelligence test to an adult Negro man who had spent most of his life on a cotton plantation in the South. One question on the test was, "If you found a sealed, stamped, addressed envelope on the street, what would you do with it?" His answer, "I wouldn't mess with it, boss," was not allowed for credit by the test manual, which preferred, "I would mail it," or something equivalent. It is by no means clear whether his answer was unintelligent, unsophisticated, uncooperative, or shrewdly adaptive. The poor fit between the man and the test-maker does not raise the examinee's score; it merely casts doubt on the entire evaluative enterprise.[22]

Even though numerous studies have measured extreme cultural differences and their effects on producing culturally biased test results, many school personnel using tests fail to profit from such findings. Instead they treat test scores as absolute determinations about individuals or groups. Recently, test-makers as well as test-users become increasingly aware of the multiplicity of factors related to test performances. Individual abilities level off within a narrowly defined range as children grow older. Thus most older children and adults show little change in test performance over a period of years. This stabilization or

[20]William Turnbull, "Influence of Cultural Background on Predictive Test Score," in Anastasi (ed.), op. cit., pp. 458–464.

[21]Gordon Fifer, "Social Class and Cultural Group Differences in Diverse Mental Abilities," in Anastasi (ed.), op. cit., pp. 481–490.

[22]Kendrick, loc. cit.

leveling off is mainly a function of motivational and personality factors, rather than any inherent qualities. Children who succeed at particular tasks are apt to maintain these skills, whereas those who are inept at them are not apt to improve. A poor reader, for example, is not likely to pursue reading exercises consciously in order to improve his skill. Rather, he will avoid or, as much as possible, abandon the task.

Attempts to Eliminate Cultural Biases.   For about 50 years social scientists have been revising (1) the meaning of intelligence, (2) the various tests and procedures for its estimation, and (3) the implications of the evidence from tests of intelligence. Attempts to produce unbiased tests that measure intellectual capacity rather than intelligence per se usually center on eliminating all individual or group differences by *adding* items. For example, since there are differences in verbal ability between male and female test-takers, one way to overcome the verbal superiority of women is by adding a sufficient amount of numerical reasoning items to make the average total score of men equal to that of women. The rationale is "no difference, ergo, no bias." Another method is to reduce group differences by *subtracting* items. This approach essentially removes the items that favor a particular group. Tests produced by subtraction, like those produced by addition, are not supposed to reflect the impact of sex, status, or culture on test performance.

Some psychometricians have attempted to produce tests that are *culture-free*. Beginning with the Army Beta Test, there have been many efforts to remove the differences attributable to culture, although none of these has been completely successful. Some tests that attempt to be culture-free are Dodd's International Group Mental Test, Cattell's Culture-Free Intelligence Test, Spearman's Visual Perception Test, the Multi-Mental Non-Language Test, and Rulon's Semantic Test of Intelligence. Each of these instruments attempts to measure intellectual performance by the manipulation of objects, pictured designs, or numbers that require "intelligent" behaviors of perception, selection, generalization, and organization. Each test is limited by the fact that different cultural experiences with the materials used significantly influence test results. "Culture-common" would more accurately fit these tests than "culture-free," since performances on such tests may be free from cultural differences, but not from cultural *influences*.

A pertinent question that might be asked about the elimination of test items differentiating subgroups of the population is, "Where should we stop?" Should we rule out items showing socioeconomic differences, sex differences, ethnic minority group differences, and educational differences? If we proceed to rule out all these, what will be left? The better solution is not to reduce bias in tests of intelligence but to use them with full knowledge that a wide range of differences may be produced as a result of physical endowment and cultural opportunities. This, then, is using tests as but one of many diagnostic tools to tell us where a particular child is in reference to others. When tests are supplemented with student and parent conferences, home visits, academic grades, and so forth, school personnel are better able to assist students in improving. Tests used in this manner become *means* to improving academic performances and not *ends* in themselves.

Tests, in other words, should not be used by teachers as instruments for predetermining a student's interest. The more effective teachers use them as but one of many diagnostic tools. Indeed, given the proper motivation and a low level of anxiety, some academically disadvantaged students have been encouraged actively to seek improvement in low-skill areas.

NATIONAL
ASSESSMENT

Articles on the national assessment of education have been appearing recently in a number of journals.[23] As a matter of fact, a storm of controversy is raging over this program. The proponents say it is a necessity in today's rapidly expanded systems of education. The opponents say it will be an unnecessary hindrance and will create many problems throughout the school systems of America. To describe it briefly, national assessment of education is simply the nationwide issuing and use of standardized tests to determine certain educational statistics. For instance, every tenth- or twelfth-grade student across the nation would be given the same test, and the tests would be different for each different grade. These standardized tests could cover reading, language arts, social studies, mathematics, citizenship, fine arts, and vocational education. The entire program would be voluntary and free from any governmental control. The National Assessment of Educational Progress (NAEP) has defined two principles on which it believes the assessment program must be based: (1) the categories and areas for which results are reported must include the states; (2) the results must then be used to compare the state school systems of this country with each other.

In April, 1969, the first phase of national assessment of education actually got underway with a minimum of problems. The first year of the program was financed by $2,560,000 from the U.S. Office of Education, the Carnegie Foundation, and the Ford Foundation and was coordinated by a quasilegal body called the Education Commission of the States (ECS); 38 states are members of ECS. Of the school systems that were asked to participate in the voluntary testing, 89 percent did so. Assessment in the summer of 1969 consisted of 17-year-olds in and out of school, plus young adults in the 25–33 age group. In the fall of 1969, the 9–13 age group was tested. The first sampling will evaluate three subject areas: science, writing, and citizenship. The total

[23]See, for instance, Lawrence Beymer, "The Pros and Cons of National Assessment," *Clearing House*, 40 (October, 1965), 137–139.

program will continue through 1971 and continue to be financed by both governmental and private funds. Almost 30,000 persons in each of the three age groups will have participated in the three-year program.

Arguments Against National Assessment
Many people fear that data from the national assessment program will be used unfairly in attacks on specific school systems and personnel. Critics say that students will not receive the "blame"; instead, it will fall on the school systems, especially the teachers. Standardized achievement tests have the capacity to measure much more than an individual's level of attainment; they may also be used to judge the competence of those responsible for the scores, including parents and teachers. As a result, externally administered achievement tests could cover entire communities with a cloud of criticism and guilt. Most of the big-city schools are against the assessment testing program for a related very important reason: They are mainly attended by low-achieving minority group students. Students in large city schools usually do rank below students in suburban schools on achievement and aptitude tests, and nonwhite students usually do test lower than white students. One opponent of the program wrote:

Negro students do not, on the average, score as high on standardized tests as white students. Today standardized test scores are used as a basis for placement in jobs, college, professional schools, and the armed forces. As long as racial disparities exist, the Negro student will receive less than his proportionate share of all the opportunities that depend on these test scores. Negro students' chances of making better test scores would be set back greatly by the proposed test program.[24]

A serious problem that will have to be faced in a national testing program is the attitude of the teachers. They fear public criticism if their students are ranked poorly. To guard against this, many teachers may ignore much of their prescribed teaching curriculum and teach the specific material on the assessment tests. If this happens, students will be deprived of the broad range of materials that are available for teaching.

Arguments for National Assessment
The national assessment program is uncovering weaknesses in education systems, but it is not the fault of the program that these weaknesses are revealed. Weaknesses obviously existed before the testing began. Individual students, schools, and communities are not identified, since all results are reported on a statewide basis. Thus individual schools are not singled out for praise or criticism. In any case, all

[24]Johnny L. Jones, "Assessing the Academic Achievement of Negro Students," *Clearing House*, 39 (October, 1964), 108.

school systems do undergo a form of national assessment—the college entrance examinations. The testing program will not correct school weaknesses, but it will report them to special committees and organizations skilled at handling such problems.

Through the earlier pilot surveys, some educational problems have already been encountered; for example, (1) the average high school student is unable to solve simple reasoning problems as well as he can read and understand directions; (2) less than half of the twelfth-grade students in the nation understand the subtler ideas in the writing of Rudyard Kipling, Sinclair Lewis, or Jules Verne. Proponents believe that additional deficits will be brought out by effective nationwide standardized tests.

The merits of national assessment and the results of efforts to devise better tests are being determined by actual trial. It is probable that more public schools will undergo advanced forms of national assessment in the near future.

SUMMARY

1. Human development is determined by *heredity* and *environment*. Heredity determines whether an individual will learn; his environment determines what he will learn.
2. The acquisition of language is crucial to human development.
3. The self is a social product, consisting of individual and group judgments about how well we fit into given situations. Students look to teachers for positive feedback.
4. Piaget's analysis of developmental periods illustrates the importance of learning correct cultural patterns of adjustment.
5. Students are likely to seek better grades and improved school task performances when teachers properly motivate and sanction them.
6. As a child becomes more socialized, he becomes less egocentric in overt patterns of interaction. Adolescents in particular are extremely peer-group conscious.
7. Intelligence tests are in reality tests of cultural adjustments and learnings. When used as a *diagnostic* tool, IQ tests can assist teachers in mitigating cultural differences.
8. National assessment has positive and negative aspects. On the one hand, it can point out curriculum weaknesses; on the other hand, it may lead to teaching primarily for favorable test results. The weaknesses revealed through such testing are not created by the tests but can be eliminated or minimized once the areas of weakness are known.

SELECTED READINGS

Bayley, Nancy, "Mental Growth During the First Three Years," in R. G. Barker, J. S. Kounin, and H. F. Wright (eds.), *Child Behavior and Development*, New York, McGraw-Hill, 1943. Bayley surveys mental development during early growth period of children.

Cattell, P., *The Measurement of Intelligence of Infants and Young Children*, New York, The Psychological Corporation, 1947. Cattell surveys various methods of intelligence measurement and postulates his own theory on the measurement of intelligence in children.

Cronbach, L. J., *Essentials of Psychological Testing* (3rd ed.), New York, Harper & Row, 1970. An overview of scientific elements and methods of testing.

Escalona, S., "The Use of Infant Tests for Predictive Purposes," Martin and Stedler (eds.), *Readings in Child Development*, New York, Harcourt, Brace & World, 1954. The author points out the strengths and weaknesses in using infant tests for predicting behaviors.

Jersild, Arthur T., *Child Psychology* (4th ed.), New York, Prentice-Hall, 1954. A complete study of child psychology which includes information on physical growth and its effect on mental development.

Mead, George Herbert, *Mind, Self, and Society*. Chicago, The University of Chicago Press, 1934. One of the earliest and most widely accepted treatments of the self in relation to society.

Watson, E. H., and G. H. Lowrey, *Growth and Development in Children* (3rd ed.), Chicago, Year Book Publishers, 1958. The authors survey studies of the complete developmental process of the child.

White, Martha S., "Social Class, Child-Rearing Practices and Child Behavior," *American Sociological Review*, 22 (December, 1957), 704–712. Students will find this brief article to be of great value in understanding the effects of child-rearing on child behavior.

Whiting, J. W. M., and I. L. Child, *Child Training and Personality*, New Haven, Conn., Yale University Press, 1953. Study of the effects of training on personality of child.

7

Socioeconomic Forces Affecting Education

*Without major changes in educational practices, greater expenditures on existing elementary schools serving disadvantaged neighborhoods will not significantly improve the quality of education. Moreover, current assessments of preschool programs indicate that their gains are lost in the elementary grades, unless the schools themselves are improved.**

In this chapter we shall consider first what happens to the family during urban and rural revolutions; then we shall discuss the changing economic foundations of education.

Each year America becomes more urban. More than half the nation now lives in urbanized areas. "Urbanization" is a complex and difficult process to define. The definitions given by a particular author are merely his way of categorizing a given community. There are, in short, no single best or innate definitions of "rural," "urban," and "urbanization." Even the United States censuses have periodically undergone official changes in definitions.

*Report of the National Advisory Commission on Civil Disorders, New York, Bantam Books, 1968, p. 447.

THE SHIFT FROM
RURAL LIVING

Urban revolution, a term coined by V. Gordon Childe, refers to changes brought about by the great discoveries and inventions between 4000 and 3000 B.C.[1] The new trades and techniques demanded specialists, and once a person became specialized he became dependent on other people. Another consequence of this revolution has been the growth of cities in which live the nonproducers of food. *Rural revolution* refers to the changes villagers face during the process of becoming urban dwellers.[2] This revolution is the result of suddenly precipitated changes in styles of life, affecting a considerable portion of a culture. One of the major problems during this transition is how to make life more satisfying for the remaining villagers, while aiding the urban adjustment of the rural migrants. Technically, the problem is how to assimilate great numbers of rural people into complex industrial communities. Modern cities, unlike the preindustrial ones, are dependent on extremely advanced technology and are extremely sensitive to malfunctions of many types. Furthermore, impersonal group interactions are becoming increasingly prevalent.

Changing Family Relationships

The shift of populations from the farm to the city has altered family members' relationships and activities. Instead of large, extended families that include many relatives, most urban families are isolated *conjugal* units, consisting only of husband, wife, and children. Other changes include the decline of male dominance and the rise in the importance of women; an increase in mobility, resulting in social distance between family members and less emphasis on a family homestead; and the transfer of work from the home to the factory, accompanied by money wages and specialization of labor.

The rural child shares in the work of the family and is given considerable responsibility at an early age; the urban child devotes most of his time and energy to play activities and is introduced to adult tasks and responsibility slowly and relatively late in childhood. In the semipatriarchal atmosphere of the rural home, the child is expected to be "seen and not heard," but generally the urban child is allowed more self-expression and, in nonlower-class homes, is a main participant in adult conversations.

Family settings differ greatly, then, in the following ways: (1) the demands for responsibility made on children, that is, the number and kinds of duties expected of them; (2) the emotionally positive behaviors of mothers to children, such as praise, absence of physical punishment, and general

---

[1] J. O. Brew, "The Metal Ages: Copper, Bronze, and Iron," in H. L. Shapiro (ed.), *Man, Culture, and Society,* New York, Oxford University Press, 1956, pp. 111–138.
[2] Joel M. Halpern, "The Rural Revolution," *Transactions of the New York Academy of Science,* 28 (1965), 60–73.

warmth; (3) the degree of control demanded over aggression toward peers both inside and outside the family; (4) the degree of aggression and obedience toward parents; (5) the extent to which the mother does the caretaking of babies; (6) the extent of her caretaking of older children; (7) the degree of the mother's emotional stability. . . .[3]

Since the skills needed in modern technology require extensive formal education, few parents can effectively train their children for economic roles. In most communities, specialized agencies, mainly the school, provide better education for children than the family can. Some school districts, for example, have gradually expanded their elementary programs to include counselors who help young people solve their personal problems and select vocations. Elementary school counselors are able to give students a wide variety of information that is not available to the average parent. Indeed, much of this special information is needed merely to help the young person adjust to the complexities of urban life. Nevertheless, this type of assistance undermines the interdependence of parents and children.

The urbanization of great numbers of people also modifies the way they are housed. The shift away from single-family dwelling units with their surrounding yards, gardens, and sometimes even orchards or fields to smaller houses and yards and to apartments in large buildings restricts the space for free movement for the entire family. Although urban children are taught to be quiet so that they will not disturb other families, their recreational activities are not easily confined to a small house or an apartment. There is little space for privacy or for the development of hobbies, indoors or out. More disruptive strains on family life include divorce, desertion, and death. More than 400,000 divorces are granted in America each year, causing some social scientists to project that the time is almost here when one out of every four marriages will end in divorce. (The divorce rate is higher among childless couples than among those with children.) In addition, many marriages are ended by desertion or death.

It is interesting to note that the children who still live in rural America are becoming urbanized not merely through mail-order catalogs, newspapers, films, and television, but also through the structure and programs of their schools. Rural public schools are imitating urban schools in their remedial programs, the content of their courses, their administrative organization, and their selection of personnel.

Functions of the Family
The modern family has relinquished some of its traditional functions and gained importance in others. The family has lost most of its economic *production* functions and is now mainly a unit of economic *consumption*. The *protective* functions have declined, giving way to

[3]William W. Lambert and Wallace E. Lambert, *Social Psychology*, Englewood Cliffs, N. J., Prentice-Hall, 1964, p. 13.

institutions outside the home. The *socialization* function is being shared largely with the school. However, the family is still the primary agent in passing on *social skills:* The child is almost totally in the care of his parents during the first few years of his life when the basic characteristics of his personality are being formed. The *sex-regulation* and *reproductive* functions have shown little change; sexual intercourse is still considered "proper" only within marriage, and every society depends primarily on the family for producing children. *Child-bearing* and *child care* also remain the primary functions of the family The *status* function continues, as families prepare children to retain their inherited social positions and, in some cases, to aspire to higher ones. A most important function is the *affectional* one; in general, this function of the family has increased.

Suburbia

The suburbs have been the most rapidly growing urban communities in the United States in the past two decades. Concurrent with the growth of the suburbs is a change in the ethnic and social class composition of the central city (see Table 2). The urban middle classes who have moved to the suburbs have been largely replaced by Negroes and Puerto Rican migrants (see Chapter 12). About half the jobs in an urban area exist to meet needs that arise because of the presence of the urban dwellers. As people move to the suburbs many jobs go with them. Industries also move outward when the central city ceases to be the only source of their labor supply. These changes have created acute problems for the central cities. Their tax bases have shrunk with the loss of industry, business, and middle-class homeowners; but demands for city services have *not* decreased proportionately.

What has happened to the central cities is now, in fact, occurring in many of the older suburbs and small cities. They too have begun to decay at the center as residents of old neighborhoods have moved out in search of more spacious, convenient, and prestigious places to live. Many urban poor whites are "leap-frogging" to the newer suburbs, where they settle near the centers of the communities; as they do, they frequently convert these neighborhoods into slums and semislums. A number of lower-class minority group people, mainly Negroes, are waiting patiently for housing to open up in the suburbs.

It is often assumed that the flight of the middle-class to the suburbs, urban sprawl, poor housing, racial hostility, and other "urban" problems exist chiefly in the large cities. Actually, studies have shown that these problems are sometimes found in a greater degree in the surburbs. These "no-problems" areas are often seething with unrecognized problems. The difference is that in the large cities there is national concern and protest about conditions that do not receive publicity in the suburbs. This can be explained partially by the existence of political forces, especially those in the large cities that are highly organized and have

Table 2
Percentage of Metropolitan White Population, in Central City and Suburbs, by Age, 1950 and 1960

| | Percentage of white population living in, | | | | Net change, 1950 to 1960 | |
| | 1950 | | 1960 | | | |
	Central city	Suburbs	Central city	Suburbs	Central city	Suburbs
23 largest metropolitan areas						
Age groups:						
0-19	54.0	46.0	42.6	57.6	+17.0	+86.4
20-40	57.3	42.7	44.9	55.1	−24.6	+24.2
41-60	56.4	43.6	48.7	51.3	− 6.4	+27.2
61 and over	57.0	43.0	55.6	44.4	+22.3	+29.8
Total	56.1	43.9	46.4	53.6	− 2.2	+44.2
19 smaller metropolitan areas						
Age groups:						
0-19	65.0	35.0	47.0	53.0	−11.8	+84.2
20-40	52.3	47.7	50.0	50.0	− 6.0	+ 3.0
41-60	58.4	41.6	51.9	48.1	+ 2.7	+34.0
61 and over	59.1	40.9	56.8	43.2	+28.3	+41.2
Total	58.9	41.1	50.2	49.8	− 2.3	+38.7

Source: Data compiled from U.S. Bureau of the Census, *1950 Census of Population* and *1960 Census of Population.*

articulate special-interest constituencies, and by a larger number of problem-oriented professionals.

SOCIAL STRATIFICATION

An individual's *socioeconomic status* determines his peer, school, and community contacts. Socioeconomic status is a broad concept; it encompasses not only social class but also education, occupation, income, and several other factors. "Low socioeconomic status" describes a consistent pattern of life: low level of education; unskilled or semiskilled work; small income; and living in a poor residential area. ("High socioeconomic status" of course means that all the elements are reversed.)

Determinants of Social Class

A child's social class is defined by the position his parents hold in society. From before he is born until after he is dead an individual's opportunities and rewards are affected by his class position. Social stratification is a condition in which a mass society is differentiated by layer upon layer of population qualities. A *stratified society* has been defined as "one in which the population has been separated into categories that are unequal in social evaluation. The greater the inequality among categories or the less the likelihood of their becoming equal, the more highly stratified the society is said to be."[4] People can be stratified according to any quality that is recognized by members of the society. That is, before groups of people can be said to be unequal they must have in common some property or factor that can be differentiated. Therefore, when a society is said to be stratified, it is so in terms of a referent—a factor in each stratum that can be graded either by some type of measurement or by judgment. The major dimensions that underline the American social class structure are prestige, occupation, possessions or income, class consciousness, value orientations, and power.

The terms "social stratum" and "social class" are in most cases synonymous. Hodgkinson defines social class as any group of people who feel socially involved with one another and who feel that in some way they are different from others who are not members of the group.[5] Warner is as responsible as anyone for stimulating research into social class in America.[6] His six-fold scale of class strata—upper-upper, lower-

[4]Bernard Barber, *Social Stratification: A Comparative Analysis of Structure and Process*, New York, Harcourt, Brace & World, 1957, p. 52.

[5]Harold L. Hodgkinson, *Education in Social and Cultural Perspectives*, Englewood Cliffs, N. J., Prentice-Hall, 1962, p. 12.

[6]W. Lloyd Warner, et al., *Social Class in America*, Chicago, Science Research Associates, 1949, p. 86.

upper, upper-middle, lower-middle, upper-lower, lower-lower—has become much used in both scientific and nonscientific contexts.

Although rural areas do not lack social class features, it is in the city where the class system appears in its most elaborate form, where social status implies extreme differences in "cultural" appreciation and in political and economic opportunities. Even though no single-objective criterion determines class status, above-average income tends to remove a person from the lowest level. But upper-class people sometimes have relatively low incomes; conversely, some persons with high incomes are excluded from the upper classes (e.g., known members of the Mafia). In the United States, occupation is the most important source of status.

An individual's social status can change for better or for worse. *Social mobility* refers to the movement of people between positions. Loss of status (downward mobility) usually comes about through improper behavior, that is, by acts that do not conform to the code of a social class. Movements up the status ladder (upward mobility) usually result from achievement. A rise from the top of lower class to the bottom of middle class is the least difficult upward move.

A high school education and the acquisition of certain social and employment skills are the usual prerequisites to securing a lower-middle-class position. To move from the lower-middle to the upper-middle class is much more difficult, since increased ability may not result in social mobility. Upper-middle-class positions are awarded in competition where factors other than ability ("whom you know," not necessarily "what you know") play a decisive role. Equally important is the fact that in many instances the number of applicants exceeds the number of available positions. The number of available positions decreases toward the top of the social class pyramid, but so too does the number of qualified competitors.

Effects of Social Class

We have noted that social class status is mainly inherited *(ascribed status)*. Even in the most mobile society, change in ascribed status is rarer than its retention. The opportunities for rising to a higher class through selective competition *(achieved status)* are limited. Effective family control over opportunities excludes most nonfamily-member competitors who have different racial, religious, or ethnic characteristics. Children of a high social class, for example, have a distinct advantage over outsiders: They are adequately prepared to move into the positions held by their parents. Access to formal education is clearly related to social class. The upper groups enjoy better educational facilities that permit them to develop their innate abilities. Social class is a nearly irreversible determinant of success in the competition for education and jobs.

Hollingshead, studying the relation between adolescents' social behavior and their class position, found that upper- and middle-class children are taught not to be aggressive, to have "good" manners, to study hard, to attend Sunday School, and to avoid making friends with lower-class children.[7] In contrast, the child in the lower class learns that he and his family are held in contempt by boys and girls in the higher classes. Frequently he comes to resent his family and his dependence upon it for food, money, clothing, and shelter. Hollingshead concluded that social class values and patterns of behavior learned in family and surrounding neighborhood subcultures not only provide the stage upon which the child acts, but also provide him with ways of acting and defining the action.

As the child participates in various social situations, he learns to act in certain ways, to regard himself as a valued member of the group or as an unwanted participant. The social class of an individual greatly limits his way of eating, what he wears, his choice of friends, selection of occupation, types of recreation, use of money, and conceptions of right and wrong. Hodgkinson noted that child-rearing practices also differ between middle- and lower-class families.[8] Fewer middle-class children were breast-fed and they were weaned earlier from either bottle or breast. Lower-class families were more lenient in their training and in their demands that a child assume responsibility. Some social scientists believe—with a large body of data for substantiation—that whether one is consciously aware of it or not, his every activity, no matter how independent he may feel, is greatly influenced and conditioned by early childhood training, growth, and development.

DOMINANT TRENDS
IN AMERICAN LIFE

We have discussed two broad aspects of American life—the shift from rural to urban living and social stratification. We now turn to some of the dominant trends in life in this country that are directly related to urban living and social classes.

The Labor Force

In 1900, more than 6 in 10 boys and 1 in 10 girls aged 14 to 19 were in the labor force. Today, children have ceased to be an important part of the labor force. They no longer have a "credit" value in the family economy; instead, they are considered expensive "deficits" who must be totally cared for. Also, families have fewer children today than in 1900. In 1964, the average size of the family was 3.7; in 1890, it was 4.5; and in 1790, it was 5.4. Women have replaced children in the labor force: In 1965, they became 34 percent of it. This trend

[7]August B. Hollingshead, *Elmtown's Youth*, New York, Wiley, 1949.
[8]Hodgkinson, op. cit., pp. 23–24.

partially reflects rising consumption standards which demand more money than many husbands can earn.

The nonwhite labor force, largely Negro, differs greatly from the white labor force in age, sex, educational, and employment characteristics. Unemployment and underemployment are consistently higher among nonwhites. Although nonwhite representation is increasing in both white collar and blue collar jobs, the largest gains are in manual and lower white collar jobs. It may be wise to consider lower-class whites as a group separate from but somewhat similar to lower-class Negroes. Certainly both groups have low socioeconomic status. Yet, largely because of their skin color, upwardly mobile whites are able to "disappear" into white middle-class cultures, whereas upwardly aspiring Negroes are unable to do so.

Another point bearing closer analysis when comparing unemployed and underemployed whites and nonwhites is the weaker psychological rationalization now available to nonwhites; conversely, the rationalization has become somewhat stronger for poor whites. In the past, nonwhites could more easily "justify" their lack of income by pointing to conditions of discrimination and segregation than could lower-class whites. Recent civil rights gains have narrowed the opportunity gap between lower-class whites and nonwhites, removing some of the discrimination against nonwhites but at the same time causing many lower-class whites to feel discriminated against.

Styles of Life
The average American family today has four times as much income as the average family in 1900. (The difference is less when adjusted for changes in the value of money.) Along with this increase has come more money for luxuries and recreation. Considerably more of the average family's budget is spent on leisure-time activities; in fact, nearly 5 percent of Americans' personal income after taxes in spent on recreation and recreational equipment. One in 10 Americans, however, does not share in this mass leisure. This group is so poverty-stricken that they cannot even be called relatively deprived—they are completely deprived. In the mass media, school textbooks, and other contacts poverty-stricken people learn how the more fortunate live; the contrast with their own existence confirms their plight. Low-income children growing up under these conditions are not the bright-eyed enthusiastic scholars children from affluent or comfortable backgrounds are likely to be.

Education as a humanization process includes learning certain social roles that allow for satisfactory cultural adjustments. As an individual changes culture, he often changes his social role. This type of adjustment begins at birth and ends at death. Therefore, education for social adjustments is not a process in which an individual participates for the first time on entering school. His family, peer groups, mass media, and all of the other informal and formal units of interpersonal behavior are vital parts of the education process. In terms of compulsory attendance, the role of the school is very significant in the total socialization process.

We might quite logically expect formal education systems in America to epitomize *democratic education*. "Democratic education recognizes as its enduring purpose the fullest development of the individual within the framework of society."[9] This ideal, however, is seldom attained in practice. Indeed, most schools perpetuate rather than ameliorate the cultural differences between the poor and the affluent. Cultural differences show up significantly in articulation of vowels, complexity of remarks and vocabulary, and recognition of words. According to one authority, the "cognitive style" of the deprived child is typically:

1. Physical and visual rather than aural.
2. Content-centered rather than form-centered.
3. Externally oriented rather than introspective.
4. Problem-centered rather than abstract-centered.
5. Inductive rather than deductive.
6. Spatial rather than temporal.
7. Slow, careful, patient, perservering (in areas of importance), rather than quick, clever, facile, flexible.[10]

Preschool experiences determine a child's *readiness* for middle-class-oriented education experiences. Few low-income students are given the readiness at home that will allow them to succeed in school. Equally important is the fact that the low-income child not only is likely to have lower verbal achievement and educational aspirations but also is likely to attend school where most of the students reflect similar low achievement and aspirations. The slum school climate, therefore, is conducive to perpetuating cultures of poverty. Furthermore, because the slum child remains isolated from the mainstream of life in the dominant society, the world of the school is inexplicable to him. This alien world usually clashes with his values; certainly it fails to open up new vistas of the "American Dream" of equal opportunity.

Social Importance of Education
Even though fewer individuals today amass great fortunes than in the nineteenth century, research indicates that there is as much economic opportunity in this country today as there was a century ago. But the ability to take advantage of economic opportunity is based to a great extent on education. This is especially true in the technical and service professions, which have grown at a rate that far exceeds the growth in

[9]Deborah P. Wolfe, "Curriculum Adaptations for the Culturally Deprived," *Journal of Negro Education*, 31 (Spring, 1952), 139.

[10]Frank Riessman, *The Culturally Deprived Child*, New York, Harper & Row, 1962, p. 73.

population. The number of executive positions, for example, is increasing so rapidly that the number of children born into middle-class families does not meet the need. As a result, some of these positions will be filled by people from the lower class.

Education has become the main road to technical and professional occupations. A college education is required for most upper-middle-class occupations, and a high school education is required for lower-middle-class occupations, such as clerical, sales, and technical jobs. The amount of education, in other words, is a good indicator of an individual's potential for achieving a particular socioeconomic status. At least, it serves as a variable that affects other factors such as choice of occupation, spouse, and place of residence.

Social class and education interact in at least two ways. First, to get a higher education takes money plus motivation. Upper-class youths have money; they also have family tradition and social encouragement. The upper-class or upper-middle-class youth asks, "What college are you going to?" Lower-middle-class and perhaps upper-lower-class youths ask one another, "What will you do after graduation?" The lower-lower-class youth asks, "How soon can I quit school?" Second, one's amount and kind of education affect the class rank he will secure. Education is one of the main levers of the ambitious. Higher education brings not only occupational skill but also changes in tastes, interests, goals, etiquette, speech—in one's total way of life.[11]

Although family background is a criterion for securing upper-upper-class status, education is an edequate substitute for family background at the intermediate social class levels. Social class determines one's life opportunities, affects his personality development, influences his social participation, and assigns responsibilities and privileges. Many differences commonly attributed to race, religion, and ethnic group are actually social class differences. For example, there are fewer differences in life styles between middle-class Negroes and middle-class whites than most people imagine.

CHANGING PATTERNS
OF SCHOOL SUPPORT
Public school education has been heralded as the single most important institution for altering the social class position of a lower-class child. This theory assumes that he is able to receive the same quality of education as other children. During the twentieth century there has been a great increase in expenditures for both public and nonpublic education; more than three times as much of the GNP was spent on education in 1969 as was spent in 1900 (see Table 3). Even so, public expenditures continue to be larger for other items, such as defense, the

[11]Paul B. Horton, *Sociology and the Health Sciences*, New York, McGraw-Hill, 1965, p. 234.

Table 3
Cost of Education in the United States, 1900–1969 (in Millions of Dollars, Current Prices)

School year	Elementary schools	Secondary schools	Colleges and universities	Total	Gross National Product (in millions of dollars)	Percentage of GNP
1899-1900	233	19	40	292	17,000	1.7
1929-1930	1,950	750	535	3,233	104,000	3.1
1959-1960	12,590	5,435	6,616	24,641	483,000	5.1
1963-1964	24,800		11,800	36,600	585,000	6.1
1964-1965	26,800		13,200	40,000	623,000	6.4
1965-1966	29,900		15,200	45,100	685,000	6.6
1966-1967	32,000		16,800	48,800	743,000	6.6
1967-1968	35,800		18,800	54,600	790,000	6.9
1968-1969	38,100		20,400	58,500	860,000	6.8

Note: The gross national product is for the calendar year in which the school year commences.
Sources: U.S. Office of Education, Digest of Educational Statistics, 1965, and 1969, and various governmental publications.

purchase and operation of automobiles, alcoholic beverages, tobacco, and various types of recreation. The more than $58 billion we spend annually on education is *less* than 7 percent of the GNP. The Russians, for example, spend about 7 percent of their GNP on education. If expenditures indicate a rank order of preferences, then Americans rank education low.

Public schools in the United States are supported by three primary sources: local, state, and federal. In 1969, local districts paid 52 percent of the cost of public elementary and secondary education; the states paid 41 percent; and the federal government paid 7 percent. Ironically, the percentages of school revenue coming from the three levels of government are inversely related to their fund-raising abilities. It seems likely that unless fundamental changes are made in the basis of support, public school systems will not be able to meet the demands society places on them.[12]

Local Support

Traditionally, the chief source of support for the public schools has come from local revenues, mainly from property tax levies. A *school district* is the basic governmental unit through which local schools are operated. Technically, it is a unit of government created and empowered by state law to administer a public school or a public school system. There are about 22,000 separate school districts in the United States. School board members are agents of the state, elected or appointed in accordance with legal provisions, and derive their authority from the state.

In financial support, school districts vary, of course. They vary in the amounts they are willing to tax themselves and they vary also in the assessment practices on which their taxation is based: some districts value property at a low rate; others use a high rate. But these variations are relatively minor compared with the very wide discrepancies in actual tax-paying ability. No matter what measuring standards are used, certain communities obviously are much less affluent than others. For instance, some are high-income suburbs, others contain much low-cost housing, and others have virtually no industrial property that can be taxed. Compounding the problem is the fact that in some states legal maximum tax rates have been established; they can be exceeded, but only by a majority vote of the voters of a district. It seems hardly necessary to add that it is often difficult to persuade a majority of the residents of a district to vote to tax themselves at a higher rate.

It is quite apparent why the local property tax, as presently administered, has been called antiquated. The burden placed on homeowners, plus the growing demands made on public schools, has served to underscore the need to find other ways to secure local sources of

---

[12]See, for instance, Orville G. Brim, *Sociology and the Field of Education*, New York, Russell Sage Foundation, 1958, p. 24.

education funds. This condition is serious for schools attended by middle- and upper-class children; it is calamitous for schools attended by lower-class children.

State Support

Most state constitutions spell out the responsibility of their state legislatures for establishing and maintaining a system of free public schools. Control over public education is also shared by the governor, the state board of education, the state department of education, and other state agencies. State departments of education are especially effective in certifying teachers, selecting textbooks, and distributing state money. State support of public education increased from one-fifth in 1920 to more than two-fifths in 1969. Whereas local school districts are empowered to levy only property taxes, the states have a much broader base of tax support—income and sales taxes. In order to correct inequalities in school funding, most states have *equalization* programs that supplement local funds in order to provide minimum support for all schools. Equalization formulas require the wealthiest districts to provide the largest part of their own financial support. Conversely, the least wealthy districts receive the greatest amount of state support. The average expenditure varies widely among states, ranging from $1,140 spent for each pupil in New York during the 1968–1969 school year to $380 in Alabama.

Some local school officials fear that increased state funds will lead to state control. With this fear in mind, one expert has said that the most valuable contribution state funds can make towards school improvement is the release of local funds for innovative programs.[13] In the final analysis, the advantages or disadvantages of equalization programs depend largely on the terms of the funding. In any case, one study concluded that fiscally dependent and independent districts did not differ greatly in their patterns of expenditure.[14] The key consideration then becomes whether the structure adopted provides a better *quality* of education.

Federal Support

The federal government has always assisted in supporting public education. This tradition started, in fact, even before the adoption of the Constitution, when the Continental Congress passed two Northwest Ordinances in 1785 and 1787. The first of these acts established the policy of reserving land for the benefit of the public schools, and both acts affirmed the necessity to encourage schools and education in

---

[13] Arvid J. Burke, *Financing Public Schools in the United States* (rev. ed.), New York, Harper & Row, 1957, p. 588.

[14] H. Thomas Jones, et al., *Wealth, Expenditures and Decision-Making for Education*, Stanford, Calif., School of Education, Stanford University, 1963, p. 99.

general. The Constitution itself does not mention education, but the federal power to aid public education is based on its general welfare clause (Article 1, section 8), which authorizes Congress to lay and collect taxes, duties, imposts, and excises and to pay the debts and provide for the common defense and the general welfare of the United States.

Federal expenditures for education are numerous. In fact, under special conditions the federal government becomes directly involved in education. Since 1804, Congress has assumed responsibility for the schools in Washington, D.C. Since 1824, the Bureau of Indian Affairs has been providing schools for Indians and natives of Alaska. In addition, the federal government has established and operated schools in foreign countries where it maintains consulates, arsenals, dockyards, and other defense-related establishments. As our defense bases around the world increase, so too do our federally operated schools for military dependents. (Dependent schools are being maintained in Europe, the British Isles, Puerto Rico, North Africa, and the Far East.)

Before 1950, federal support of education in this country was mainly concerned with vocational education. By 1965, however, broad federal programs were operating under the Vocational Education Act of 1963, the Manpower Development and Training Act, the expanded National Defense Education Act, and the Economic Opportunity Act of 1964. Even broader and more far-reaching programs were made possible by the Elementary and Secondary Education Act of 1965, which extended federal support for the first time down through elementary schools.

The case for federal support of public education is similar to the rationalization for state support. Just as local school districts are limited in their revenue sources, so too are the states. Some states, for example, have higher average per capita incomes than others, ranging from Connecticut with the highest ($3,969 in 1967) to Mississippi with the lowest ($1,896 in 1967). Although most school districts accept state equalization plans, they nevertheless resist national equalization proposals. The federal government assists public elementary and secondary schools in the following ways:

Innovation and improvement.   Money administered by the U. S. Office of Education and the National Science Foundation is used for educational research. For example, four major centers of research and development were founded in the early 1960s at Harvard and the Universities of Pittsburgh, Wisconsin, and Oregon. Similarly, the Elementary and Secondary Education Act of 1965 provided $100 million to start a number of *regional* centers for educational research and development. About 30 to 40 such centers will have been established by 1970.

Training of personnel.   The federal government also provides money for the advanced training of various specialists. Most of this money goes for training research workers in the natural sciences, but large sums have also been provided (through the U. S. Office of Education and the National Defense Education Act) for training school counselors and for the retraining of classroom teachers in science, mathematics, foreign languages, and work with handicapped children.

Education of the underprivileged and the handicapped. The federal government is continuing its programs for the education and re-habilitation of physically handicapped people; the retraining of people whose jobs have been eliminated by automation; the education of adult illiterates; work-experience and related education for unemployed youth; compensatory education for disadvantaged preschool and school-age children. It also provides funds for research on the causes of mental deficiency.

A comprehensive program of federal aid to the culturally dis-advantaged began with the Economic Opportunity Act of 1964. This act provided federal funds for many activities, including community action programs, youth employment opportunities, and training of adults who are recipients or potential recipients of public welfare. Specific programs include Head Start, the Job Corps, Neighborhood Youth Corps, and Work-Study programs. It is mainly through these programs that cultural differences are expected to be minimized.

Aid to Parochial Schools

Whether or not to give federal funds to private and parochial schools is a growing problem that is the subject of continuing controversy. There are valid arguments on both sides. Since Catholic schools com-prise 90 percent of the private schools, most of our comments will focus on Catholic schools and the church versus state issue.

Parochial schools educate 14 percent of the total enrolled students. Proponents of federal aid point out that if these schools abandoned this function, the public schools would not be able to absorb the additional students. For example, in Pittsburgh and Chicago, nearly 50 percent and 35 percent, respectively, of the children are in parochial schools. Advocates of federal aid argue that since these schools perform a public service, they should receive public funds in order to eliminate what is in effect double taxation of the parents of parochial school children.

Opponents of federal aid acknowledge the public service aspect but maintain that providing federal funds for parochial schools is uncon-stitutional. The Supreme Court has often reaffirmed the American tradition of keeping church and state separate, most recently in the Abington School District case.[15] The Court ruled that prayers and Bible reading in public schools and the laws requiring them are un-constitutional. As for double taxation, it has been justified on the

[15]School District of Abington Township, Pennsylvania, et al., *v.* Schempp, et al., 374 U.S. 203 (1963).

ground that the cost of public education must be borne by all citizens because it is available to all citizens and because all citizens govern and control it. If citizens are dissatisfied with the way the schools are operated, they can vote to change them.[16]

Despite unyielding opposition, federal funds *are* being used to assist some parochial school programs, for instance, cultural enrichment for low-income students and improvement of science, mathematics, and language arts programs. When federal efforts make public school desegregation even more widespread, it is possible that improved parochial schools will become even more attractive to those who wish to escape racial integration. If this does happen, we will see a sadly ironic situation—highly segregated religious schools in a nation committed to integrated public schools.

School Facilities
The growing need for better educational facilities reflects insufficient expenditures for new construction, modernization, and maintenance. School buildings must change architecturally to meet changing instructional demands. Early schools consisted of only one large classroom that accommodated a single teacher with a group of ungraded students. The shift to grading brought a shift to the traditional building with an individual room for each class. In recent years, the concepts of flexible scheduling and nongrading have made traditional buildings no longer functional.

Few school districts are able to keep up, structurally, with their growing populations. Though nearly $25 billion was spent on public school construction during the 1950s, schools began the 1960–1961 academic year with a shortage of 132,000 classrooms. By 2000, this shortage is likely to have doubled. School construction costs are borne mainly by local districts. The local burden is compounded because the allocation of land and buildings for school use removes them from local tax rolls. As in many other areas of education, low-income communities and their students are the most seriously lacking in adequate school buildings and facilities.

SUMMARY
1. The shift from rural to urban living has altered the patterns of family living in America. The family is no longer the center of work activities.
2. Many of the functions traditionally performed by the family such as formal education, recreation, and welfare are being shared with other social institutions, especially the school.
3. Children born in nonlower-class homes have the greatest probability of

[16]Leo Pfeffer and W. G. McCluskey, "Federal Aid for Private and Parochial Schools? Yes—No," *Current History*, August, 1961, 70–81.

achieving academic and occupational success. The ascribed status into which a child is born is difficult to overcome. The social class of a child's family largely determines the roles, values, and aspirations that he will learn.

4. Despite a hardening of social class lines, education is still an important factor in altering an individual's social class. Although the family background is a criterion for securing upper-upper-class status, education is an adequate substitute for family background at the intermediate social class levels.

5. Public schools in America are supported by three major sources: local, state, and federal. The main source of school support is local revenues; the least amount of funds comes from federal sources. Most states have equalization programs that supplement local funds in order to provide minimum support for all schools within the state.

6. Federal aid for parochial schools is still unconstitutional. However, some federal funds are made available to parochial schools in order to improve education in "nonreligious" areas.

7. Unless sources of revenue other than local taxes are found and used, few school districts will be able to keep up, instructionally and structurally, with their growing populations.

SELECTED READINGS

Allen, Francis K., et al., *Technology and Social Change*, New York, Appleton-Century-Crofts, 1957. A concise treatment of both the theory and the "content" of social change, especially in America.

Cooley, Charles Horton, *Human Nature and Social Order* (rev. ed.), New York, Scribner, 1922. A classical comment on the relationship between man and society.

Elkin, Frederick, *The Child and Society*, New York, Random House, 1960. The author assesses the impact of society upon the socialization of the child.

Gottman, Jean, *Megalopolis: The Urbanized Northeastern Seaboard of the United States*, New York, The Twentieth Century Fund, 1961. Those interested in a discussion of rapidly emerging urban areas that encompass urban and suburban cities will find this book worth reading.

Hodges, Harold M., Jr., *Social Stratification: Class in America*, Cambridge, Mass., Schenkman, 1964. A current perspective of elements of American stratification.

Jones, Howard R., *Financing Public Elementary and Secondary Education*, New York, Applied Research Center, 1966. An analysis of factors affecting school funding and operational needs.

Kenkel, William F., *The Family in Perspective*, New York, Appleton-Century-Crofts, 1966. One of the better reference books on the study of the family.

Meranto, Philip, *Politics of Federal Aid to Education*, Syracuse, N.Y., Syracuse University Press, 1967. The author examines practical considerations that shape federal aid to education. Students get an understanding of the concept "political expediency."

Shryrock, Henry S., Jr., *Population Mobility Within the United States*, Chicago, Community and Family Study Center, The University of Chicago, 1964. An excellent overview of the patterns and magnitudes of population redistribution in the United States.

Part III
ISSUES AND INNOVATIONS IN AMERICAN EDUCATION

Curriculum Reforms in Public Schools

Innovations in Grouping for Instruction

Higher Education in Transition

Racial Integration of the Public Schools

Part III begins with an examination of curriculum reforms that represent the response of the school to the fast-moving events in our society. It also examines innovations and issues in grouping for instruction, in higher education, and in the racial integration of schools.

The text can only provide an introduction to these topics. The student should consult the readings listed at the end of each chapter to supplement the text. He will, no doubt, want to explore other issues and innovations in American education that cannot even be touched on in these chapters.

8

Curriculum Reforms
in Public Schools

Even if all the proposed reforms continue to expand at the present speed, it will take a decade or more for the school curriculum to catch up with the fast-moving events on the frontiers of knowledge. Clearly the time has come for an educational revolution.*

After the student has examined the new circumstances surrounding the American school, he will want to know how the schools have responded to these new challenges. A study of the "foundations of American education" would have little meaning if it did not include significant changes in the school as a social institution.

Significant changes have been taking place in elementary and secondary schools and in higher education. Even more spectacular changes seem to be in the offing; perhaps the schools of the year 2000 will differ as much from those we now know as today's schools differ from those of 1890.

*Paul Woodring, "Introduction," in Robert W. Heath (ed.), New Curricula, New York, Harper & Row, 1964, p. 2.

Assessing the future, two educational experts recently wrote,

We foresee even more rapid changes in curriculum content, methodology, and the educational setting. We think that schools need to make better use of the professional talents of teachers and principals, the potential talents of learners, the purchasing power of school monies, the resources of communities, and the findings of educational research.[1]

Although curriculum reform has been underway for a long time, the tempo of change increased rapidly after the launching of the first Sputnik by Soviet Russia in 1957. The massive curriculum reform movement began with mathematics, science, and foreign languages; it soon spread to other curriculum areas, such as the language arts and social studies. There is abundant evidence that the need for national survival in a troubled world has been a compelling motive for curriculum reform, but this has not been the only motive. Also influential has been the need to have the schools contribute to the solution of critical problems on the domestic scene such as the urban crisis, unemployment and poverty, racial discrimination, and unequal educational opportunities. (These are treated elsewhere in this text.)

While these social and economic forces were calling for curriculum reforms, new insights into human growth and learning were undermining traditional teaching procedures. The volume of research in this field has been increasing rapidly in recent decades, and the importance of using data dealing with human development in curriculum planning has been given increasing attention.

NEW
CURRICULA

Americans have traditionally viewed the public elementary and secondary schools as belonging to the people of local communities; indeed, the conviction was firmly held that these schools could remain truly American only as long as they remained responsive to the wishes of the people in the communities. Until recently, no one seriously questioned the idea that local control of the curriculum was desirable. Curriculum reforms have, therefore, been initiated primarily at the state and local school district levels.

Since 1957, however, the major changes in the curriculum have been initiated by curriculum improvement projects at the national level. This radical change in the direction of curriculum reform cannot be attributed entirely to the influence of the first Sputnik. For example, three years after Sputnik, Lieberman pointed out that mobility and interdependence had completely undermined the notion that local communities should have a free hand in educating their children.[2] Although

---

[1]J. Lloyd Trump and Delmas F. Miller, *Secondary School Curriculum Improvement*, Boston, Allyn & Bacon, 1968, p. 16.

[2]Myron Lieberman, *The Future of Public Education*, Chicago, The University of Chicago Press, 1960, p. 34.

most of the curriculum improvement projects at the national level have been initiated since Sputnik, the movement was already underway in some areas before 1957.

Salient Features of the New Curricula

The interesting story of how "curriculum reform from the top down" came to be the prevailing pattern during the postwar period need not be repeated in detail here. Some highlights may, however, serve as a suitable preface to the analysis of some of the new curricula that follows.

1. National curriculum improvement projects, located on university campuses throughout the country, have been generously supported with funds from the federal government and from private foundations.

2. Attention has been sharply focused on single subjects, so that local school systems have been left with the problem of maintaining balance in the curriculum. Many school systems have therefore found it necessary to adapt, rather than adopt, the materials produced by these projects.

3. The groups that have been responsible for directing these projects have generally included staff members from colleges of liberal arts and sciences; colleges of education, and the public schools.

4. Although the movement began with mathematics, science, and foreign languages, new courses have also been developed in English, social studies, anthropology, geography, and economics.

5. The sponsors of the new curricula generally advocate a "spiral" arrangement for the grade placement of content in the various curriculum areas. For example, instead of teaching geometry only in the tenth grade, elements of this subject are introduced in the elementary school and the subject is "revisited" at successive grade levels. The same arrangement is used for economics, geography, and other subjects.

6. Most of the new curricula expect more of students than the mere acquisition of information; they are expected to learn the structure of each discipline and thus to think like a scientist, a mathematician, or an economist. Something more lasting than the learning of bits of information has been sought; the new procedures emphasize concept formation, learning by discovery, and the development of the ability to think. A kind of education that will enable students to become increasingly self-propelling during a lifetime of learning is the goal.

7. There is little question that these national projects have developed vastly improved content and procedures in many curriculum areas; the questions that are raised generally deal with how these new programs can be *implemented* in elementary and secondary schools. Since most of the teachers now employed in the schools have not been taught the new science and the new mathematics, the new curricula place a heavy burden on the in-service education budgets of the public school sys-

tems. Summer institutes, operating under federal grants, have helped.

8. Teaching procedures necessary to implement the new curricula involve an understanding of newer insights into the nature of the learning process; if the new programs are to achieve their maximum potentials, classroom teachers must become much more proficient as practicing psychologists.

Intellectual Development

Chapter 6 was devoted to the psychological and behavioral aspects of American education, but it now seems appropriate to relate new developments in learning theory to the process of curriculum planning; as curriculum specialists, principals, and teachers learn more about learning, they become more proficient in curriculum development.

Concept development.   The role of concepts in intellectual development has been studied intensively for many years. Because there are several kinds of concepts, it is difficult to formulate a single definition that will fit all situations in which concepts are developed. The definition given by Woodruff is a useful one, however, in terms of the problem with which this chapter is concerned.

For purposes of talking about curriculum planning in general, a concept may be defined as some amount of meaning more or less organized in an individual mind as a result of sensory perception of external objects or events and the cognitive interpretation of the perceived data. A concept is important because it is the internal mediating variable that accounts for the direction of a person's response to a situation.[3]

One clue to an understanding of the new curricula is the emphasis placed on concept development. Observations in hundreds of traditional classrooms have revealed that the dominant activity was information-giving; the teacher presented information and the students memorized it.[4] The new curricula are designed to foster the development of concepts around which information can be organized and *used* in the solution of problems. Curriculum guides developed for the purpose of helping teachers implement the new curricula generally present a conceptual framework for the various subjects. The explosion of knowledge in practically every field of learning has made this arrangement necessary. The newer explanations of the learning process also support this practice. In other words, the role of the school has become increasingly that of providing the students with the skills, understanding, and concepts that will make it possible for him to explore a field of knowledge on his own and to continue to educate himself.

Woodruff has presented propositions relating to concepts that are supported by psychological research and that seem to be useful in

---

[3]A. D. Woodruff, "The Use of Concepts in Teaching and Learning," *Journal of Teacher Education*, March, 1964, 84.

[4]Ibid., p. 81.

curriculum planning. He suggests that (1) subject matter becomes more meaningful when it is presented in conceptual form, (2) students need to develop concepts in order to engage in problem-solving activities, (3) concept-forming and concept-using are interdependent, and (4) serious consideration should be given to readiness for concepts.[5]

Organizing learning experiences in any subject in terms of the basic concepts to be learned is an important step in curriculum development, but this is only the first step. The next step that confronts the classroom teacher is that of learning how the concepts of adult specialists become the concepts of students—how students come to *own* concepts. This involves a thorough exploration of the new research on learning, including the work of a group of psychologists who specialize in the psychology of cognition—how we know and how we teach others to know.[6] Jean Piaget, developmental psychologist at the University of Geneva, Jerome S. Bruner, director of the Center for Cognitive Studies at Harvard University, and Robert M. Gagné, director of research at the American Institute for Research, are prominent members of this group of psychologists.

Bruner called attention to an important principle of concept development when he wrote: "What is most important for teaching basic concepts is that the child be helped to pass progressively from concrete thinking to the utilization of more conceptually adequate modes of thought."[7] He has drawn upon the experimental work of Piaget and others to identify three stages of concept development: the "preoperational" stage, the stage of "concrete operations," and the "formal operations" stage.

During the first stage, which generally ends about age 5 or 6, the child is concerned with manipulating objects on a trial-and-error basis. During the second stage, which begins after the child enters school, the ability to organize the data acquired through contact with concrete objects emerges, and the child learns to use organized data in the solution of problems. During the third stage, which generally begins between the ages of 10 and 14, the child acquires the ability to operate on hypothetical propositions, without having the concrete objects before him. This process approximates the kind of intellectual activity that is the stock in trade of the mature scientist and the abstract thinker.

Although it is useful for those who participate in the development of curriculum guides to recognize that children generally pass through these three stages of concept development, the classroom teacher soon discovers that all children do not pass from one stage to another at the same age. Bruner has recognized the responsibility of the classroom teacher as follows:

[5]Ibid., pp. 95–96.
[6]Richard C. Anderson and David P. Ausubel (eds.), *Readings in the Psychology of Cognition*, New York, Holt, 1965.
[7]Jerome S. Bruner, *The Process of Education*, Cambridge, Mass., Harvard University Press, 1962, p. 38.

Precisely what kinds of material should be used at what age with what effect is a subject for research. . . . Nor need we wait for all the research findings to be in before proceeding, for a skillful teacher can also experiment by attempting to teach what seems to be intuitively right for children of different ages, correcting as he goes.[8]

New dimensions of the problem of readiness.   New insights into intellectual development and information gained from curriculum improvement projects have altered traditional ideas about readiness for learning. It is no longer thought to be feasible to assign an absolute level of difficulty to any topic or subject; the difficulty depends on the previous learning experiences of the pupil and the methods and materials used in presenting it. The "ladder" system of grade placement—geometry in the tenth grade, chemistry in the eleventh grade, physics in the twelfth grade, and economics at the college level—is now regarded as out of harmony with what is known about the continuous growth of mental capabilities. As we have mentioned, the new curricula introduce pupils to elements of these subjects as soon as they enter school, "revisiting" them in successively more complex and difficult forms as long as they remain in school (the "spiral" system).

A new aspect of readiness, called "content" or "subject-matter" readiness, has also become widely recognized. Gagné has explained this as follows:

The planning that precedes effective design for learning is a matter of specifying with some care what may be called the learning structure of any subject to be acquired. In order to determine what comes before what, the subject must be analyzed in terms of the types of learning involved in it.[9]

Instead of assuming that a child is not ready to begin the study of a subject until he has reached a certain age, this interpretation of readiness assumes that he is ready to learn something new as soon as he has acquired the necessary capabilities through preceding learning. Curriculum workers have, therefore, been turning to scholars in the various disciplines for information about the structure of knowledge in their various fields.

Learning by discovery.   It has been stated earlier in this chapter that the new curricula emphasize learning by discovery. Renner and Ragan have pointed out that (1) the act of discovery includes all forms of obtaining knowledge or insight for oneself by the use of one's own mental powers; (2) the discovery method allows pupils to arrive at generalizations that are truly their own; and (3) the method helps the pupil develop his rational powers, gain understanding of content, and learn how to learn.[10] Lindberg has stated that helping children discover knowledge and ways of working for themselves eliminates the necessity of finding

[8]Ibid., p. 53.
[9]Robert M. Gagné, *The Conditions of Learning,* New York, Holt, 1965, p. 25.
[10]John W. Renner and William B. Ragan, *Teaching Science in the Elementary School,* New York, Harper & Row, 1968, p. 111.

ways to hold their attention—that the urge to pursue learning comes from within.[11] There will always be a need for information-giving by the teacher, but teaching that consists primarily of exposition robs students of the opportunity to learn how to learn.

Games with simulated environments. The use of games that simulate real-life situations has been increasing in American classrooms. There is evidence that when this technique is used, (1) students become highly motivated; (2) they learn more; (3) they learn the need for cooperation; (4) they get a more realistic understanding of how things are done in life outside the school; and (5) they gain an appreciation of the complexity of real-life situations.[12]

THE NEW
MATHEMATICS PROGRAMS

The curriculum reform movement in mathematics is not new; its antecedents can be traced back at least to the 1930s. For instance, one expert wrote in 1935: "The basic tenet in the proposed instructional reorganization is to make arithmetic less a challenge to the pupil's memory and more a challenge to his intelligence."[13] It has been reported that, by 1953, 1,100 studies of the teaching of arithmetic had been made.[14] The curriculum improvement projects in mathematics at the national level have, however, introduced new topics, emphasized the structure of the discipline of mathematics, introduced elements of algebra and geometry into the elementary school program, given greater priority to the mathematical phases of the program and less to the social applications, fostered a more precise use of mathematical language, developed more appropriate instructional materials, and demonstrated the use of procedures designed to facilitate learning by discovery.

UICSM. In 1952, a group at the University of Illinois, under the leadership of Max Beberman, began to develop materials of instruction that they believed would help students understand and become enthusiastic about mathematics; they also developed methods of training high school teachers in the use of the new materials. An advisory board, the University of Illinois Committee on School Mathematics, drew its members from the colleges of education, engineering, and liberal arts and sciences. Beberman reported in 1958: "We now have

[11]Lucile Lindberg, "Learning Through Searching," *Childhood Education*, October, 1961, 58–60.
[12]S. Boocock and James S. Coleman, "Games with Simulated Environments in Learning," *Sociology of Education*, 39 (Summer, 1966), 215–237.
[13]William A. Brownell, "Psychological Considerations in the Learning and Teaching of Arithmetic," in *The Teaching of Arithmetic*, Washington, D.C., National Council of the Teachers of Mathematics, 1935, p. 10.
[14]William Van Til, *Research Affecting Education*, Washington, D.C., Association for Supervision and Curriculum Development, 1953, p. 120.

courses for the four high school grades on trial in classrooms in a dozen pilot schools. Some forty teachers and over seventeen hundred students are participating."[15]

The UICSM project was the first of its kind in this country; it provided a model for other curriculum improvement projects in mathematics that started in 1957 or later. A careful examination of Beberman's description of this project reveals the extent to which it incorporated the basic principles on which the new curricula are based.[16] One writer has stated: "UICSM may properly be regarded as the progenitor of all the current curricular projects in mathematics."[17]

Since 1957, many more national curriculum improvement projects in mathematics have been set up, and several publishers have produced series of textbooks incorporating their findings. Most of the references listed at the end of this chapter give detailed descriptions of these projects. We will now, therefore, describe briefly only one project and merely list some others, with a few essential facts about each.

SMSG. The materials produced by the School Mathematics Study Group are among the most widely used of all the new mathematics programs. E. G. Begle of Stanford University was director of the project, which grew out of a conference sponsored by the American Mathematical Society in February, 1958; the National Science Foundation provided approximately $8 million to finance SMSG. This project prepared preliminary and revised editions of sample textbooks for grades K–12. The work of SMSG assumes that basic mathematical concepts are central to the effective teaching of mathematics; that the program should develop an awareness of the basic properties of mathematics; and that, while students manipulate numbers, they should move to progressively higher levels of abstraction. The basic texts are written by teams composed of college mathematicians, mathematics educators, and classroom teachers of mathematics.

Boston College Mathematics Institute's Contemporary Mathematics Program. This secondary school mathematics project is also sponsored by the National Science Foundation; it has prepared a series of textbooks that use the new terminology of mathematics and emphasize the unifying concepts; since 1960 it has sponsored a home study program designed to strengthen the understanding of modern mathematics by elementary and secondary teachers.

Greater Cleveland Mathematics Program. This K–12 program was initiated in 1959 by the Educational Research Council of Greater Cleveland. It has prepared both teacher and pupil materials (published by

---

[15]Max Beberman, "An Emerging Program of Secondary School Mathematics," in R. W. Heath (ed.), *New Curricula*, New York, Harper & Row, 1964, p. 10.
[16]Ibid., pp. 9–11.
[17]Kenneth B. Henderson, "Mathematics," in *Using Current Curriculum Developments*, Washington, D.C., Association for Supervision and Curriculum Development, 1963, p. 57.

Science Research Associates, Inc., Chicago). The materials emphasize the "guided discovery" approach and are designed to help students gain an understanding of the structure of mathematics.

Syracuse University-Webster College Madison Project. This project began at the Madison School in Syracuse, New York, with financial support from the Marcel Holzer and Alfred P. Sloan Foundations. It was sponsored by the mathematics department of Syracuse University. The project, during the early years, worked with culturally deprived children; the emphasis later shifted to work with children of above-average ability living in "overprivileged" homes. A second project center was opened in Weston, Connecticut, and a third at Webster College, St. Louis, Missouri. Since 1961 the project has been supported by funds from the National Science Foundation and the U.S. Office of Education. Teacher preparation has been a central activity of the Madison project; in Chicago alone 18,000 teachers have been involved. The project has sought to broaden the curriculum for Grades 2–8 by introducing elements of algebra, geometry, and logic.

University of Illinois Arithmetic Project. This project, under the direction of David Page, received support from the University of Illinois, the Carnegie Corporation, and the National Science Foundation. It is now operating in connection with Educational Services, Inc. It is designed to help children develop a sense of power with respect to mathematical properties and operations. It places major emphasis on teacher preparation; some 500 teachers have attended the institutes sponsored by the project.

University of Maryland Mathematics Project. This project was established in 1957 with financial support from the Carnegie Corporation. It was designed to prepare experimental mathematics courses for Grades 7 and 8. *Mathematics for the Junior High School,* published in 1961, placed great emphasis on number systems and mathematical structure. Students in courses using these materials have scored as high in traditional standardized tests as students who used traditional materials, and they have made even better scores in tests prepared specifically to test achievement in the new courses.

NEW CURRICULA
IN SCIENCE
Since 1957, more attention has been given to the improvement of the curriculum in science than any other field. Progress in science and technology has brought about drastic changes in how people live and in how they make a living; a higher level of literacy in science than ever before is needed to make decisions about problems of living. The new programs in science place more emphasis on the processes of science and less emphasis on the products, they involve more learning by discovery and less dependence on exposition, and they require students

to learn how a scientist thinks and acts. Curriculum improvement projects at the national level, supported by funds from the National Science Foundation and the foundations, have conducted experiments and produced materials for use in elementary and secondary schools. Local school systems have in turn developed curriculum guides that implement the principal features of these programs. Most school systems elect to *adapt* rather than to *adopt* the programs developed by these projects. The National Science Foundation, which has sponsored most of the projects, has stated: "Decisions on what to teach remain, in the healthy American tradition, the exclusive responsibility of individual schools and teachers."[18]

PSSC.   Experimentation with new curricula in high school science began in the mid-1950s. Jerrold Zacharias of the Massachusetts Institute of Technology provided the leadership from which a pattern of cooperation between scientists and teachers emerged to develop new curricula in physics, biology, and chemistry. The Physical Science Study Committee, initiated in 1956, was the first of the new science programs.

The high school physics program includes a study of the universe, optics and waves, mechanics, and electricity and modern physics. The program, sponsored by the National Science Foundation, the Fund for the Advancement of Education, and the Alfred P. Sloan Foundation, emphasizes learning the structure of physics and the processes of inquiry and developing concepts through experimentation. It also stresses the interconnections between physics and other sciences.

Goodlad and others state that there is no evidence that students who complete the PSSC physics courses in high school are in any way at a disadvantage when they move on to college courses based primarily on the old materials. They comment on the need for revised college courses in physics as follows:

The Physical Science Study Committee points to the need for revising the college physics curriculum if PSSC students are to be adequately challenged, and if college courses are to keep pace with current thought in physics education. There are increasing signs that this collegiate reform has started.[19]

Other high school science projects include: The Biological Sciences Curriculum Study (BSCS), the Chemical Bond Approach project (CBA), and the Earth Science Curriculum Project (ESCP). These projects are described in the references listed at the end of this chapter.

SCIS.   The Science Curriculum Improvement Study has received financial support from the National Science Foundation since 1959; the director is Robert Karplus of the University of California at Berkeley. Instructional units for Grades K–6 have been tried out in selected

[18]Bowen C. Dees, *Science Course Improvement Projects*, Washington, D.C.: National Science Foundation, 1962, p. 1.

[19]John I. Goodlad, Renata Von Stoephasius, and M. Frances Klein, *The Changing Curriculum*, New York, The Fund for the Advancement of Education, 1966, p. 49.

schools in the San Francisco Bay area and in several schools in the area of Teachers College, Columbia University, the University of California at Los Angeles, the University of Oklahoma, and the University of Hawaii.

The staff of SCIS has sponsored orientation conferences, conducted in-service education courses, and prepared instructional units for Grades K–6. A teacher education package containing students' and teachers' manuals for certain topics such as "material objects" and "interaction," audiovisual aids, and kits of equipment for experiments is published by D. C. Heath and Company. A college text, *Teaching Science in the Elementary School*, provides detailed suggestions for using the SCIS approach. The authors state:

Thus, the work of the SCIS group could be thought of as being a program for elementary-school science which teaches a child science through investigation. Such experiences will, according to the SCIS group, provide a child with intellectual development (rational powers) and assist him in building a conceptual structure of the discipline.[20]

Other elementary school science projects include: *Science: A Process Approach*, developed by the American Association for the Advancement of Science; the Elementary Science Study of Educational Services, Inc.; the Minnesota Mathematics and Science Teaching Project; the Elementary School Science Project of Utah State University; and the Elementary School Science Project of the University of California. These programs are described in detail in the references listed at the end of this chapter.

ENGLISH-LANGUAGE
ARTS PROJECT
Project English is sponsored by the U.S. Office of Education and the National Council of Teachers of English; 16 universities throughout the country are participating in the program, which is concerned with language arts curriculum improvement from kindergarten through the second year of college. The program, supported by National Defense Education Act funds, has updated the knowledge of about 4000 English teachers, primarily through summer institutes. Goodlad and others comment on the work of curriculum improvement centers as follows:

There is little doubt that the "new" English will be characterized by carefully structured curricula taught inductively; by literature courses that emphasize depth and analysis, and lead the student to appreciate literary craftsmanship and its relation to meaning; and by an interest in structural linguistics, in generative grammar, and in speech as an integral part of the curriculum.[21]

[20]Renner and Ragan, op. cit., p. 259.
[21]Goodlad, et al., op. cit., p. 76.

PROJECTS IN
THE SOCIAL SCIENCES

Very few social science disciplines received grants from the National Science Foundation; the U.S. Office of Education began to finance social studies projects in 1962. By 1966, 14 curriculum development centers had been established at universities. These projects had these obejctives in common: (1) to clarify the scope and purposes of the social studies program, (2) to develop materials and procedures for the achievement of these objectives, (3) to submit these productions to experimentation, evaluation, and revision, and (4) to disseminate materials and information. The centers include Carnegie Institute of Technology, the University of Minnesota, Harvard University, Syracuse University, the University of Illinois, the Ohio State University, Amherst College, and the University of Georgia.

The Greater Cleveland Social Science Program was initiated in 1961. This program is developed around concepts from history, geography, philosophy, economics, political science, psychology, sociology, and anthropology. The program has been used by schools in the Cleveland area, enrolling some 90,000 students. The Elkhart (Indiana) Experiment in Economic Education was established in 1958; it is funded by the Elkhart Public Schools, Purdue University, and the Carnegie Corporation. The director is Lawrence Senesh of Purdue; Science Research Associates of Chicago publishes materials produced by the project.

Curriculum improvement projects in other school subject areas are described in the references listed at the end of this chapter. Obviously, only a few aspects of the massive curriculum reform movement of the 1950s and 1960s can be discussed within the limits of a single chapter. Moreover, it should come as no surprise to learn that neither the psychological foundations of the "new" curricula nor the programs themselves are universally accepted. Criticisms of the programs arise from (1) resistance to change, (2) lack of understanding of the psychological foundations and the programs themselves, and (3) the fact that the programs are still in a transitional stage and are not to be regarded as fixed and final solutions.

A research psychologist has examined recent innovations in teaching for the purpose of stating a few words of caution "that may prevent some excellent notions on teaching and learning from becoming unexamined fixtures of sacred ritual."[22] He points out: (1) Some of the new programs overlook the fact that "skill in performing routine operations may be the learner's key to comprehending concepts." (2) "Much of our faith in the discovery method of learning is based on the assumption that the student is more likely to retain insights he has developed on his own. I know of no extensive 'hard' evidence to support this view."

[22]Bernard Z. Friedlander, "Today's Innovations in Teaching," *NEA Journal*, March, 1966, 11–14.

Again, if the student is to evaluate these criticisms, he must become thoroughly familiar with the meanings of "the discovery method" and "concept learning" and with the ways these are used in the "new" curricula. He may find, for example, that these programs make adequate provision for the development of skills; that they do not depend exclusively on learning by discovery; and that the discovery method is subject to gross misinterpretations in practice.[23]

SUMMARY

1. A massive curriculum reform movement gained momentum in this country between 1950 and 1969; scholars foresee even more rapid changes in curriculum content and methodology in the next few decades.
2. The need for national survival in a troubled world, the rapid expansion of knowledge, and the desire to have the schools contribute to the solution of critical problems on the domestic scene have been influential in the initiation of new instructional programs.
3. New insights into human growth, development, and learning have undermined traditional instructional practices.
4. Since 1950, the major changes in the curriculum of elementary and secondary schools have been initiated at the national level.
5. National curriculum improvement projects have generally been located on university campuses; they have been supported by funds from the federal government and from the foundations.
6. Attention has been sharply focused on single subjects; local school systems have had to assume responsibility for maintaining balance in the curriculum; and most school systems have *adapted* rather than *adopted* the programs developed by national projects.
7. The "new" curricula generally employ the "spiral" rather than the "ladder" system of grade placement of content; elements of a subject are introduced during the child's first year in school and "revisited" at successive grade levels.
8. Most of the "new" curricula emphasize the development of the ability to think rather than to memorize, concept learning rather than the acquisition of isolated bits of information, and learning by discovery.
9. Teachers need greater insight into the nature of the learning process if the "new" curricula are to achieve their maximum potentials.
10. The role of the school has become increasingly that of providing the student with skills, understandings, and concepts that will make him increasingly independent in the exploration of a field of knowledge.
11. The experimental work of Piaget and other psychologists has identified the stages in concept development, but precisely what materials should be used with children at a particular stage of development is still the responsibility of a skillful teacher.
12. There will always be a need for exposition or information-giving on the part of the teacher, but the principal responsibility of the teacher is to help the student learn how to learn.
13. The new mathematics programs introduce algebra and geometry into the

[23]Gagné, op. cit., p. 165.

elementary school program, emphasize the structure of the discipline, foster more precise use of mathematical language, and place more emphasis on the mathematical phases of the program and less emphasis on its social applications.

14. The new program in science places more emphasis on the processes of science and less emphasis on its products, involves more learning by discovery and less learning by exposition, and expects students to learn how to think like a scientist.

15. Project English is designed to develop a more effective program in language arts from kindergarten through the second year of college; more emphasis is being placed on structural linguistics, appreciation of literary craftsmanship, and more recognition of speech as an integral part of the curriculum.

16. The U.S. Office of Education began to finance social studies projects in 1962; by 1966, curriculum improvement centers had been established at 14 universities. The objectives of these projects included: (1) clarification of the scope and functions of the social studies program, (2) development of materials and procedures to achieve these objectives, (3) submission of these productions to experimentation, evaluation, and revision, and (4) dissemination of materials and procedures.

17. The "new" social studies programs are built around concepts drawn from social science disciplines and expect students to be active in the identification of problems, the collection of data, and the forming of conclusions based on evidence.

SELECTED READINGS

Anderson, Richard C., and David P. Ausubel (eds.), *Readings in the Psychology of Cognition,* New York, Holt, 1965. Parts 3 and 4 of this book of readings deal with concept formation, thinking, problem-solving, and the act of discovery—processes that play a major role in the "new" curricula.

Association for Supervision and Curriculum Development, *Using Current Curriculum Developments,* Washington, D.C., The Association, 1963. Besides providing an analysis of the major curriculum improvements projects, this pamphlet contains chapters on instructional technology and learning theory.

Bruner, Jerome S., *The Process of Education,* Cambridge, Mass., Harvard University Press, 1962. Chapter 3 presents valuable information on concept information.

Dees, Bowen C., *Science Course Improvement Projects,* Washington, D.C., National Science Foundation, 1962. Presents an analysis of the science projects sponsored by the National Science Foundation.

Friedlander, Bernard Z., "Today's Innovations in Teaching," *NEA Journal,* March, 1966. Presents some interesting criticisms of learning by discovery, concept learning, and curiosity.

Gagné, Robert M., *The Conditions of Learning,* New York, Holt, 1965. Explains clearly the meaning of "learning." Clarifies the meaning of the discovery method (p. 165); says that discovery is only the final step in a sequence of learning.

Goodlad, John I., Renata Von Stoephasius, and M. Frances Klein, *The Changing Curriculum,* New York, The Fund for the Advancement of Education, 1966. Provides an excellent analysis of the major curriculum improvement projects.

Heath, Robert W. (ed.), *New Curricula*, New York, Harper & Row, 1964. Presents an excellent analysis of the "new" curricula in various subject areas.

Hillson, Maurie (ed.), *Current Issues and Research in Education: Elementary Education*, New York, The Free Press, 1967. Contains a series of articles dealing with innovations in reading, mathematics, science, and foreign languages.

Renner, John W., and William B. Ragan, *Teaching Science in the Elementary School*, New York, Harper & Row, 1968. Explains how the inquiry-discovery method is used in teaching science.

Trump, J. Lloyd, and D. F. Miller, *Secondary School Curriculum Improvement*, Boston, Allyn & Bacon, 1968. Describes curriculum improvement projects in secondary school subjects.

9

Innovations
in Grouping for Instruction

*Different children, or the same children at different age levels, need different activities in order to maximize their well-rounded development; hence various groups must be organized. Through grouping, in its multiple forms, the school endeavors to place each child in varying environmental and learning situations to enhance this development.**

School organization is not an end in itself; it is a means of releasing the potential of each teacher and of facilitating the achievement of the objectives of the school. Grouping pupils for instruction is an important facet of the internal organization of a school. Innovations in grouping for instruction began in this country early in the nineteenth century; they have multiplied steadily through the years. Any history of American education is likely to include an analysis of two pioneering developments in grouping: the Lancastrian or monitorial plan, which was first established in the schools of New York City in 1806 and which spread to many other city school systems during the

*Henry J. Otto and David C. Sanders, *Elementary School Organization and Administration* (4th ed.), New York, Appleton-Century-Crofts, 1964, p. 94.

first decade of the nineteenth century; and the first graded elementary school in America, established at the Quincy School in Boston in 1848.

The graded school soon spread to urban school systems throughout the country and is still the type of organization used in the great majority of elementary schools. Some of the factors that have caused this form of regimentation to persist despite its obvious weaknesses are: the publication of graded series of textbooks; the relative simplicity of giving the same assignment to all members of a class; the use of standardized achievement tests with norms established in terms of grade levels; the necessity to report attendance to state departments of education in terms of grades; and, in general, the factory-like precision made possible by the system. As the Lynds put it in their famous *Middletown*, a study of Muncie, Indiana, the typical school of 1925 was ". . . like a factory—a thoroughly regimented affair."[1]

The consequences of the effort to regiment children became apparent many years ago: increasing dropout rates, high percentages of children not promoted, and bright students unchallenged by the standard curriculum. As a matter of fact, even before the end of the nineteenth century, some school systems began to try to break this lock step. For instance, in Saint Louis, Pueblo, Portland, North Denver, and other cities, the schools adopted innovations as early as the 1890s. A few famous plans, such as the Gary Plan, the Dalton Plan, and the Winnetka Plan, appeared during the first few decades of this century. In general, however, the period since 1940 has been the one when many new plans for grouping children for instruction have emerged. The rest of this chapter is devoted to an examination of the advantages and limitations of some of these plans.

THE NONGRADED
PLAN
The use of the nongraded plan for grouping pupils for instruction has been increasing since 1950. One study of a sample of 600 elementary schools (out of a total of 85,000) reported that 6 percent were using some nongraded sequences in 1956, 12 percent were doing so in 1961, and 26 percent of the principals reporting said that they expected to be using the plan by 1966.[2] In 1960 it was predicted that the decade of the 1950s would be recorded in history texts of the future as one of great ferment in elementary and secondary schools. The same authority pointed out that, during the 1950s, instead of centering on curriculum reform, the elementary school had largely concerned itself with or-

[1]Robert S. Lynd and Helen Lynd, *Middletown*, New York, Harcourt, Brace & World, 1929, p. 188.
[2]Project on the Instructional Program of the Public Schools, *The Principals Look at the Schools*, Washington, D.C., National Education Association, 1962, preface and pp. 39–40.

ganizational changes designed to group children more efficiently for individual differences.[3]

The nongraded plan is primarily a development of the 1950s and 1960s—at least in terms of the number of schools using the plan and of the space devoted to it in educational publications. As early as 1940, however, a "Primary Unit" plan was used in Pittsburgh, and an "Early Elementary School" system was adopted in Minneapolis. Both of these plans eliminated annual promotions during the first three years the child was in school or during the first four years in schools maintaining kindergartens.[4] The reports on these two plans indicate that they were intended to achieve more than the elimination of annual promotions. For instance, the report of a survey of the Pittsburgh schools thus commented on the Primary Unit: "Combined with the activity curriculum or variations of this approach to curriculum development, it is a superior basis for advancing curriculum practice in the city."[5] A bulletin of the Minneapolis schools made this comment on the Early Elementary School: "In each year, the teacher will adapt the curriculum to the needs of each child."[6] These statements are particularly pertinent to any evaluation of nongraded plans as they exist today, for it is generally recognized that a change in the organization of a school without corresponding changes in the curriculum and in teaching may result in merely substituting one form of regimentation for another—substituting uniform materials and standards for each *level* for uniform materials and standards for each *grade*.

The motivation for developing the nongraded school has come primarily from two sources. The first source is the increasing amount of information about the wide variations that exist among children at any grade level. Pupils who enter the first grade generally range over a four-year spread in mental age; the longer they remain in school, the wider these variations become. Our democratic ideals demand equality of educational opportunity; they do not demand identical achievement at any age or grade level. The second source is the increasing acceptance of the philosophy of continuous growth, which holds that the school should assist each child in growing according to his natural pattern, without depriving the bright child of the opportunity of making the most of his talents or forcing the slow child to experience failure if he cannot advance as rapidly as others.

Characteristics of the Nongraded Plan

The nongraded plan varies from one school system to another and from one year to the next in the same school system. It is possible, therefore,

[3]Celia B. Stendler, "Grouping Practices," in National Elementary Principal, *Those First Years at School*, Washington, D.C., National Education Association, 1960, pp. 147–148.

[4]Hollis L. Caswell and Arthur W. Foshay, *Education in the Elementary School* (3rd ed.), New York, American Book, 1957, pp. 361–363.

[5]Ibid.

[6]Ibid.

to mention only some common characteristics that apply to most non-graded plans.

1. The plan is used most extensively in the primary division (Grades 1–3 in the graded school). In some schools, it has been extended to the kindergarten, the intermediate division, and the high school.
2. The content of the curriculum for the primary unit is divided into eight or nine levels, and pupils progress from one level to the next in terms of their rates of achievement. Each child begins in September where he left off the previous June, without repeating the work he has completed.
3. Charts are developed showing what achievement each child must attain before he moves from one level to the next. These charts are generally geared to reading achievement, but some schools also include levels for arithmetic and language usage.
4. A teacher is generally given a group of pupils who do not vary by more than two progress levels in achievement.
5. Teachers must become very proficient in the use of tests and other evaluation procedures in order to determine when a pupil has completed one of the levels.
6. Teachers and parents must become familiar with an entirely different form of reporting pupil progress.

Advantages of the Nongraded Plan
1. It permits each child to progress at his own rate of learning.
2. It reduces the emotional tensions that develop when a child is forced into learning situations before he is ready.
3. It requires teachers to become more explicit concerning objectives, materials, and procedures.
4. It promotes cooperative planning on the part of teachers.

Limitations of the Nongraded Plan
1. The plan is not a panacea; it is merely a step in the right direction.
2. The plan cannot achieve its greatest potential if it is merely an administrative device for regulating pupil progress through a school. It requires considerable modification in instructional materials, including both locally prepared materials and textbooks.[7]
3. It does not give the teacher a group of pupils who are alike with respect to all the factors that influence their progress in school. No plan of grouping has been devised that relieves the teacher of the responsibility of recognizing and making provision for individual differences.
4. When the plan requires all pupils to move through a preplanned, prescribed sequence of content and skills, it becomes another form

[7]Richard I. Miller, *The Nongraded School: Analysis and Study*, New York, Harper & Row, 1967, p. 13.

of regimentation in which standards for levels are substituted for standards for grades. Some learnings are needed by all pupils; others are unique to the individual. Pupils, therefore, need opportunities to participate in the selection of some materials and the planning of some learning activities.

5. There is little evidence from research that the use of the nongraded plan improves the achievement of pupils. Some studies show a slight gain in reading for nongraded schools over graded schools; other studies do not. Although the studies were controlled for academic aptitude, they do not reveal whether the amount of time spent on reading was the same under both programs.[8]

6. Since the nongraded plan is based on ability grouping, it may penalize lower-class children who are bright but not as verbal as their middle-class peers.

7. As Goodlad and Anderson put it in their pioneering publication on the nongraded school, "Teachers in nongraded schools who have not yet faced up to the inappropriateness of graded content for this new pattern are only beginning the process of school improvement."[9]

THE APPROPRIATE
PLACEMENT SCHOOL

A school using the nongraded plan combined with a multiphased curriculum is known as an *Appropriate Placement School*. This plan has been described as a sophisticated nongraded curriculum, because it is much more than just another way of grouping students. It has been adopted in a number of high schools, notably the Melbourne (Florida) High School, which is widely known in the education profession for its pioneering and successful use of it.

The appropriate placement plan was developed as a result of a conference held at the Massachusetts Institute of Technology in May, 1963, under the auspices of the President's Science Advisory Committee. The conference, which was headed by B. Frank Brown, sought to determine the effectiveness of the nongraded plan in salvaging the 30 percent of American school children who become educational failures. After the meeting, Brown traveled more than 100,000 miles, visiting nongraded schools throughout the nation. He spent more than a year working on a new curriculum model for nongraded schools. He characterized the plan as follows:

This new modus operandi can no longer be properly called a nongraded school. The nongraded school implies a change in school organization with minor curriculum adjustments. In its more sophisticated form, the nongraded school has become the Appropriate Placement School. This is a

---

[8]Stendler, op. cit., pp. 155–157.
[9]John I. Goodlad and Robert H. Anderson, *The Nongraded Elementary School*, New York, Harcourt, Brace & World, 1959, p. 214.

*revolutionary new organization which calls for both a new organization and
a corresponding revolution in curriculum.*[10]

The "revolution in curriculum"—the multiphased curriculum—is described thus:

Phase 1—*Subjects are provided for students who perform from 0–20th percentile on standardized achievement tests, indicating that they need special assistance in small classes.*

Phase 2—*Subjects are organized for students who range between the 20th and 40th percentile in achievement and who need more emphasis on fundamentals.*

Phase 3—*Courses are arranged for students who score between the 40th and 60th percentile on standardized achievement tests, indicating that they have an average background of accomplishment.*

Phase 4—*Subject matter is planned for extremely well prepared students who achieve between the 60th and 80th percentile and desire education in depth.*

Phase 5—*Courses are available for students who attain above the 80th percentile and are willing to assume responsibility for their own learning, pursuing college level courses while still in high school.*

Phase Q—*Students whose creative talents are well developed should give consideration to the Quest phase of the curriculum. This is an important dimension of the phased organization which gives thrust in the direction of individual fulfillment. In this phase, a student may research any area in which he is deeply and sincerely interested.*[11]

Class time in the multiphased classroom is distributed as follows:

1. *Presentation of materials comprises approximately 20 percent of the time in the course. (This includes time spent in viewing films as well as lecturing.)*
2. *Discussion in analysis groups constitutes approximately 40 percent of the class time.*
3. *Individual work and reading encompasses roughly 40 percent of the class time.*[12]

THE DUAL
PROGRESS PLAN

The *Dual Progress Plan* was initiated in 1958 in the schools of two suburban towns, Long Beach and Ossining, New York. At first it was limited to Grades 3–6, but by 1960 it had been extended to include Grades 7 and 8. The plan was developed cooperatively by the Experimental Teaching Center at New York University and the two school systems. George D. Stoddard, chancellor of New York University, was in general charge of the study, which received financial

[10]B. Frank Brown, *The Appropriate Placement School: A Sophisticated Nongraded Curriculum*, West Nyack, N.Y., Parker, 1965, pp. 3–4.

[11]Ibid., pp. 26–27.

[12]Ibid., p. 28.

support from the Ford Foundation. Stoddard wrote a book that contains the most extensive description of the plan that is available.[13] As the subtitle of his book, *A New Philosophy and Program in Elementary Education*, indicates, he regards the plan as much more than a device for grouping pupils for instruction.

The Dual Progress Plan offers a semidepartmentalized arrangement as a substitute for the self-contained classroom. The self-contained classroom, which has for many years been the type of organization used by most elementary schools for grouping pupils, is the familiar one that involves one teacher teaching all or almost all the subjects taken by one group of children in one general-purpose classroom. The proponents of this plan point out that it enables the teacher to learn a great deal about each pupil through long association and through observing him in a wide variety of situations and that it permits a more flexible use of time, since learning activities are not brought to an abrupt end because pupils must go to another classroom.[14]

There are serious limitations to the self-contained classroom plan, however, and it was in an effort to overcome them that the Dual Progress Plan was developed. Under it, the language arts, social studies, and physical education are called "cultural imperatives," those subjects that everyone in our society needs as a basis for effective social living. Mathematics, science, and the arts are called "cultural electives." Pupils spend one-half day on the cultural imperatives with a homeroom teacher and a core specialist in physical education; they spend the other half-day on the cultural electives, taught by specialists in the various areas. The cultural imperatives portion of the program is graded; the cultural electives portion is nongraded. Promotion is generally determined by the homeroom teacher.

Advantages Claimed for the Dual Progress Plan
1. Every pupil is taught each of the curriculum areas each year by a teacher who knows the area well.
2. The plan makes better provision for developing the intellectual potentialities and the personalities of pupils than does the self-contained classroom plan.
3. The plan offers a more satisfying professional role for elementary teachers.
4. The plan offers individualized learning programs for the slow, the average, and the gifted pupils.
5. Pupils profit from having several teachers, each of whom has a different personality and uses different methods.
6. Pupils who have special interests and talents can progress more

---

[13]George D. Stoddard, *The Dual Progress Plan: A New Philosophy and Program in Elementary Education*, New York, Harper & Row, 1961.
[14]Association for Supervision and Curriculum Development, *The Self-Contained Classroom*, Washington, D.C., ASCD, 1960.

rapidly in the appropriate areas than they can in a conventional school.

Limitations of the Dual Progress Plan

1. The division of curriculum areas into cultural imperatives and cultural electives is an arbitrary one; a more defensible position would seem to be that everything taught in an elementary school should be regarded as a cultural imperative.
2. The plan limits the opportunity for the teacher to know each pupil well and to make provisions for his individual needs; the mathematics teacher, for example, who meets a different group of pupils every 40 minutes (so that during the day he meets more than 150 pupils) has little opportunity to know each pupil well.
3. The scheduling of so many classes during the school day, each meeting with a different teacher in a different room, limits the opportunity for cultural tours and other out-of-class activities. The result is a reduction of enrichment experience for pupils, a greater adherence to a rigid, preplanned curriculum.
4. The plan limits the opportunities for pupils to see the relationships existing among school subjects and makes it difficult to devote time to unified learning activities that center around problems or concepts that cut across subject-matter boundaries.
5. "Today's secondary schools are struggling with their problems created by over-departmentalization and subject-centeredness. It is a shame to impose the old organizational pattern of secondary education upon the elementary school."[15]

TEAM TEACHING

Although team teaching has as its primary purpose a better utilization of the special talents of teachers, it does involve a unique procedure for grouping students for instruction: It provides for large-group learning situations, small-group learning situations, and individual learning situations.

The first experimental team teaching was done at the Franklin Elementary School in Lexington, Massachusetts, in 1957, but by 1960 more secondary schools than elementary schools were experimenting with the plan. The rationale for team teaching and an outline of the structure of teaching teams to be formed were contained in a proposal made to the Fund for the Advancement of Education by Dean Francis Keppel of Harvard's Graduate School of Education in 1956. Among the points Keppel made were these: A new pattern of cooperation between uni-

[15]Robert S. Fleming, et al., "Reactions to the Dual Progress Plan," in Maurie Hillson, *Change and Innovation in Elementary School Organization*, New York, Holt, 1965, p. 262.

versities and school systems is needed; half the children in America are being taught by relatively inexperienced teachers; the difference between those who make a lifetime career of teaching and those who teach for only a few years must be recognized. The proposal resulted in a grant for the establishment of the School and University Program for Research and Development (SUPRAD), which developed the team-teaching concept in detail, evolved methods of applying it, and directed the program in Lexington and later ones in Newton and Concord, Massachusetts.

Types of Teaching Teams

The types of teaching teams vary from one school system to another. Cunningham has divided the teaching teams described in the literature into four categories: the team leader type, the associate type, the master teacher-beginning teacher type, and the coordinated type.[16]

The team leader type.   More schools use this type than use any of the others. A large group of students is assigned to a team composed of two or more certified teachers, one or more nonprofessionals, and, in some cases, a student teacher or two. A team leader is selected to coordinate the work of the team. The team leader presides over planning sessions, exercises varying degrees of leadership over the team, and generally does some teaching. In most cases the team leader receives a higher salary than other members of the team; he is responsible for assigning pupils to groups, for developing a suitable curriculum, and for supervising the less experienced members of the team. The nonprofessionals perform nonteaching tasks. The student teachers have an opportunity to observe more than one teacher, teach certain topics for which they have special preparation, and join in the planning and evaluation of learning activities.

The associate type.   Most of the teaching teams of this type work with large classes. Opportunities are provided for large-group learning situations, small-group learning situations, and independent study. No teacher is designated as team leader; planning for instruction is worked out cooperatively so that the best talents of each member of the team are used. Sometimes the members of the teaching team represent only one subject area and sometimes more than one. Some of the teaching teams have nonprofessional adults and student teachers assigned to them.

The master teacher-beginning teacher type.   Beginning teachers and teachers who are new to the school system are sometimes teamed with one or two master teachers to share the responsibility for teaching a

---

[16]Luverne L. Cunningham, "Team Teaching: Where Do We Stand?" *The Administrator's Notebook*, Midwest Administration Center, The University of Chicago, April, 1960.

large group of students. This plan, which has been used most frequently in secondary schools, has not generally involved the designation of a team leader. It offers an excellent opportunity for less experienced teachers to mature under the guidance of experienced teachers.

The coordinated team type.   This variation of team teaching does not assign joint responsibility for a large group of students to members of the team. Instead, teachers who have different sections of the same course meet regularly to coordinate methods and materials used in the various sections of the course. Sometimes the students in all sections of the course are brought together in an auditorium for lectures or other large-group presentations. (Cunningham and others question whether this arrangement should be called team teaching at all.)

Advantages of Team Teaching
1. The plan makes better use of the talents of master teachers; more students are able to profit from their teaching, and their leadership makes it possible to develop better programs of instruction.
2. It enables superior teachers to gain recognition and increases in salaries without leaving the classroom for administrative positions.
3. It facilitates the orientation of new teachers to the school system and to the community.
4. When noncertificated personnel and clerical help are available, teachers are relieved of many nonteaching chores.
5. Beginning teachers have better opportunities for professional growth than they do when they are isolated in one room.
6. The plan makes it possible for members of the teaching team to concentrate more on their areas of specialization.
7. It makes it unnecessary for any group of students to receive all their instruction from an inexperienced teacher.
8. Students gain valuable experience from opportunities for learning in large-group situations, small-group situations, and individual learning situations.
9. The plan provides opportunities for student teachers to observe the work of several teachers and to participate in cooperative planning activities.
10. Sharing the teaching of a class with other teachers results in a higher quality of teaching than can be achieved in the conventional one-teacher classroom.

Factors Influencing the Success of the Plan
Team teaching is not a panacea. Its success depends on the thoroughness with which administrators, teachers, and parents have been prepared for its introduction; the expertness of members of the teaching team; the availability of adequate space and materials; and the ability

of the team leader to release the talents of all members of the teaching team. Following are some of the hazards to be overcome in the operation of the plan:

1. The members of the teaching team must be able to work together harmoniously and productively; friction in interpersonal relations can destroy the effectiveness of the plan.
2. The large-group learning situations may become formal lecture sessions in which students have little opportunity to ask questions or to make contributions.
3. Unless the superior teachers who serve as team leaders do some teaching, the plan may result in the loss of expert teaching talent in the interest of the performance of semiadministrative tasks.
4. The plan can operate at its highest level of effectiveness only in a building that has been planned specifically for this type of organization.

SOME GENERALIZATIONS
ABOUT GROUPING

1. Grouping students for instruction is only one aspect of school organization. Developing the over-all design of the curriculum, developing an effective organization within the individual classroom, and organizing the staff for the improvement of instruction are other important facets of organization.
2. The best type of grouping for instruction is the one that is most compatible with the major beliefs and goals of the school staff.
3. Under no type of organization yet devised can the individual teacher ignore his responsibility for recognizing and making provision for individual differences among pupils.
4. It is generally unwise for one school system to take over some "package plan" that has worked well in another system; the plan should be tailor-made by the local school staff within the total situation in which it must function.
5. The installation of a new plan for grouping students for instruction must also make curriculum adaptations for different types of students; otherwise, the new plan is not likely to have much impact on the problem of meeting individual needs.
6. No organizational plan can serve as a substitute for competent teachers; the most that any plan can accomplish is to "set the stage"—to provide the situation in which it is possible for the teacher to perform as well as he is capable of performing.

The discussion of innovations in grouping students for instruction presented in this chapter is not definitive or complete. There are many other types of vertical and horizontal organizations. Enough has been said, however, to indicate the general direction that practice has been taking. (The references listed at the end of this chapter permit the student to pursue the problem in greater detail.)

SUMMARY

1. Innovations in grouping pupils for instruction began in this country during the early years of the nineteenth century; they have continued to appear ever since then.
2. The graded elementary school was established in 1848; it continues to be the prevailing type of elementary school organization.
3. The weaknesses of the graded school system were highlighted by high dropout rates, increasing percentages of nonpromotion, and failure to challenge capable students.
4. The period since 1940 has witnessed the emergence of many plans for grouping students for instruction.
5. Annual promotions during the child's first three years in school were eliminated in Minneapolis and Pittsburgh as early as 1940.
6. The rationale for the nongraded plan comes primarily from increased recognition of individual differences and from increasing acceptance of the philosophy of continuous growth.
7. The nongraded plan permits each pupil to begin each school year where he left off the previous year, without repeating any of the work he has completed.
8. The nongraded plan promotes cooperative planning on the part of the staff of the school.
9. The nongraded plan cannot achieve its greatest potential unless modifications are made in instructional materials, including both locally prepared materials and textbooks.
10. The Appropriate Placement School calls for both a new organization and a corresponding revolution in the curriculum.
11. One outstanding feature of the Appropriate Placement School is its multi-phased curriculum.
12. The Dual Progress Plan offers a semidepartmentalized arrangement as a substitute for the self-contained classroom plan.
13. The Dual Progress Plan makes it possible for each child to be taught each year by teachers who know their subjects well.
14. Team teaching was developed primarily to make better use of the talents of superior teachers.
15. Team teaching makes it possible for superior teachers to gain recognition and increased salaries without leaving the classroom for administrative positions.

SELECTED READINGS

Association for Supervision and Curriculum Development, *The Self-Contained Classroom*, Washington, D.C., The Association, 1960. A pamphlet devoted entirely to a discussion of the advantages of the self-contained classroom plan.

Beggs, D. W., *Team Teaching: Bold New Venture*, Bloomington, Ind., Indiana University Press, 1964. An excellent treatment of team teaching.

Blair, Medill, and Richard G. Woodward, *Team Teaching in Action*, Boston, Houghton Mifflin, 1964. Gives the rationale for team teaching, characteristics, space requirements, functions of team leaders, suggestions for planning, and other information.

Brown, B. Frank, *The Appropriate Placement School: A Sophisticated Nongraded Curriculum*, West Nyack, N.Y., Parker, 1965. Holds that the major roadblock to the acceptance of the nongraded school lies in the absence of an orderly curriculum scheme. Presents a multiphased curriculum.

Caswell, Hollis L., and Arthur W. Foshay, *Education in the Elementary School* (3rd ed.), New York, American Book, 1957. Chapter 13 presents information about early experiments with nongradedness in Minneapolis and Pittsburgh.

Goodlad, John I., and Robert H. Anderson, *The Nongraded Elementary School*, New York, Harcourt, Brace & World, 1959. Perhaps the most widely known book on the nongraded school.

Hillson, Maurie, *Change and Innovation in Elementary School Organization, Selected Readings*, New York, Holt, 1965. Perhaps the most complete treatment of innovations in grouping that has been published.

Miller, Richard I., *The Nongraded School: Analysis and Study*, New York, Harper & Row, 1967. Presents the historical and sociological perspectives on the nongraded school, the administrators role in initiating the plan, and criteria for evaluating a nongraded program.

Morse, Arthur D., *Schools of Tomorrow—Today*, Garden City, N.Y., Doubleday, 1960. The first two chapters deal with team teaching and nongraded schools.

Otto, Henry J., and David C. Sanders, *Elementary School Organization and Administration* (4th ed.), New York, Appleton-Century-Crofts, 1964. Chapters 3 and 4 deal with "Organization for Instruction" and "Grouping Children for Wholesome Development."

Project on the Instructional Program of the Public Schools, *The Principals Look at the Schools*, Washington, D.C., National Education Association, 1962. Provides data on the extent of use of innovations in grouping.

Ragan, William B., *Modern Elementary Curriculum* (3rd ed.), New York, Holt, 1966. Chapter 5 deals with innovations in grouping for instruction.

Stendler, Celia B., "Grouping Practices," in *National Elementary Principal, Those First Years at School*, Washington, D.C., National Education Association, 1960. An excellent discussion of the status of innovations in grouping.

Stoddard, George W., *The Dual Progress Plan: A New Philosophy and Program in Elementary Education*, New York, Harper & Row, 1961. States the philosophy of the Dual Progress Plan, explains a new approach to subject matter, and reports on the operation of the plan in two schools in New York.

Trump, J. Lloyd, and Delmas F. Miller, *Secondary School Curriculum Improvement*, Boston, Allyn & Bacon, 1968. Chapter 24, "Team Teaching and Improved Staff Utilization," explains what team teaching is, how teams operate, and the provisions that are necessary to facilitate team teaching.

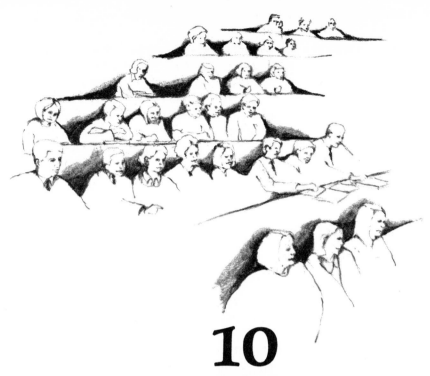

10

Higher Education in Transition

*Those of us relegated to administration must count on the action intellectual on campus to make the university dynamic, relevant, and significant in western culture. The whole business comes to a focus in the faculty-student encounter, the academic dialogue, the learning process.**

The University of Santo Domingo, founded in the Dominican Republic in 1538, was the first institution of higher learning in the Western Hemisphere. The first in the North American Colonies was Harvard College, established by the Puritans in Massachusetts in 1636. Harvard, whose primary purpose was to prepare ministers for the church, remained the only institution of higher learning in North America until near the end of the seventeenth century.

The church college was the capstone of the colonial school system. Like Harvard, the next institutions all had denominational connections. William and Mary was established in Virginia in 1693; Yale in Connecticut in 1701; Princeton in New Jersey in 1746; King's

*John F. Olson, President, Oklahoma City University, "Action Intellectuals on Campus" (address to the faculty, September 1, 1967).

College (later Columbia University) in New York in 1754; Brown in Rhode Island in 1764; Rutgers in New Jersey in 1766; and Dartmouth in New Hampshire in 1769. Other types of institutions came later. Only two states—Georgia and North Carolina—had chartered state universities by the end of the eighteenth century. In the nineteenth century, however, many new types of collegiate institutions were founded: state universities, land-grant colleges, institutions established by philanthropies, Negro colleges and universities, colleges for women, coeducational institutions, technological institutes, and many types of professional schools. The junior college did not appear until 1902.

INCREASING MAGNITUDE OF THE ENTERPRISE

Harvard College never had more than 20 students enrolled at one time during the first 64 years of its existence. The situation became very different in later years. There were 238,000 students enrolled in colleges and universities in 1900; 598,000 in 1920; 1,494,000 in 1940; 5,300,000 in 1964; and 7,100,000 in 1969–1970. It took about three centuries for this country to reach an enrollment in higher education of 1.5 million students; it took only 30 years to increase this figure to 7.1 million. The president of Harvard taught all the courses during its first 64 years; in 1970, there were 532,000 college and university teachers in the United States. The U. S. Office of Education estimated that in 1970 the total cost of public and nonpublic institutions of higher education, including both current operating expenditures and capital outlay, was $22.7 billion.[1]

There were more than 2000 colleges and universities in the United States in 1965. The classification according to type of institution and source of control was as follows:

Type	
Four-year institutions	792
Junior colleges	644
Institutions offering work through the master's level	455
Institutions granting the doctorate	223
Unclassified	25
Control	
Private and nondenominational	507
State	405
Local government units	357
Protestant	438
Roman Catholic	361
Federal	12
Jewish	8

Source: Logan Wilson (ed.), *Emerging Patterns in American Higher Education*, Washington, D.C., American Council on Education, 1965, pp. 1–2.

[1]"The Magnitude of the American Educational Establishment," *Saturday Review*, October 18, 1969, 83.

Several factors have contributed to the recent rapid increase in the magnitude of the higher education enterprise: the growth in the population of the United States; the increasing percentage of high school graduates who enter colleges and universities; the increasing dependence of industry and government on higher education institutions for research and for the preparation of specialized personnel; and the increasing recognition that the "life chances" of young people growing up in our kind of society are enhanced by a college education. In other words, the increases in enrollments and the expansion of programs in higher education have reflected the changes in American life summarized in earlier chapters of this text.

Expanding Programs in Higher Education

As we have noted, colonial colleges, like the common schools and the grammar schools, were dominated by the religious motive; established to prepare ministers, they were controlled by denominational boards. Their programs were, to a great extent, patterned after the old English universities—Oxford and Cambridge—from which most of their faculties had graduated. The curricula consisted of the liberal arts, philosophy, and the classical languages. The students were listed in the order of the social rank of their parents.

Universities established in this country during the nineteenth century continued the liberal arts program, with the addition of new subjects, such as biological and physical sciences, geography, history, surveying, and navigation. The professional goal of the colonial colleges was expanded to include the preparation of lawyers, physicians, teachers, engineers, and others.

Many new subjects have been added to the liberal arts curriculum in higher education since the beginning of the twentieth century; many new professional schools, such as journalism, social work, business administration, and geology, have also been established. As Figure 3 indicates, the modern university also maintains many service departments that were unknown in earlier universities. The student will find it interesting to examine the general catalog and the student-faculty directory of his own university and to compare the enterprises in which it is engaged with those listed in Figure 3.

HIGHER EDUCATION TODAY

Living in a nation whose future is both lighted by promises and clouded by threats, living in an age when the individual must pass judgment on increasingly complicated issues, every citizen has, in the words of John Erskine, "the moral obligation to be intelligent." Yet the magnitude of our higher education enterprise alone will not ensure that future citizens will be intelligent or that their intelligence will be directed toward the creation of a better tomorrow.

It is certainly true that colleges and universities have served America well. They have been a principal source of strength for government; they have provided specialized personnel, research facilities, and competent managers for industry; and they have opened the doors of opportunity to millions of American youth. Nevertheless, there is widespread concern about the ability of this huge enterprise to put into practice the principle of self-renewal to such an extent that it will be able to perform the tasks expected of it in an age of accelerated change—its ability, in fact, to bring about the internal reforms that will be needed to make it more relevant to the realities of the next few decades. The rest of this chapter considers needed reforms and promising innovations in the internal structure of institutions of higher education connected with efforts to improve instruction and efforts to develop a coordinated system of higher education within states and regions.

Inside the Individual Institution

Our 2480 colleges and universities have grown up independently; each has been relatively free to develop its own pattern of operation. The U. S. Office of Education has exercised less authority over higher education than has the ministry of education in any other country. Because research relating to college and university organization and administration has been relatively neglected, we have little objective knowledge on which to base decisions about the operation of a college or a university. One observer has commented on this situation as follows:

The managerial revolution which has long been under way in business, industry, and government has been slow to start in the groves of academe. I would urge that it is high time for us to allocate more time and energy to the structural and functional problems of educational institutions and to develop a more efficient and effective system of higher education better suited to its own ends and the needs of society.[2]

It is difficult, therefore, to generalize about the internal arrangements in American colleges and universities. Nevertheless, certain conditions that exist in most of them can be identified.

Administration.   Colleges and universities are under the general control and supervision of boards of trustees or boards of regents. These boards generally delegate much authority to a chief administrative official, the president. The president, in turn, generally delegates much responsibility to vice-presidents, deans, chairmen of departments, directors of various enterprises, and other administrative officers.

As colleges and universities become larger, the degree of specialization increases; as specialization increases, the task of supervision by

[2]Logan Wilson (ed.), *Emerging Patterns in American Higher Education*, Washington, D.C., American Council on Education, 1965, p. 28.

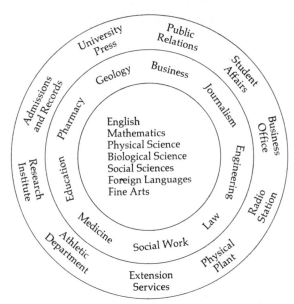

Figure 3. Typical Enterprises of a Modern University. The inner circle lists some typical courses generally offered in the liberal arts or general education program of a modern university. The second ring lists some of the professional schools that are frequently maintained. The outer ring represents the rapidly expanding group of service operations in which universities are engaged.

the president and his central office staff becomes more difficult. As another writer has aptly said, "I might pause to observe that it takes a courageous dean and fearless president to deal firmly with budgetary requests from a speciality they can neither pronounce nor spell."[3]

Many institutions have made attempts to remedy the chaos that arose from excessive diffusion of power in the area of decision-making. Organizations composed of representatives from the various colleges and departments have been developed for the purpose of recommending to the president and the board of trustees certain major goals and policies and for the purpose of mobilizing the resources of the entire institution to achieve these goals. The faculty senate, the budget council, the council on teacher education, and the council on instruction are illustrations. Somewhat similar organizations are frequently set up *within* colleges and departments to provide a means for faculty participation in decision-making at the same time that sound policies and consistent practices are maintained. The success of these organizations in achieving coordination of the activities of a college or university varies from one institution to another. They soon degenerate into mere debating societies unless the administration has a genuine interest in their operation, provides the supervision and encouragement that is needed, and has high-level competence in human relations.

[3]James Perkins in ibid., p. 10.

Faculty. There are many myths about college and university professors. One view holds that the comparative security and established routine of the campus provide a safe retreat from the harsh competition of other occupations. Other views are that (1) professors live in an "ivory tower" and deal with abstractions that have little value for the "practical" man; (2) they know and care little about anything that is outside their fields of specialization; and (3) they have little interest in students. A few individuals distrust the professor as an intellectual who disturbs the status quo by pointing out conditions in our society that call for reforms.

Whatever may be said for these views, a surprising number of successful men and women in all walks of life give credit to a college or university professor who helped them to gain confidence in themselves, to respect intellectual attainments, and to develop the tools for a lifetime of learning.

The "ivory tower" type of professor can still be found occasionally, but his breed is almost extinct. The "action intellectual" is a much more prevalent type; it is he who keeps the university "dynamic, relevant, and significant in western culture."[4] The action intellectual keeps himself well informed about a wide range of issues before the American people; he is actively engaged in discussions with other members of the faculty about the mission and performance of the institution; he strives to invent ways to involve students in the learning process.

In addition to playing an active role in the academic life of the campus, many college and university professors are active participants in the life of the community, state, and nation. They serve on boards of education, city councils, church boards, and civic club boards and committees. They conduct important research for government and industry; provide factual information and guidance for the legislature; conduct surveys; serve as consultants for public school systems; participate actively in political campaigns; and, in some cases, are elected to important offices in government. As Woodrow Wilson, a noted example of the last category of professors, said, "We were not put into the world to sit still and know; we were put into the world to act."

Curriculum and instruction. The curriculum in most colleges and universities came into existence by historical accretion rather than by any carefully developed plan. As institutions become larger, new courses are added, but few courses are discarded. The relative autonomy of departments has led to much duplication; it is not unusual for essentially the same course to be offered in two or more departments. The rigidity of the departmental structure makes it difficult to develop courses dealing with problems that cut across departmental lines. For example, it has become common in recent decades to make teacher

[4]Olson, op. cit.

education a university-wide responsibility. Although it is relatively simple to develop a "paper" organization for this purpose, many difficulties are encountered in putting such a plan into actual operation. One typical difficulty involves students preparing to teach in elementary and secondary schools who need to learn about the content and procedures involved in the "new" mathematics and the "new" science; the courses they take in colleges and universities, however, seldom incorporate the new content and procedures. Many college and university courses deal with conditions that existed when the professor was receiving his own education. Once the professor has developed his lecture on the basis of these conditions, too often he is reluctant to change it. College students want professors to "tell it like it is." They want to know about conditions that exist now. Those who have talked with students themselves about "student unrest" have been told that much of what they have been expected to learn has little relevance to issues and problems with which Americans must deal today.

Although the projects that have revolutionized instruction in elementary and secondary school have been located on university campuses and directed by university professors, universities as a whole have been slow to adopt newer teaching procedures. Involving students in the teaching-learning process; arranging learning situations so that students discover concepts and principles rather than having these handed to them "ready-made"; making provision for individual differences; experimenting with team teaching and the use of new instructional media; discovering the use of questions—these are some of the hallmarks of effective teaching procedures. Nevertheless, the lecture method still dominates the instructional scene in most, but not all, institutions of higher education (although it can be effective when it is supplemented by other procedures). Moreover, the professor who is regarded as an excellent lecturer generally receives the highest awards from the university.

Again, student unrest can be explained, at least in part, by failure to provide classroom situations that cause students to feel that they play a significant role in their own education. The fact that research is given greater recognition than excellent teaching, the "publish or perish" policy, the increasing extent to which faculty members are drawn from the classroom to work on projects financed by grants from various sources, and the increasing use of graduate students for classroom instruction also cause concern about the quality of instruction provided by colleges and universities.

These comments do not imply that no progress has been made in improving instruction in higher education. Several colleges and universities have conducted experiments designed to improve teaching arrangements and procedures; some have made excellent provision for the use of newer instructional media; and most of them are engaged in self-study programs for the purpose of identifying weaknesses and developing plans for the future.

Outside the Individual Institution

As enrollments in higher education increase, as new institutions are established, and as the functions colleges and universities are expected to perform multiply, the need for coordination of programs of higher education becomes imperative. If it is difficult to coordinate the efforts of various segments within a university, it is to be expected that the task of coordinating the activities of institutions within a state or region will be even more difficult. The rationale for state, regional, and national coordination of programs of higher education is not difficult to understand: Each institution surrenders a part of its independence in order to gain greater strength by blending its activities with those of other institutions. What is more difficult to understand or defend is the fact that the principle of coordination has not been more widely implemented in the United States.

State agencies for coordinating higher education. In 1965, 9 states had single boards for governing all public higher education and 12 other states had boards with more limited authority over institutions, each of which had its own board of trustees. These "master" boards generally allocate a budget to each institution from the general appropriation for higher education; exercise some control over the curricula offered by each institution; issue regulations concerning admission, degree-granting standards, and reporting practices; and make studies of the future needs of higher education in the state. (The most fully developed master board for higher education is the Coordinating Council for Higher Education in California.)

Regional agencies for coordinating higher education. Agencies for accrediting institutions of higher education have been in existence for many decades. The North Central Association of Secondary Schools and Colleges, the Southern Association of Secondary Schools and Colleges, and similar associations in six regions of the United States publish standards for accreditation and send visitation teams to high schools, colleges, and universities periodically to evaluate the institutions in terms of the published criteria.

A development of the last few decades has been consortium arrangements, which have evolved in virtually every region. Their activities include procedures for exchange of student credits, joint faculty appointments, pooling of library and audiovisual resources, and coordination of extension programs. Regional compacts, such as the Southern Regional Education Board, the Western Interstate Commission for Higher Education, and the New England Board of Higher Education, constitute another form of joint action in higher education. The tremendous increases in enrollments and the increasing costs of higher education in the next decade will, no doubt, hasten efforts to avoid the costly blunders connected with the location of new institutions, wasteful duplication of curricula, and general lack of coordination that have characterized higher education in the past.

National agencies affecting higher education. Voluntary organizations at the national level set standards for various professional schools that the local university must meet. Examples are the American Medical Association, the American Library Association, the National Commission on Teacher Education and Professional Standards, and the American Association of School Administrators. These and many similar associations serve the useful function of preventing substandard programs from springing up in institutions that lack the facilities for providing the preparation needed by members of these strategic professions. Other national organizations providing services for college and university faculty members include the American Association of University Professors, the American Council on Education, the American Chemical Society, the American Council of Learned Societies, and the American Council for the Advancement of Science. The federal government includes dozens of agencies that affect higher education; many universities receive the bulk of their research funds from these sources.

The Two-Year College
The first junior college was established in this country in 1902. Until comparatively recent years, the principal function of this institution was to prepare students to enter four-year colleges and universities. A new kind of two-year college has made its appearance in recent decades —the community college. This type of college has grown rapidly in recent years and seems destined to play an increasing role in higher education in the years ahead. The President's Commission on National Goals recommended in 1960 that two-year colleges should be within commuting distance of most high school graduates and that they should give adult education a vital role, offering new values throughout the life span.[5] In 1962, more than 400 public community colleges and 270 private junior colleges served 748,619 students.

The community college makes a unique contribution by admitting all students who can profit from its program; by maintaining a multiphased curriculum that provides opportunities for both the academically talented student and the nonacademic, vocationally oriented student; and by serving adults in the community who have not had an opportunity to attend college.

Student Unrest
Student unrest on the campus is not a new development in American higher education; students openly rebelled against college authorities during the early decades of the nineteenth century, and they have at times ever since. Historians have generally attributed these revolts to

[5]President's Commission on National Goals, *Goals for Americans*, Englewood Cliffs, N. J., Prentice-Hall, 1960, pp. 81–100.

the slowness of colleges and universities to respond to the changing conditions of American life. The increase in the number and violence of student demonstrations, riots, and protests during the last few years, however, has been marked, not only in the United States but throughout the world. (At least twenty-five nations have experienced student uprisings in recent years.)[6]

Sociologists and psychologists have been giving a great deal of study to the causes of student unrest. These studies indicate that most of the "activist" students come from rather stable families and that most of them are among the most capable students on the campus. Frustration over the Vietnam war and a desire to make the university a more humane place in which to live are identified as leading causes. Other factors include the conviction that the curriculum has too little relevance to present problems of living; the desire to have more opportunities to participate in the decision-making affecting their education; and the fact that students have been taught in high schools to think for themselves, to work out their own solutions to problems, and to take an active interest in public affairs. How the problem will be solved remains to be seen. However, these young people can no longer be pushed aside and told to wait until they are more mature before they can take any part in the life of the universities or of the nation.

HIGHER EDUCATION
TOMORROW

The future of higher education can already be glimpsed in some of the new colleges. At the University of South Florida, students are expected to assume responsibility for their own education; at Monteith College of Wayne State University, independent study is emphasized; at New College of Hofstra University, interdisciplinary and seminar-type courses are provided for students; and at Florida Presbyterian College, students are given time for individual research by holding no classes during the month of January. Many other innovations have been initiated at these and other colleges and universities throughout the country.[7]

Scientists predict that amazing technological advances will have occurred by the beginning of the twenty-first century. They expect some of these to supply teaching tools that will enhance the effectiveness of the teaching-learning process. For instance, one writer has stated:

Thus, one can visualize a world in which anyone anywhere might have ready access to great libraries and their books, to videotape or film libraries

---

[6]Many general newspapers and magazines and most educational journals have carried, and are continuing to carry, articles on student unrest. See, for example, the *NEA Journal*, September, 1968.

[7] Samuel Baskin (ed.), *Higher Education: Some Newer Developments*, New York, McGraw-Hill, 1968, chap. 1.

containing lessons on specialized topics, to records of significant present or past events, to outstanding dramatic productions, to a difficult operation particularly well performed in a leading hospital, and to a particularly smooth negotiation by particularly wise diplomats.[8]

The same writer points out that the underdeveloped countries may, with the aid of educational technology, attain universal education in less time than it has taken Western nations and that educational technology will affect international diplomacy in proportion to the extent to which formal education in this nation and others can adopt changes necessary for its use.

As enrollments in higher education continue to increase at a constantly accelerating rate, it will become too costly to have a professor give the same lecture to several sections of a course. Television provides one obvious solution, although college professors have resisted it. In a comment on the situation, Eurich predicts that the resistance will have virtually disappeared by the twenty-first century:

The use of television as an educational medium in colleges developed swiftly after it was introduced in the 1950s. Educators resisted, but demonstration after demonstration, such as those carried on at Pennsylvania State University, established the truth that televised instruction was educationally effective and economically feasible. In 1962 some 30,000 courses were given over television in the United States. But more years were to elapse before colleges recognized that television had made the standard lecture obsolete and the conventional laboratory demonstration inadequate and costly.[9]

Other predictions about higher education in the next century include:

1. There will be a two-year college within commuting distance of the home of every young man and woman.

2. The first two years of higher education will be eliminated from universities and liberal arts colleges.

3. The large universities will become larger; some of them will enroll more than 200,000 students.

4. The practice of processing all students through the same series of lectures and courses will be eliminated. Each student will progress at his own rate; he will spend much time on his own doing individual research or working with a group of other students with interests similar to his own; and he will have access to a wide range of learning resources.

5. Cooperative arrangements among colleges and universities will bring competent instructors and adequate learning resources within reach of more students.

6. University libraries will contain as any as 300 million volumes in miniaturized form, and a multichannel cable will instantly transmit

[8] Foreign Policy Association, *Toward the Year 2018*, New York, Cowles Education Corporation, 1968, p. 76.

[9] Alvin C. Eurich, "Higher Education in the 21st Century," in Glen Haas and Kimball Wiles (eds.), *Readings in Curriculum*, Boston, Allyn & Bacon, 1965, p. 564.

information from these volumes to reading groups on campuses through-out the country.

7. The practice of recording the lectures of outstanding scholars of the world on electronic tapes began systematically in the middle of the 1960s. In the twenty-first century, students will be able to study such taped lectures at their own rate and to review them on kinescopes as often as necessary.

SUMMARY

1. Higher education in North America began in 1636, with the establishment of Harvard College; the church college was the capstone of the colonial school system.
2. During the nineteenth century, many types of collegiate institutions were established: state universities, land-grant colleges, colleges for Negroes and for women, colleges established by philanthropies, and coeducational colleges.
3. It took approximately 300 years for this country to reach an enrollment of 1.5 million in higher education; it took only 30 years (1940–1970) to increase this figure to 7.1 million.
4. There were more than 2000 colleges and universities in the United States in 1965.
5. The core of the program of the modern university is the liberal arts college; professional schools and service enterprises have grown up around this core in most universities.
6. Colleges and universities have served the nation well: They have been a source of strength for government, they have provided industry with specialized personnel and research facilities, and they have opened the doors of opportunity for millions of American youth.
7. Within the individual institution, decentralization in decision-making has been the watchword until recently.
8. The faculty senate, the budget council, the council on instruction, and the council on teacher education are examples of organizations that have been developed in universities for the purpose of mobilizing the resources of the entire university for achieving certain goals.
9. The "ivory tower" university professor has been replaced to a large extent by the "action intellectual," who participates actively in the academic affairs of the campus and also provides important services to the community, state, and nation.
10. The curriculum in most colleges and universities has come into existence by historical accretion rather than by any carefully developed plan; students frequently are concerned about the fact that what they are expected to learn has little relevance to issues and problems with which Americans have to deal today.
11. University professors have, as a rule, been slow to adopt newer teaching procedures such as team teaching, to involve students in the teaching-learning process, to make provision for individual differences, and to use newer instructional media.
12. The "publish or perish" policy and the prestige awarded to research as

opposed to excellent teaching are factors that operate to lower the quality of teaching.

13. State agencies, regional agencies, and national organizations have been developed to bring about more coordination among colleges and universities.

14. The first junior college was established in the United States in 1902; in 1962 there were more than 400 public community colleges and 270 private junior colleges, serving 748,619 students.

15. The community college makes a unique contribution by admitting all students who can profit from its program, by providing opportunities for the vocationally oriented student as well as the academically talented one, and by serving adults in the community.

16. Higher education in the twenty-first century will use many tools provided by educational technology to enhance the effectiveness of the teaching-learning process: It will provide two-year colleges within commuting distance of the home of every young man and woman; will provide more time for students to do individual research; and will develop cooperative arrangements to bring competent instructors and adequate learning resources within reach of more students.

SELECTED READINGS

Baskin, Samuel (ed.), *Higher Education: Some Newer Developments*, New York, McGraw-Hill, 1965. Chapter I, "The New Colleges," explains in detail innovations in several colleges.

Foreign Policy Association (eds.), *Toward the Year 2018*, New York, Cowles Education Corporation, 1968. Chapter 7 predicts the effects of educational technology on higher education in the twenty-first century.

Haas, Glen, and Kimball Wiles (eds.), *Readings in Curriculum*, Boston, Allyn & Bacon, 1965. Section 8 deals with the community college and higher education in the twenty-first century.

Stickler, W. Hugh (ed.), *Experimental Colleges*, Tallahassee, Florida State University Press, 1964. A book of readings describing experimental programs in a dozen colleges.

Wilson, Logan (ed.), *Emerging Patterns in American Higher Education*, Washington, D.C., American Council on Education, 1965. Deals with new patterns of internal organization, state systems of higher education, and unified approaches to national problems.

11

Racial Integration of the Public Schools

It would be impossible for a white person to understand what happened within black breasts on that Monday [May 17, 1954]. An ardent segregationist has called it "Black Monday." He was so right, but for reasons other than the ones he advances: That was the day we won; the day we took the white man's laws and won our case before an all-white Supreme Court with a Negro lawyer, Thurgood Marshall, as our chief counsel. And we were proud. But we were also naive.*

Racial segregation parallels poverty as the most explosive issue of our time. While we are accelerating our efforts to abolish poverty, racial integration is taking place much more slowly. Population growth and urbanization, accompanied by the exodus of white citizens to the suburbs, have resulted in most Americans living in segregated communities where race is the major criterion for residence. This is not solely a black versus white issue; concentrations of other groups are vividly illustrated by Mexican-American and American Indian communities in the Southwest and Puerto Rican communities in New York. These segregated communities produce racial isolation of our schools, which in turn perpetuates prejudicial attitudes and behaviors.

*Louis E. Lomax, *The Negro Revolt*, New York, New American Library, 1962, pp. 84–85.

LEGAL
FOUNDATIONS

On May 17, 1954, the United States Supreme Court ruled unanimously, in Brown et al. *v.* the Board of Education of Topeka et al. that the U.S. Constitution is violated when a state operates racially segregated public schools. Segregationists reacted to the decision with a combination of frustration, resentment, anger, and resignation. Civil rights advocates, on the other hand, hailed the decision as a giant step toward equal educational opportunities for all people.

Certain earlier Supreme Court decisions and the Civil Rights Act of 1964 also are important legal foundations for efforts to integrate the public schools.

Supreme Court Cases

The seeds of the Brown case were sown in 1896 in the Plessy *v.* Ferguson case. Its issue was whether a state could, without violating the equal protection clause of the Constitution, require by law that passengers in railroad cars be segregated according to race. Louisiana provided "separate but equal" railroad accommodations for black and white passengers. The Supreme Court upheld the statute, asserting that the Fourteenth Amendment had intended to accord political but not social equality to Negroes.

In the only dissenting opinion, Justice John Marshall Harlan said:

Our Constitution is color-blind, and neither knows nor tolerates classes among citizens. In respect of civil rights, all citizens are equal before the law. The humblest is the peer of the most powerful. The law regards man as man, and takes no account of his surroundings or of his color when his civil rights as guaranteed by the supreme law of the land are involved.[1]

Harlan argued that the Plessy decision did not merely sanction an existing practice of racial segregation but also placed the stamp of judicial approval on *all* types of racial segregation. Indeed, the Plessy doctrine did just that.

The first major departures from approval of "separate but equal" practices came in two key cases. In 1938, the Supreme Court ruled in Gaines *v.* Missouri that Missouri was not providing Negroes with equal professional education by paying for them to attend law school outside the state. The state responded by setting up a separate law school for Negroes in St. Louis. The Court issued a similar ruling in 1948 in Sipuel *v.* Board of Regents of the University of Oklahoma. Oklahoma, however, decided to admit Negroes to its regular law school rather than establish a separate black institution.

Most jurists agree that the Brown decision is one of the most spectacular and significant judicial decisions of the century. In essence, the Supreme Court reversed the Plessy decision, ruling that racial

[1]Plessy *v.* Ferguson, 163 U.S. 537 (1896).

segregation of children in the public schools denies them equal protection of the laws guaranteed by the Fourteenth Amendment. Chief Justice Earl Warren wrote:

1. *The history of the Fourteenth Amendment is inconclusive as to its intended effect on public education.*
2. *The question presented in these cases must be determined, not on the basis of conditions existing when the Fourteenth Amendment was adopted, but in the light of the full development of public education and its present place in American life throughout the Nation.*
3. *Where a state has undertaken to provide an opportunity for an education in its public schools, such an opportunity is a right which must be made available to all on equal terms.*
4. *Segregation of children in public schools solely on the basis of race deprives children of the minority groups of equal educational opportunities, even though the physical facilities and other "tangible" factors may be equal.*
5. *The "separate but equal" doctrine adopted in Plessy v. Ferguson, 163 U.S. 537, has no place in the field of public education.*[2]

The Court's opinion was not cluttered with legal citations. Instead, it was based on the belief that human rights should transcend legal precedents. For the first time in the history of a country's highest court, a child's social growth and development overshadowed court precedents and procedures.

Civil Rights Act of 1964
Title IV of the Civil Rights Act of 1964 authorizes the Commissioner of Education to provide technical assistance and financial aid to assist in solving problems dealing with public school desegregation and authorizes the Attorney General to require desegregation in interstate commerce activities. Title VI of the same law and the regulations issued under it stipulate that no person shall, on the ground of race, color, or national origin, be subjected to discrimination in *any* program receiving federal financial assistance. In March, 1966, the U. S. Office of Education released a "Revised Statement of Policies for School Desegregation Plans" under Title VI of the Civil Rights Act of 1964. The sections concerning desegregation of the faculties of public schools are significant:

1. Desegregation of staff.   The racial composition of the professional staff of a school system, and of the schools in the system, must be considered in determining whether students are subjected to discrimination in educational programs. Each school system is responsible for correcting the effects of all past discriminatory practices in the assignment of teachers and other professional staff.

2. New assignments.   Race, color, or national origin may not be a factor in the hiring or assignment to schools or within schools of teachers and other professional staff, including student teachers and staff serving two

[2]Brown et al. *v.* Board of Education of Topeka et al., 347 U.S. 483 (1954).

*or more schools, except to correct the effects of past discriminatory
assignments.*

*3. Dismissals.   Teachers and other professional staff may not be
dismissed, demoted, or passed over for retention, promotion, or rehiring,
on the ground of race, color, or national origin. In any instance where one
or more teachers or other professional staff members are to be displaced
as a result of desegregation, no staff vacancy in the school system may be
filled through recruitment from outside the system unless the school
officials can show that no such displaced staff member is qualified to fill
the vacancy. If, as a result of desegregation, there is to be a reduction in
the total professional staff of the school system, the qualifications of all
staff members in the system must be evaluated in selecting the staff
members to be released.*

*4. Past assignments.   The pattern of assignment of teachers and other
professional staff among the various schools of a system may not be such
that schools are identifiable as intended for students of a particular race,
color, or such that teachers or other professional staff of a particular race
are concentrated in those schools where all, or the majority of, the students
are of that race. Each school system has a positive duty to make staff
assignments and reassignments necessary to eliminate past discriminatory
assignment patterns. . . .*[3]

Despite the decisions, laws, and regulations applying to the schools
and their faculties, racial isolation in the public schools persists as a
prevalent pattern throughout the United States, especially in the
metropolitan areas, which include two-thirds of the population. Furthermore, as metropolitan populations increase, they are becoming more
separated by race: four of every five white children live in the
suburbs.[4] The picture is even bleaker in the elementary schools. Almost
80 percent of the Negro elementary students in the nation's cities are
in schools with all-Negro enrollments, and nearly 90 percent of them
attend predominantly Negro schools On the other hand, more than
80 percent of the white elementary students are in all-white schools.
The U. S. Commission on Civil Rights reports that in southern and
border states, although the *proportion* of Negroes in all-Negro schools
has decreased since the Brown decision, a rising Negro enrollment,
combined with only slight desegregation, has produced a substantial
increase in the *number* of "Negro" schools. Another factor contributing
to this problem is the increase in private, all-white schools.

MAJOR
ISSUES
Compared with suburbs, cities spend a third more per capita for welfare and twice as much per capita for public safety; the suburbs, however, spend nearly twice as much in proportion for education as the

[3]U.S. Commissioner of Education, "Revised Statement of Policies for School Desegregation Plans," March, 1966, Section 181.13.
[4]U.S. Commission on Civil Rights, *Racial Isolation in the Public Schools*, Washington, D.C., U.S. Government Printing Office, 1967, p. 260.

cities. For a number of reasons, more disadvantaged children are non-white than white; the nonwhite children are also more likely to live in the cities. Thus, racial separation and economic factors result in more serious handicaps for nonwhite students than for white students. For instance, although both nonwhite and white children are likely to attend schools with libraries, white children attend schools that have more library volumes per student; their schools also have better science laboratories and equipment and more advanced science and language courses.[5]

Schools are unique as social agencies working for the maximum total development of each individual's intellectual, moral, emotional, and physical potential. Although the family has the major role in this process, schools remain the primary socializing influence outside the family. There is general agreement, therefore, that in attempting to diminish and eventually abolish the academic disadvantages of Negro and other minority group children, it is most practical and logical to work through the schools. There is no general agreement among educators and concerned citizens, however, on the best way. Faced with this crisis, school systems generally have taken one of two basic approaches: *compensatory education,* or school *desegregation* leading to *integration.*

Desegregation is accomplished by placing two or more racial groups together within the same school. Integration, on the other hand, requires a more intimate and lasting contact between the groups. Few schools are desegregated, and fewer still are integrated. In some de-segregated schools, white and black students voluntarily maintain caste-like cleavages. Court orders can cause various racial groups to attend the same school, but it takes great skill in human relations for school officials to bring about integration.

Compensatory Education

Compensatory education refers to programs aimed at the rehabilitation of culturally disadvantaged children. Much attention is being given to correcting conditions of poverty. School are being called on to provide special services to minority group children in low-income families. These services are designed to close the gap caused by segregated schools. The public schools have developed and implemented a wide variety of compensatory education programs (see Table 4), but because local school funds are extremely limited, compensatory measures financed from property taxes have not been able to break the cycle of poverty significantly.

Recently, the federal government has begun attacking the problem at the national level, particularly through the Elementary and Secondary Education Act of 1965 (ESEA). In Title I of ESEA, the federal

[5]Ibid., p. 199.

Table 4
Distribution of Compensatory Education Funds Among Elementary Schools
in Twelve City School Systems, by Racial Composition of Schools—1965–1966

City	Total number of schools using compensatory education funds	Number of schools more than 50 percent Negro	Number of schools 11 to 50 percent Negro	Number of schools 0 to 10 percent Negro
Buffalo	30	17	7	6
Pittsburgh[a]	51	25	19	7
Philadelphia	65	59	5	1
Oakland	26	23	3	0
Cincinnati	30	21	5	4
Boston	45	31	5	9
Atlanta	40	31	0	9
San Francisco	47	20	9	18
New Haven	14	11	3	0
Milwaukee[a]	46	19	9	18
Baltimore[a]	105	77	11	17
Detroit[a]	130	101	18	11

[a] Figures for 1966–1967.
Source: U.S. Commission on Civil Rights, Racial Isolation in the Public Schools, Washington, D.C., U.S. Government Printing Office, 1967, p. 118.

government acknowledged that the special needs of children of low-income families and the impact of concentrations of low-income families on the schools necessitate additional financial assistance. By the end of its second academic year (1966–1967), Title I officials reported that 16,400 school districts had spent more than $1 billion on Title I programs involving 9.2 million children. The same officials noted, however, that only half the children needing such programs were actually involved and that the billion dollars could not, by itself, meet the educational needs of culturally disadvantaged children.[6]

All compensatory education programs have in common dual goals— remedial work and prevention. They are remedial in that they attempt to fill gaps (whether social, cultural, or academic) in a child's total experience; they are preventive in that by doing remedial work they are trying to break the pattern of continuing failures. Compensatory education has been called "privileged education for the underprivileged."

Within a relatively short time, the programs for the disadvantaged began to fall into a general pattern, including: (1) preschool and early education programs aimed at compensating for early experiential deficits, primarily in language and cognitive development; (2) remedial programs in the basic skill areas; (3) individual and small-group tutoring programs conducted by professionals, paraprofessionals, and volunteers; (4) enrichment programs to overcome cultural differences, enhance motiva-

[6]U.S. Office of Education, Title I: Year II, Washington, D.C., U.S. Government Printing Office, 1968.

tion, and otherwise widen the horizons of students from low-income areas; (5) pre-service and in-service training of teachers to familiarize them with the life styles and growth patterns of children from depressed areas; (6) special guidance programs to extend counseling and therapy services to disadvantaged children and adults; (7) lengthening of the school day and year in an effort to provide community programs; (8) work-study programs involving subsidized on-the-job training; (9) development of special remedial materials; and (10) assignment of additional "special service personnel" (e.g., social workers, nurses, teacher aides) to schools with high ratios of disadvantaged students.

A fundamental question, however, underlies all these efforts at rehabilitation: Can we salvage the all-black schools? There are many schemes and proposals for upgrading and compensation, for "higher horizons," for keeping the schools open a few hours longer, for special textbooks, for appeals to the middle-class conscience, for recruiting devoted teachers, and for model schools. Their main goal is to make the schools good while they remain black or predominantly black.[7] Joseph Alsop typifies those who believe the practical solution does not lie in integration but in improving education in the ghetto schools:

> . . . the overwhelming majority of the children of the ghettos are going to be educated exclusively in ghetto schools . . . for many years to come, no matter how much politicking and patching and court ordering we may do. . . . No integration measures can ever do more than fray the fringes of the ghetto school problem in cities with school populations 50 percent Negro and above. . . . Education is the key to the whole problem, because it leads to jobs; jobs lead to achievement and achievement reduces discrimination. . . . White prejudice will surely be eroded, in every area where Negroes are enabled to achieve highly.[8]

In some communities black parents are just as much set against integration as white parents. Both groups argue that school distribution on the basis of race does not directly attack the educational problems found in depressed socioeconomic neighborhoods. In some instances, they state, forced integration detracts from efforts to improve the quality of education in segregated neighborhoods. In any case, we should be realistic—the reality is that our communities are becoming not less segregated, but more. Livingston Wingate, a black leader, put it this way:

> The greatest need today is the immediate establishment of quality education in the ghetto. We must no longer pursue the myth that integrated education is equated with quality education. Busing a disadvantaged and isolated child out of Harlem on a segregated bus to an "integrated" classroom downtown will not give him quality education. Once in the classroom downtown, the disadvantaged Harlem pupil would find himself below the achievement level

---

[7]James W. Guthrie and James A. Kelly, "Compensatory Education—Some Answers for a Skeptic," *Phi Delta Kappan*, 46 (October, 1965), 70–74.

[8]Joseph Alsop, "No More Nonsense About Ghetto Education!" *New Republic*, 157 (July, 1967), 18–23.

*of his white classmates and suffer a more demoralizing experience of
frustration than he had in the ghetto inferior school. Moreover, he would
return at night to the same ghetto conditions he left in the morning.*[9]

Other critics of school integration maintain that placing black students in white schools will: (1) emphasize Negro pupils' low achievement, (2) suggest the superiority of whites, (3) cause Negro pupils to be rejected by whites, and (4) decrease the number of adult role models for Negroes.

Advocates of compensatory education admit that the cost of establishing superior schools in the inner-cities would be high. The price, they argue, is justifiable, considering the nation's social debt to disadvantaged citizens. As a matter of fact, the U.S. Office of Education Study of Title I cited earlier concluded that concentrated remedial assistance *can* help raise the level of academic achievement. However, such programs are very expensive in terms of teachers, materials, and space. Inadequate funds have resulted in what frequently are referred to as "band-aid programs" that inadequately cover what is actually a cancerous sore. The advocates of compensatory education say we simply must provide the money for really comprehensive programs. As they see it, failure to provide superior education for the culturally disadvantaged will result in continued national educational stagnation, perpetuation of conditions that lead to social disruption and political conflicts, and the continuation of cultures of poverty.

Integration

Most Americans still believe that social inequalities can be corrected through improved integrated education. This dominant ethos provides a grand formula by which they hope to perpetuate and perfect our culture. One authority, however, arguing that the American faith in the efficacy of education rests on dubious grounds, offers four discouraging propositions: (1) the control of American education is generally in the hands of conservative elements in society; (2) the control of education is exerted to prevent change except in the areas where the dominant group desires change; (3) as an integral part of the society, education can function as an agency of change only within the structure of the society, and not as an external agency; and (4) the American faith in education as the creator of a better world can be realized only as the other forces also function as agencies of change.[10] It seems likely that a number of changes in attitude are necessary. In other words, if the schools are to be effective in helping society implement integration, Americans must answer two fundamental questions:

[9]Livingston L. Wingate, "Statement of Livingston L. Wingate, Executive Director of HARYOU-ACT," 25th Annual Conference for Superintendents, New York, Teachers College, July 9, 1966, p. 3.

[10]Wilbur B. Brookover, *A Sociology of Education*, New York, American Book, 1955, p. 76.

Do they agree with the preamble to the Declaration of Independence, which states that all men are created equal and that they are endowed by the Creator with certain inalienable rights? Do they believe that equal educational opportunity is an inalienable right?

Four basic reasons are usually given for supporting *quality integrated education* as the best way to provide equal educational opportunities:

1. The amount of money needed for really far-reaching compensatory programs is vast—much more than any community (even with enormous federal aid) will agree to invest in an exclusive nonwhite network of schools.

2. The influence of other deprived children and of the ghetto culture in an all-black, lower-class school is so powerful that it largely offsets the effects of academic and technological upgrading.

3. The teachers in all-black schools often are poorly trained middle-class Negroes (they themselves the products of an inferior education) who frequently show quite rigid and hostile attitudes toward lower-class Negro children; the prevailing atmosphere in these schools often is cold and authoritarian, emphasizing unthinking conformity to the values of the "black bourgeoisie."

4. The absence in all-black schools of a mixed population of children (white, middle-class, differing national origins and religions, varied vocational status of parents) itself symbolizes the ghettoized and segregated life of the big-city Negro child and impresses on him constantly—no matter what the teachers do or say—that he is basically different and inferior, that he is not being brought up to take his place in the mainstream of American life.

Most proponents of school integration argue that the schools must prepare all students for life in an integrated society. They also conclude that compensatory efforts alone will not produce a significant amount of racial integration. As Kenneth Clark, noted Negro psychologist, put it, segregated schools are symbols of discrimination and make a mockery of our democratic ideals. Even if all-black schools were made equal or superior to the white schools, he surmised, they would remain visible reminders of the alleged inferiority of the Negro; they would in fact be reminders of a situation that is incompatible with the goals of democratic education.[11] Charles Silberman adds this somber thought: "Failure to do *anything* about *de facto* segregation will poison the atmosphere of race relations in any community. . . . What a community does about school integration is generally regarded as the ultimate measure of white sincerity and of white willingness to share power."[12] These statements clearly reflect opposition to those who believe that there are no politically and educationally feasible alterna-

[11]Kenneth B. Clark, *Prejudice and Your Child*, Boston, Beacon, 1966, pp. 32–33.
[12]Charles E. Silberman, *Crisis in Black and White*, New York, Random House, 1964, p. 292.

tives to "black but better" schools. (The social effects of racial isolation are equally applicable to white students who are in all-white schools.)

Research Findings
Systematic study of the impact of desegregation and improved educational opportunity is limited, although it does seem likely that improved opportunities that include school desegregation efforts have resulted in improved school achievement by Negro pupils.[13] In general, however, the compensatory programs that have been tried have not enabled large numbers of students to reach and sustain grade-level achievement. For instance, a study of school achievement in the recently integrated Louisville public schools did show gains in median scores for all grades tested; furthermore, the degree of improvement in achievement levels over the year before school desegregation was greater for Negro pupils than for white pupils. The Negro pupils' level of achievement nevertheless did not equal that of the white pupils.[14] In other cities, academic progress in schools following integration has showed consistent gains for the Negro pupils.[15] There usually are initial declines for white pupils, followed by a return to previous rates of academic achievement. The achievement level for white pupils, however, tends to remain somewhat higher than that for Negro pupils.

The so-called "Coleman Report" (*Equality of Educational Opportunity*) of 1966 focused on four significant issues: (1) the extent to which racial and ethnic groups are segregated in the public schools; (2) the extent to which schools offer equal educational opportunities to the various groups; (3) student academic achievement as measured by performance on standardized tests; and (4) the relationships between student achievement and the racial composition of the schools students attend. The report noted that more than two-thirds of all Negro first-graders attended schools that were 90 percent or more Negro, and about the same proportion of Negro twelfth-graders attended schools that were 50 percent or more black. Teachers and other staff members showed comparable racial isolation. In terms of academic achievement, the report suggested that most Negro students attend low-quality schools and that only through integration—not compensatory education —will they be able substantially to raise their academic achievement, as well as their self-conceptions.[16]

The general picture of integration, then, is one of achievement gains

[13]U.S. Commission on Civil Rights, op. cit., chap. IV.

[14]Frank H. Stallings, "A Study of the Immediate Effects of Integration on Scholastic Achievement in the Louisville Public Schools," *Journal of Negro Education,* 28 (Fall, 1959), 439–444.

[15]See, for example, Carl F. Hansen, "The Scholastic Performance of Negro and White Pupils in the Integrated Public Schools of the District of Columbia," *Harvard Educational Review*, 30 (Summer, 1960), 216–236.

[16]James S. Coleman, et al., *Equality of Educational Opportunity*, Washington, D.C., U.S. Government Printing Office, 1966. This view was supported by U.S. Commission on Civil Rights, op. cit.

for Negro pupils without losses for white students. Available research does not indicate clearly whether these gains result from the simple act of integration or from improved teaching techniques. Of even greater concern to those committed to equality of educational achievement is the negative fact that Negro pupils continue to be academically outdistanced by their white counterparts despite improvements in educational opportunities and desegregation efforts. A multifaceted approach probably is necessary. One authority has summarized the components of such an approach as follows:

1. *Standards of Negro schools should be raised so that integrated students will have a better chance of success.*
2. *Parents should be brought into school programs and their aid enlisted.*
3. *Integrated schools need in-service training for teachers.*
4. *Ability grouping within schools should be abandoned or seriously modified.*
5. *Desegregation should proceed from the lowest grades to the highest to optimize chances of success.*[17]

The best course to follow seems to be desegregation that leads to integration, *coupled with* compensatory programs so that "disadvantaged" students will be better able to adjust to integrated classrooms. Once schools are racially integrated, compensatory programs should be continued as part of the pupil personnel services. A major reason for this need is the fact that long after racial or ethnic differences are diminished, social class differences continue to produce different educational levels of achievement. The social class composition of a student body is more highly related to achievement than any other single characteristic. Children of middle-class or higher backgrounds tend to do well in school regardless of racial or ethnic differences.

Viewing desegregation of the public schools as a vital condition to resolving the nation's racial crisis, the National Advisory Commission on Civil Disorders observed that none of us can escape the consequences of the continuing economic and social decay of the central city and the closely related problem of rural poverty. Noting that overcoming segregation and racial isolation is only the first step toward equalizing education, the Commission concluded that integration should be the final goal in our schools.[18] To accomplish this end, we will need dedicated school personnel, especially teachers. Thus, we now consider the role of teachers.

Teachers Make the Difference

The teacher's role in school integration is crucial. He helps or hinders the adjustment of each child to the desegregated classroom. He also

---

[17]Irwin Katz, "Review of Evidence Relating to Effects of Desegregation Performance of Negroes," *American Psychologist*, 19 (June, 1964), 381–399.

[18]*Report of the National Advisory Commission on Civil Disorders*, New York, Bantam Books, 1968, p. 438.

helps parents form their attitudes toward school desegregation. Obviously, not all teachers respond in the same way. Some are extremely liberal in their racial views; others are quite prejudiced. As a group, they are likely to be similar in their attitudes to most of the resident in the communities where they teach. In many communities, it is only adherence to the "letter of the law" that keeps the desegregation effort alive at all.

Most teachers accept assignments to desegregated schools with much anxiety. White teachers seem to be no better prepared for school desegregation than nonwhite teachers. Both exhibit what may be called a "fear of the unknown." They fear that, once hired, they will lose their jobs to better prepared individuals of the other group. Both groups are unsure about the reactions of community residents and their fellow faculty members. In addition, they fear that they will be confronted by children and adults whose goals, value systems, and behaviors are different from their own.[19] This condition of temporary normlessness comes from their having learned behavior appropriate in segregated situations but inappropriate in integrated situations.[20] *Peer* relationships are vastly different from *caste* relationships. Both majority- and minority-group people must learn new roles.

As black teachers in particular move into schools with recently desegregated staffs, they carry with them intense minority sensitivities and behaviors appropriate to their past lives. This is especially true in situations centering around social activities. The slowness, reluctance, and even outright refusal of some school districts to desegregate is caused in part by a strong opinion that blacks in predominantly white schools would be very uncomfortable. The "concerned" community leaders erroneously believe that black Americans can only be happy with "their own kind." Fortunately, once schools actually are desegregated, anxieties tend to give way to reasonably well-defined cooperative integrated activities.

PLANS FOR PUPIL
INTEGRATION
There are no sure-fire ways to integrate our schools. Faculty integration is much easier to accomplish than pupil integration. After all, most parents are not employees of school systems; therefore, the integration of pupils is not the relatively simple matter of assignment and training that it is with teachers. Quotas, redrawing attendance boundaries, reorganization of grades, open enrollment, and educational parks are some of the plans that have been tried. What works well in one community

19James H. Bash, *Effective Teaching in the Desegregated School*, Bloomington, Ind., Phi Delta Kappa, 1966, p. 8.
20Nebraska Mays, "Behavioral Expectations of Negro and White Teachers on Recently Desegregated Public School Faculties," *Journal of Negro Education*, 32 (Summer, 1963), 218.

may not work well in another. Some communities adopt a plan and proceed gradually; others move quickly. We shall describe the plans in terms of black-white interrelationships.

Quotas

Dispersing *all* black students on a quota basis to white schools is believed by some educators to be the only way to integrate all schools quickly. Ideally, the plan calls for some white students to be transferred to "Negro" schools. Bus transportation is likely to be involved in either case. But this plan—usually referred to simply as "busing"—is both expensive and socially irritating. Opponents say that small children are forced to travel long distances from their homes. Proponents maintain that this method insures racial balance and is more comprehensive than any other plan.

Redrawing Attendance Boundaries

Redrawing attendance boundaries to split Negro neighborhoods and attach them to adjoining white neighborhoods has worked in some communities. This plan does not affect as many students as the quota plan. The schools remain essentially neighborhood schools. Very little money is needed for transportation. The disadvantages are mainly two: (1) Even a relatively small number of black students in a few white schools may panic the white residents; and (2) shifts in population would necessitate a continual redrawing of boundaries.

Reorganization of Grades (Princeton Plan)

The Princeton Plan, in which two attendance districts not necessarily adjoining are merged with all children in certain grades going to one school, affects more students than redrawing attendance boundaries. This plan is especially successful in small school districts. Opponents argue that when schools are not adjoining, transportation expenses generally must be borne by the parents. Proponents argue that this plan is fairer than most others because schools within both black and white districts are involved. Thus white students are also transported, breaking the usual pattern of black students going to white schools.

Open Enrollment

Open enrollment permits Negroes in predominantly Negro schools to transfer to under-used white schools until a predetermined percentage of the student body of the receiving school is Negro. Voluntary transfer of white students to predominantly Negro schools is allowed on the same basis. Proponents maintain that open enrollment will be used by highly motivated, mainly academically successful students and that the result will be the integration of highly competitive black students. Opponents note that this plan tends to drain black schools of top scholars and articulate parents. In addition, few poverty-stricken parents can pay for their children to attend out-of-district schools. This plan is one of the least effective in integrating schools.

Educational Parks

Placing together on one site all schools serving an entire school district or a large section of a city is known as the educational park or "school village" plan. The costs are quite high—existing buildings must be abandoned and a campus erected; in fact, for most school districts, they are prohibitive. Such a consolidation of school districts can, of course, lead to urban-suburban or black-white integration—or both.

Whichever plan is used, it is clear that racial integration is more than placing black and white bodies within close proximity. Integration is *involvement*. It is white and nonwhite students and faculties interacting in a lasting and positive manner. When this happens, they become participants in a common culture.

SUMMARY

1. The 1954 Brown decision was the first time in the history of a country's highest court that a child's social growth and development was placed above legal precedents.
2. Both white and nonwhite students are socially disadvantaged when they must attend racially segregated schools. Students attending segregated schools are not being adequately prepared to live in an integrated world.
3. Our public schools are more segregated today than they were in 1954.
4. Our public schools are becoming more racially segregated each year. Proponents of *compensatory education* say that racial integration is not a realistic goal for most inner-city schools and, therefore, that these schools must be given adequate funds to improve the quality of segregated education. Proponents of *integrated* schools argue that only integration itself can provide students with a top-quality education. Current school conditions require both approaches.
5. In general, integration seems to result in achievement gains for Negro pupils without losses for white pupils.
6. No matter which actual plan is used to achieve integration, the result must be involvement and interaction among blacks and whites.

SELECTED READINGS

Coleman, James S., et al., *Equality of Educational Opportunity*, Washington, D.C., U.S. Government Printing Office, 1966. Sometimes referred to as the "Coleman Report," this report analyzes the social, psychological, and economic effects of racial integration of the public schools. Pupil, teacher, and administrator attitudes are also included.

Educational Policies Commission, *American Education and the Search for Equal Opportunity*, Washington, D.C., National Education Association, 1965. A review of problems of disadvantaged children and guides for corrective and preventive school programs.

Giles, Hermann H., *The Integrated Classroom*, New York, Basic Books, 1959. One of the few books to stress what is needed to integrate a classroom. The reader will be impressed by the many different kinds of challenges facing teachers.

Holt, John, *How Children Fail*, New York, Pitman, 1964. A case study of ways in which schools fail children without regard to race.

Humphrey, Hubert H., *School Desegregation: Documents and Commentaries*, New York, Crowell, 1964. Students interested in excerpts of famous court cases, reactions to the Brown decision, and the effects of private education on desegregation will fnd this book a valuable source of reference.

Mack, Raymond W. (ed.), *Our Children's Burden: Desegregation in Ten American Communities*, New York, Random House, 1968. Case studies of public school desegregation efforts in large and small cities.

Noar, Gertrude, *The Teacher and Integration*, Washington, D.C., National Education Association, 1966. A book of practical and precious suggestions by a master teacher and national consultant.

U.S. Commission on Civil Rights, *Racial Isolation in the Public Schools*, Washington, D.C.: U.S. Government Printing Office, 1967. One of the most comprehensive studies on problems inherent in school segregation and integration. This publication also devotes an entire section to plans for integration.

Part IV
EDUCATION IN
THE INNER CITIES

Part IV describes life and learning in America's inner cities. The following are discussed in terms of people: the effects of poverty and alienation; the circumstances that influence the development of attitudes toward self and others; role models; the life chances of inner-city children and youth.

12

Beyond Poverty
of Income

Human beings who are forced to live under ghetto conditions and whose daily experience tells them that almost nowhere in society are they respected and granted the ordinary dignity and courtesy accorded to others will, as a matter of course, begin to doubt their own worth.*

CHARACTERISTICS
OF POVERTY

One-fifth to one-fourth of the United States population is poverty-stricken.[1] The exact proportion varies according to the criteria used. For example, the National Policy Committee on Pockets of Poverty set three ceilings on poverty for a family of four: *minimum subsistence* ($2,500 a year), *minimum adequacy* ($3,500 a year), and *minimum comfort* ($5,500 a year).[2] Whatever the exact criteria, the poor are simply those who are unable to maintain a decent standard of living with respect to their society. In actual numbers, more than

*Kenneth B. Clark, *Dark Ghetto*, New York, Harper & Row, 1965, p. 64.

[1]See Michael Harrington, *The Other America*, New York, Macmillan, 1962.

[2]Other ceilings used to determine poverty include less than $1,500 annual income for single persons and less than $3,000 annual income for families.

twice as many white as nonwhite families are poverty-stricken. In terms of percentages, however, a larger proportion of nonwhite families lives in poverty; Negroes comprise the largest nonwhite poverty group, but a substantial number of Puerto Ricans and American Indians are also included. The economic disparities between Negroes and whites have been succinctly outlined as follows:

1. *In 1964, the rate at which unemployed Negroes had involuntarily lost their jobs (as distinct from the rate of unemployment for all reasons) was at least two and one-half times that of unemployed whites. While slightly more than three-fifths of all unemployed white males 20 years old or more involuntarily lost their jobs, the proportion for Negro males was closed to four-fifths. This type of statistic belies any stereotype of high Negro unemployment as being due to an unusual degree of unwillingness to work.*

2. *In 1964, nonwhites made up 11 percent of the labor force but 21 percent of the unemployed. Their unemployment was at least twice that of whites. While they made up only 11 percent of the labor force, they constituted one-fourth of all long-term unemployed (six months or longer). . . .*

3. *During the 1960–1965 period of high economic growth in this country, the economic status of Negroes in the labor market did not improve to the same degree as that of whites. In some ways it actually worsened. The disparity is partly related to the concentration of Negroes in occupations and industries which are not expanding in a long-run sense.*

4. *Much of the unemployment problem is hidden, since many Negroes, especially the long-term unemployed who have simply given up the search for jobs and the teenagers who have hardly entered the labor market, are not counted officially as unemployed. . . .*

5. *The problems associated with the job status of Negroes are greater than the observation of simple statistics might lead us to believe. One expert has estimated that roughly 50 percent of all Negro workers require upgrading of one sort or another. . . .*[3]

Obviously, there is hardly any foundation of truth in the widespread notions that most people receiving public subsidy could earn their living if they had more initiative, that a family can live comfortably on a welfare budget, and that most relief recipients are employable but innately lazy.

Income levels serve as valuable guides for social planning, but if we assume that the lack of funds for minimum subsistence is the only characteristic of poverty, our "vision" is greatly limited. Some other specific characteristics are shown in Table 5. There also are many general conditions associated with poverty that are even more degrading and infectious than a severely limited income in itself.

Job Restrictions
It has often been suggested that all we need to do to eliminate poverty is provide more jobs. That solution sounds conveniently simple, but

[3]Harold L. Sheppard and Herbert E. Striner, *Civil Rights, Employment and Social Status of American Negroes*, Kalamazoo, Mich., The Upjohn Institute, 1966, pp. 6–9.

Table 5
Selected Characteristics of All Families and of Poor Families, 1962

	All families		Poor families	
	Number (millions)	Percentage of total	Number (millions)	Percentage of total
Total	47.0	100	9.3	100
Age of head				
14–24 years	2.5	5	.8	8
25–54 years	30.4	65	3.9	42
55–64 years	7.3	16	1.4	15
65 years and over	6.8	14	3.2	34
Education of head				
8 years or less	16.3	35	6.0	61
9–11 years	8.6	19	1.7	17
12 years	12.2	26	1.5	15
More than 12 years	9.3	20	.7	7
Sex of head				
Male	42.3	90	7.0	75
Female	4.7	10	2.3	25
Labor force status of head[a]				
Not in civilian labor force	8.4	18	4.1	44
Employed	36.9	78	4.6	49
Unemployed	1.7	4	.6	6
Color of family				
White	42.4	90	7.3	78
Nonwhite	4.6	10	2.0	22
Children under 18 years of age in family				
None	18.8	40	4.9	52
One to three	22.7	48	3.3	36
Four or more	5.5	12	1.1	11
Earners in family				
None	3.8	8	2.8	30
One	21.1	45	4.3	46
Two or more	22.1	47	2.2	23
Regional location of family[b, c]				
Northeast	11.5	25	1.6	17
North Central	13.1	29	2.3	25
South	13.5	30	4.3	57
West	7.0	16	1.0	11

[a] Labor force status relates to survey week of March, 1963.

[b] Based on 1960 residence and 1959 income (1962 prices).

[c] Data are from 1960 Census and are therefore not strictly comparable to the other data in this table.

Note: Data related to families and exclude unrelated individuals. Poor families are defined as all families with total money income of less than $3,000 (based on 1961 income and 1962 prices).

Source: Current Population Reports (but see note c).

Table 6
Unemployment Rates of Experienced Workers, by Color and Occupation, 1963

Major occupation group	White	Nonwhite
All occupation groups[a]	4.4	9.3
Clerical and sales workers	3.9	7.4
Craftsmen and foremen	4.6	8.2
Operatives	6.9	11.1
Private household workers	3.1	7.7
Other service workers	5.3	10.0
Farm laborers and foremen	5.0	7.1
Laborers, except farm and mine	11.0	15.2

[a] Includes the following groups not shown separately: Professional and technical workers; managers, officials, and proprietors; and farmers and farm managers.

Note: The base for the unemployment rate includes the employed, classified according to their current jobs, and the unemployed, classified according to their latest civilian job, if any; excluding unemployed persons who have never had a full-time civilian job.

Source: U.S. Department of Labor statistics.

the actual situation is far too complicated for any simple solutions. For one thing, about 40 percent of the adults living in poverty are in effect unemployable, because of "old" age or physical or mental handicaps. Even when poverty-stricken people do find jobs, their limited skills usually doom them to substandard wages. And even when such people do receive standard wages, they often receive them only part of the time: They are the first victims of seasonal and other lay-offs. In other words, *for nearly half the families living in poverty, their condition is not a lack of employment, but, instead, a lack of adequate wages, job security, job upgrading, and training or retraining.* This marginal employment is a key factor in the perpetuation of poverty.

There are many skilled jobs going unfilled because of the lack of "qualified" workers, and this situation particularly reflects the fact that the poor are seriously disadvantaged in the job market. Their educational, racial, and physiological handicaps prevent them from getting and keeping the kinds of employment that would enable them to become self-supporting (see Table 6). A study of poverty in Detroit concluded that the poorest households were most frequently headed by a person with one or more of the following characteristics: female, nonwhite, less than a sixth-grade education, over 60 years of age.[4] In addition, the poorest households most frequently had extreme health, family, school, and housing problems. A man who is the head of his household and yet does not have adequate means of support is considered both an economic and a social failure. The tendency of unemployed and marginally employed men to withdraw from community activities affects their civic participation and thus weakens their com-

[4]Greenleigh Associates, *A Study of Services To Deal with Poverty in Detroit,* New York, 1965.

munity ties. In this respect they become analogous to urban nomads, constantly moving from place to place without becoming active participants in any neighborhood affairs.

Slums

Because of distinctive patterns of growth, many large urban cities consist of three separate cities within one: an "old" city, a "middle-aged" city, and a "new" city.[5]

Old city. Built before community building codes and zoning regulations, most of the structures in this area originally did not have modern plumbing, lighting, or heating facilities. Houses with wooden foundation posts and narrow (thirty feet) lots add to the irregularity of the streets; industrial and commercial establishments are scattered capriciously throughout residential neighborhoods. The majority of old city residents live in dilapidated, insect- and rodent-invested multiple-family dwellings; streets are congested and parking space is insufficient; school and recreation facilities are inadequate. This area is occupied by predominantly low-income whites and nonwhites, with the majority being nonwhite. Old city is sometimes referred to as "inner-city."

Middle-aged city. Most of the structures in this area were built under some kind of building code and are physically sound. Yet, as in old city, most of the buildings—mainly multiple-dwelling units—were built on narrow lots (many with less than six feet of yard space between them). By comparison, middle-aged city is better developed than old city. However, it too is characterized by congested streets, insufficient parking space, and inadequate education and recreation facilities. Middle-aged city is occupied by predominantly lower-middle-income whites and nonwhites, with the majority being nonwhite. As this area undergoes racial and economic changes, it usually becomes a part of the inner city.

New city. Built after 1930, under both building and zoning codes, most of the structures in new city are in very good repair. Nearest to the suburbs, this area is primarily a single-family residential district. Compared with old and middle-aged cities, new city has larger lots, fewer congested streets, and more nearly adequate recreation and school facilities. This area is occupied by predominantly upper-middle-income white residents.

Since 1950, many urban neighborhoods have seen a large exodus of white residents, along with a still larger in-migration of nonwhites, especially Negroes (see Table 7). Sociologists call this phenomenon an

[5]For a comprehensive analysis of the cities-within-a-city approach, see Maurice F. Parkins, *Neighborhood Conservation: A Pilot Study*, Detroit, Detroit City Plan Commission, 1958.

Table 7
Nonwhite Population Trends in Large Cities
(Percentage of the City's Population)

	1920	1940	1960	1965 (esti- mates)
New York	2.7	6.1	14.0	18.0
Chicago	4.1	8.2	22.9	28.0
Philadelphia–Camden	7.4	13.0	26.4	31.0
Los Angeles–Long Beach	2.5	3.9	12.2	17.0
San Francisco–Oakland	1.1	1.4	14.3	16.0
Detroit	4.1	9.2	28.9	34.0
Boston	2.2	3.1	9.1	13.0
Pittsburgh	6.4	9.3	16.7	20.0
Washington	25.1	28.0	53.9	66.0
Atlanta	31.3	34.6	38.3	44.0
Birmingham	39.3	40.7	39.6	39.0

Note: Nonwhite includes Orientals, who are present in significant numbers in San Francisco and Los Angeles, but not in other cities on this list.
Source: Data compiled by U.S. Bureau of the Census for years cited.

ecological invasion. But more than racial composition is changing in the cities. Mainly because of urban renewal and state highway expansions, urban neighborhoods are changing from middle-class white to middle-class nonwhite to lower-class nonwhite. As middle-aged city neighborhoods change in occupancy to lower-class residents, large and structurally sound single-family dwellings are converted to multiple-family uses; soon they too begin to deteriorate. Maintenance (plumbing, wiring, heating, plaster, and painting) is generally neglected. Renters blame the slum landlords; the landlords blame the renters. Most frequently, landlords fail to comply with city property maintenance regulations. On the other hand, when landlords do attempt to prevent their properties from deteriorating, their efforts often are negated by tenants who fail to maintain the premises. Along with the physical changes go an increase in adult and juvenile crime rates and changes in such interrelated factors as unemployment and underemployment, school dropouts, population per household, and number of broken homes.

Public housing projects are being built in an effort to alleviate slum conditions. Critics of public housing contend that these projects correct only the physical aspects of slums; they replace the blight with new landscaping and architecture, but the major problem, the slum-dwellers themselves, remains unaffected. When this happens, a massive public housing project is in effect merely transferring a slum environment from, say, 20 square blocks to 20 stories. In fact, federally sponsored housing programs intensify concentrations of the poor within the central cities.

Negative Life Themes

A foremost disadvantage of being poverty-stricken is the negative definition that individuals, whatever their incomes, attach to poverty. The words to the song "Dead-End Street" are only too well understood by many of the poor:

They say this a big rich town,
But I live in the poorest part.
I know I'm on a dead-end street
In a city without a heart.

I learned to fight before I was six—
The only way I could get along.
When you're raised on a dead-end street
You've gotta be tough and strong.

All the guys go get in trouble—
That's how it's always been.
When the odds are all against you,
How can you win?

The song accurately reflects the despair, loneliness, and cynicism of the slums—the cultural and social impoverishment that comes from economic deprivation. Children who grow up in such an atmosphere in turn become unskilled and unemployed adults. Thus the cycle of poverty continually renews itself.

Out of poverty comes insecurity. Prolonged conditions of insecurity lead to feelings of *alienation*. These "anomic" aspects of alienation shown in the beliefs of the poor have been described: The individual believes that (1) community leaders are indifferent to and detached from his needs, (2) his social conditions and those of people like him are getting progressively worse, (3) life is meaningless, and (4) his immediate circle of relationships is not comfortable or supportive.[6] The life themes of the poor also include a preference for *fatalism* and an *orientation to the present*. Feeling helpless in an unpredictable world, the poor resort to a "live for today" philosophy that leaves little room for projecting long-range goals such as completing educational courses. Dropping out of school and getting a job seem to "make more sense" to them.

Defeatist attitudes partially explain why the poor pay more for consumer goods. Rather than shop around for bargains, they pay more not only for their few luxuries, but also for their necessities—housing, food, clothing. Neighborhood merchants realize large profits by offering slum-dwellers credit for goods that have high marks-ups and hidden installment, finance, and service charges. As for the programs that do enable the poor to save money—for example, public housing, surplus goods, food stamps, free legal aid—relatively few poverty-stricken people make use of them. Bureaucratic red tape and social workers

[6]David Hunter, *The Slums: Challenge and Response*, New York, Macmillan, 1962, p. 89.

frighten them, and the means test used in determining the need for public aid is often degrading or time-consuming or both.

Within the perspective of middle-class rewards and punishments, it is economically "bad" to be poor and it is socially "bad" to be a member of a racial minority group. There are ample studies to support the contention that poverty-stricken minority-group people are by far the most economically and socially disadvantaged.

What about all the social-action programs that have been initiated? Minority groups have made gains, of course, but even the most ardent supporters of the programs admit that so far the improvements in employment, housing, and education have been almost entirely limited to middle-income minorities. Many informed people believe it will be a number of years before the gains begin to filter down to poverty-stricken minority groups. Indeed, our antipoverty efforts seem to have been more successful in recruiting previously underemployed minority-group administrators than in finding jobs for unemployed slum-dwellers. It is depressingly apparent that the vicious circle of inferior education, low-paying jobs, and segregated neighborhoods, difficult enough at best for racial minorities to get out of, is becoming even more difficult to escape. Racial ghettos are inexorably expanding, and public schools are inexorably becoming more segregated.

For an explanation of these grim facts, we must face the grim reality of race prejudice. Although from a scientific point of view the concept of "race" is as irrational as a primitive taboo, its actual effects are as deadly as modern combat weapons. Metaphorically, one shot from the race-prejudice cannon results in the economic, social, and psychological deaths of millions of minority-group Americans. Civil rights leaders lament that black Americans have the highest casualty rate.

Self-Fulfilling Prophecy

Many of the disadvantages of the poor stem from middle-class opinions of them. This is one example of the effects of prejudice. The effect is particularly tragic in the case of education. Specifically, when middle-class teachers unequivocally state that poverty-stricken children cannot learn standardized materials and then proceed to deny them the opportunity to learn, the children do *not* learn. In sociological terms, by accepting an initially false definition and behaving as though it were true, a *self-fulfilling prophecy* is created and perpetuated. (This is discussed in more detail in Chapter 15.)

POOR
NEGROES

The past and present negative definitions of the word "Negro" make it difficult for most Americans to give it positive meanings. By current definitions "Negro" *denotes* dark skin. Also by current definitions

"Negro" *connotes* inferiority. Daily, our mass media alert us to the realities of a Negro Revolution and its possible counterreaction of white backlash. When some people think or see black, they either consciously or subconsciously think of black as the antonym of white. Historically, Americans have associated white with "good"—with Christ and the angels, cleanliness, virtue. On the other hand, through the ages black has been associated with "bad"—with the devil, dirt, sin. We can even find such comparative usages in our dictionaries, ranging from "white hope" to "whitewash," from "black arts" to "blackmail."

In some literary contexts the Negro is a contrast to the white man; he is a member of the opposite race, the enemy. Social scientists use the war term "invasion" when Negroes move into white neighborhoods, but—reflecting "superiority"—they call it "integration" when whites move into Negro neighborhoods. Less subtle than definitions of changing neighborhoods are white opinions of Negroes. Tumin found that no matter how he divided a sample of white respondents, whether by education, income, occupation, or whatever, a majority viewed Negroes as inferior to whites in certain essential respects, such as intelligence, morality, responsibility, and ambition.[7] Of course, there are non-Negroes who accept or reject Negroes on their merits and not prejudicially. Civil rights leaders argue, however, that the relative deprivation of Negroes in America suggests that such views are still in a minority.

Views from the Inside

The Negro in America very early discovers that he is a Negro and as a result is denied access to much that the dominant white society considers desirable. James Baldwin has eloquently portrayed this:

At home one's hair was always being attacked with hard brushes and combs and Vaseline; it was shameful to have "nappy" hair. . . . One was always being mercilessly scrubbed and polished as though in hope that a stain could thus be washed away. . . . The women were forever straightening and curling their hair, and using bleaching creams. And yet, it was clear that none of this would release one from the stigma of being a Negro; this effort merely increased the shame and rage. There was not, no matter where one turned, any acceptable image of oneself, no proof of one's existence. One had the choice, either of "acting just like a nigger" or of not acting just like a nigger and only those who have tried it know how impossible it is to tell the difference.[8]

Other writers have observed that Negroes are constantly exposed to assurances of their inferiority that verge on brainwashing. The brainwashing is said to be revealed in the Negro slang of the streets. "This

[7]Melvin M. Tumin, *Desegregation*, Princeton, N. J., Princeton University Press, 1958, p. 190. See also George Henderson, "Understanding the Negro Revolt," *Social Studies*, 58 (April, 1967), 145–153.

[8]James Baldwin, *Nobody Knows My Name*, New York, Dell, 1963, p. 73.

is the white man's world" or "We can only go as far as the [white] Man lets us." Isaacs concluded:

Every "black" person obviously has been called upon to reject or somehow deflect from himself the associations of evil and inferiority so powerfully attached to blackness. He has been called upon to do this, moreover, under conditions in which his ego was kept under constant assault from all the conditions of his life. That so many Negroes in every successive generation found the ego strength to meet and resist these indentifications is in itself no small miracle. That a greater number accepted the white man's images as the truth about themselves is no wonder at all.[9]

But it is not merely a problem of black and white; variations in skin color among Negroes add to an already complicated social situation. Historically, Negroes have reacted in a discriminatory manner to their own darker-skinned members: "If you're white, you're right; if you're brown, stick around; if you're yellow, you're mellow; if you're black, get back!" Recently, color prejudice among Negroes has diminished. A major reason for this has been the emergence of independent African nations abroad and the growth of black nationalism at home (see Chapter 16). Thus, more American Negroes are pointing to black people with pride and, to some extent, identity. Almost as if it were a fad, it is now quite fashionable to be black. This search for *negritude* or blackness is altering theories of the "Negro personality." Nevertheless, it is difficult for some personality theorists to accept as sincere the statements of Negroes who stand before large audiences and proclaim their pride in having a dark hue. And it is paradoxical that black children quickly discover that color pride alone will not allow them to overcome racial barriers.

Seldom have writers been able to capture the feeling of life from the Negro's viewpoint as objectively but sensitively as Whitney Young in *To Be Equal*.[10] The Negro begins life with much higher odds against him. He is more likely to die in infancy than the white baby. If the Negro baby lives, the chances of losing his mother in childbirth are relatively high; the maternal mortality rate is four times as high as for white mothers. The Negro baby is born into a family that lives in the inner city (over 70 percent of the Negro population does), usually in the Negro ghetto. It is a family that is larger than its white counterpart, and it is crowded into housing that is dilapidated—quarters structurally unsound or unable to keep out cold, rain, snow, rats, or pests. With more mouths to feed, more babies to clothe, and more needs to satisfy, the Negro family is forced to exist on a median family income of barely half the median white family income. When the Negro youngster goes to school, he is usually aware that he is starting down a path that has proved no avenue to adequate living, much less to fame or fortune. And because Negro children are generally taught in slum schools, usually with inferior teachers, equipment, and facilities, the real gap between

[9]Harold R. Isaacs, *The New World of Negro Americans*, New York, John Day, 1963, pp. 80–81.

[10]Whitney M. Young, Jr., *To Be Equal*, New York, McGraw-Hill, 1964, pp. 67–68.

Negro and white students of the same age often approaches five or six years.

Most Negroes look at all these conditions, but not all of them see the same social implications. For some, the conditions require a change; for others, the status quo is fine. *The conflicts that center on color do not lead to a single response: Many Negroes withdraw, others clown, others assume proud mannerisms, and still others become aggressive or highly suspicious of non-Negroes.* Those who run to a pride in blackness do not find Utopia. Once inside the winner's circle of blackness, an invisible veil seems to enshroud both the light-skinned and the dark-skinned "victors." This invisible veil, as Ellison pointed out, is not physical invisibility:

That invisibility to which I refer occurs because of a peculiar disposition of the eyes of those with whom I come in contact. A matter of the construction of their inner eyes, those eyes with which they look through their physical eyes upon reality. . . . It is sometimes advantageous to be unseen, although it is most often rather wearing on the nerves. . . . You ache with the need to convince yourself that you do exist in the real world, that you're a part of all the sound and anguish, and you strike out with your fists, you curse and you swear to make them recognize you. And, alas, it's seldom successful.[11]

To many readers Baldwin may seem too hostile, Young too academic, and Ellison too dramatic. But each captures some of the ingredients that go into making a Negro slum. This is the reality of being a black man in a white society.

Marginality

In most communities heavily populated by Negroes, low- and middle-income groups live within extremely close proximity to each other. This situation is not caused primarily by a natural selection process but by de facto housing segregation. Consequently, the plight of poverty-stricken Negroes is distorted if only census data are considered. Negro "haves" appear less affluent and the "have nots" seem less disadvantaged than they are. There is, in short, a much wider gap between Negro middle- and lower-classes than is apparent. Both groups closely approximate their white counterparts in income and living styles.

Now let us consider the fact that most Negroes are *marginal* in the dominant white culture.[12] Add to this disadvantage by making them marginal compared with their white socioeconomic counterparts. Finally, make poverty-stricken Negroes marginal compared with surrounding middle-income Negroes. When all these facts coalesce, one will have a picture of poverty-stricken Negroes—a minority group within a minor-

---

[11]Ralph Ellison, *Invisible Man*, New York, New American Library, 1964, pp. 7–8.

[12]At one time or another adolescents, career women, migrants, chiropractors, bilingual persons, monks, the hard of hearing, middle-income groups, Catholics, factory foremen, druggists, and sociologists have all been situationally marginal. See J. W. Mann, "Group Relations of the Marginal Personality," *Human Relations*, 11 (1958), 77–92.

ity group. Marginality, therefore, is characterized by the following conditions: (1) There must be a situation that places two cultures (or subcultures) in lasting contact. (2) One culture must be dominant in terms of power and reward potential. This is the nonmarginal of the two cultures; its members are not particularly influenced by or attracted to the marginal culture. (3) The boundaries between the two cultures are sufficiently defined for the members of the marginal culture to internalize the patterns of the dominant group and not be satisfied with the "inferior" group. Although not all poverty-stricken Negroes are marginal people, many exhibit marginal characteristics, such as high juvenile delinquency and adult crime rates. It is likely that those who are marginal have become victims of aspirations that they will never achieve and hopes that they will never satisfy.

APPALACHIAN WHITES

During the course of investigating the nature of urban communities, it has become evident that there is a substantial poverty-stricken white population. A large number of the urban poor whites came from the rural Appalachian mountain areas of Kentucky, Tennessee, West Virginia, Arkansas, Georgia, and Alabama.[13] For years, the emigration rate from these states to other parts of the country has been very high. During the 1950s, 1.5 million people left the Appalachians; most of them became economically secure. Like their Negro counterparts, they moved to northern cities primarily for economic reasons. They were attracted by the growing northern industries as contrasted with a comparatively stagnant southern economy.

Most studies indicate that the southern whites moved to urban communities in order to improve their economic conditions, but recent documentation of those who failed to achieve middle-classness illustrates a seemingly low respect for money. A few writers have observed the lower-class southern white's lack of commitment to the thrift theme that permeates our country's basic middle-class orientation. They usually do not put anything away for a "rainy day." Money for them appears to be inordinately "easy come" and easier to go. Mountain people usually return "home" not because they have accumulated enough money to buy a small farm or business but, instead, because they are broke. Home is the migrant's place of origin in the South; "home folks" are those with similar rural backgrounds.

Primary Group Relationships

The southern migrant brings with him rural culture patterns that are vastly different from those he finds in urban communities. Often, his

[13]See W. D. Weatherford and E. Brewer, *Life and Religion in Southern Appalachia*, New York, Friendship, 1962.

behavior is so different from that of indigenous urban residents that conflict rather than assimilation is the dominant pattern of adjustment. Both groups, when thrown into sudden contact, have been known to experience severe *culture shock*.[14] That is, they are unprepared to interact in a positive manner with members of the other culture.

The central focus of the Appalachian white is his family. Having strong family and kinship ties, he often practices voluntary segregation in his urban place of residence. Family cohesiveness is a shield against the large, overpowering, and impersonal city. Clustering together gives southern white migrants a sense of protection against the many disorganizing experiences rural newcomers find in big cities. This voluntary "togetherness" provides an outlet for their basic needs for recognition, affection, and security.

Both objective research and subjective novels reveal a harsh, authoritarian relationship between the father and children in low-income southern white families.[15] Out of this relationship come awe and fear, but seldom love. Traditionally, the father is the disciplinarian and the mother is the emotional (love) center of the Appalachian family. But, as more mothers find employment outside the home, these roles are being filled by parent surrogates.

Health Conditions

Except during religious services, southern whites normally do not openly express fear, pain, or hardship. This suppression of emotions causes some observers mistakenly to stereotype mountain people as having an unlimited amount of strength and patience. In reality, they have a very limiting set of folkways. Taught not to express fear or pain and believing that illness is quite unavoidable, poor whites—like poor nonwhites—fail to take preventive health measures or use health-care social agencies. Low-income mothers, for example, are not likely to have their children immunized in free health programs; the mothers themselves do not take advantage of free medical services. Symptoms of illness are often ignored. Spending money for daily needs is more likely than using it for abstract preventive medical care. Only when an illness is quite severe does the sick poor person begin even self-medication (the poor tend to have well-stocked home medicine chests). When self-help has proved useless, friends and relatives are called in. If they are of no avail, then paraprofessionals like druggists or spiritual healers are most often consulted. Only after all home remedy measures have failed will the poverty-stricken sick person consult a medical doctor. Private doctors and free clinic personnel are much too cold and

14George Henderson, "Poor Southern Whites: A Neglected Urban Problem," *Journal of Secondary Education*, 41 (March, 1966), 111–114.

15See Harriette Arnow, *The Dollmaker*, New York, Macmillan, 1954; Henry Hill Collins, Jr., *America's Own Refugees*, Princeton, N. J., Princeton University Press, 1957.

Table 8
Percentage of Respondents in Each Social Class Recognizing
Specified Symptoms as Needing Medical Attention

Symptom	Upper class (N = 51)	Middle class (N = 335)	Lower class (N = 128)
Loss of appetite	57	50	20
Persistent backache	33	44	19
Continued coughing	77	78	23
Persistent joint and muscle pains	80	47	19
Blood in stool	98	89	60
Excessive vaginal bleeding	92	83	54
Blood in urine	100	93	69
Swelling of ankles	77	76	23
Loss of weight	80	51	21
Bleeding gums	79	51	20
Chronic fatigue	80	53	19
Shortness of breath	77	55	21
Persistent headaches	80	56	22
Fainting spells	80	51	33
Pain in chest	80	51	31
Lump in breast	94	71	44
Lump in abdomen	92	65	34

Note: Percentages are rounded to nearest whole numbers. N signifies number of respondents.

Source: The Health of Regionville by Earl Loman Koos. Copyright 1954 by Columbia University Press and reproduced with their permission.

businesslike for the rather frightened and unsophisticated poor white patient, at least until he is so sick that he is desperate (see Table 8).

Educational Goals

The lack of cultural aspirations to formal education makes difficult the successful urban adjustment of low-income southern whites. "A little readin' and writin' " seems sufficient for most of them. Only a few urban schools have been able to reach out effectively and pull in southern white parents in order to raise the educational goals of their children. The parents do not seem to be against the educational system: They are *indifferent* to it. Their children enter school ready to drop out and susceptible to being pushed out. The heterogeneity of the student population, the large size of the physical plants, and the more or less sterile decorum of urban schools quickly crush what little emotional security southern white students have on first entering school. The formality in schools is likely to accentuate their shyness and reticence.

Some teachers have observed that, unlike low-income Negro students, who tend to become verbally or physically aggressive, southern white students tend to withdraw and become passive when angered. "They are like vegetables. They just sit and stare. And if the pressure becomes too great, they merely get up and leave," a puzzled Detroit teacher commented at a workshop. Many southern white students respond in this manner because they do not internalize a dialogue that convinces them that they are active school participants. *School is something that is happening to them and not for them.* In a "Poor Scholar's Soliloquy" some of the possible negative effects of a rigid curriculum on the motivation and achievement of urban school students with rural backgrounds are vividly portrayed:

No, I'm not very good in school. This is my second year in the seventh grade and I'm bigger and taller than the other kids. They like me all right, though, even if I don't say much in the schoolroom because outside I can tell them how to do a lot of things. They tag me around and that sort of makes up for what goes on in school.

I don't know why teachers don't like me. They never have very much. Seems like they don't think you know anything unless they can name the book it comes out of. I've got a lot of books in my room at home—books like Popular Science Mechanical Encyclopedia, *and the Sear's and Ward's catalogues, but I don't very often just sit down and read them through like they make us do in school. I use my books when I want to find something out, like whenever Mom buys anything secondhand I look it up in Sears or Wards first and tell her if she's getting stung or not. I can use the index in a hurry to find the things that I want.*

In school, though, we've got to learn whatever is in the book and I just can't memorize the stuff. Last year I stayed after school every night for two weeks trying to learn the names of the Presidents. Of course I knew some of them like Washington and Jefferson and Lincoln, but there must have been thirty altogether and I never did get them straight.

I'm not too sorry though because the kids who learned the Presidents had to turn right around and learn all the Vice Presidents. I am taking the seventh grade over but our teacher this year isn't so interested in the names of the Presidents. She has us trying to learn the names of all the great American inventors. . . .

Dad says I can quit school when I'm fifteen and I'm sort of anxious to because there are a lot of things I want to learn how to do and my uncle says, I'm not getting any younger.[16]

Teachers who believe that such students are innately incapable of memorizing facts because they cannot memorize the names of presidents, vice presidents, and inventors might be surprised to learn that the same students have memorized the names of famous athletes and hundreds of cars. Once the basic skills of reading and writing are learned, school loses its functional value for such pupils. Many youths state that they do not need a high school diploma in order to get a job somewhere; "somewhere," of course, usually means in an unskilled or semiskilled capacity.

[16]Stephen M. Corey, "Poor Scholar's Soliloquy," *Childhood Education*, 20 (January, 1944), 219–220.

Table 9
Relationship of Education to White and Nonwhite Earnings

	Expected lifetime earnings		Nonwhite as percentage of white
School years completed	White	Nonwhite	
Less than 8	$157,000	$ 95,000	61
8	191,000	123,000	64
9 to 11	221,000	132,000	60
12	253,000	151,000	60
13 to 15	301,000	162,000	54
16	395,000	185,000	47
17 or more	466,000	246,000	53

Source: From *Rich Man, Poor Man* by Herman P. Miller, published 1965 by Thomas Y. Crowell Company; reproduced with their permission.

OTHER
MINORITIES

As most cities become ever more populated with disadvantaged nonwhite families, their educational offerings become less relevant for the students. One reason for this is that what has been called "meaningless education" is not related to their community and adjustment patterns.[17] Nor is education an automatic income equalizer even when nonwhites do stay in school. As Table 9 shows, nonwhite high school graduates earn much less than their white classmates.

The negative effects of ghetto life are evident in the nonwhite child who comes to school tired and hungry, from a home barren of reading materials and lacking in contact with the world beyond the immediate neighborhood. His preschool conditioning usually does not include being taught to respond to oral or written stimuli, and he must rely on less complex visual stimuli. He is likely to point, push, shove, or grimace instead of using verbal skills. He may even be unprepared to sit quietly in a classroom. The ability to sit and listen does not come automatically with maturation but, rather, with a child's experiences in a "sitting" atmosphere. Many of those who can sit quietly at their desks are severely limited in their ability to solve "middle-class" abstract reasoning problems, and of those few who can, the majority are not in one school long enough to complete a planned sequence of work.

Middle- and upper-class nonwhite children generally view school as an extension of home, whereas lower-class nonwhite children view school as an environment separate from and, often, antagonistic to the home. To the lower-class child—regardless of color—home is home and school is school, and it is difficult for educators to cause the two to meet

[17]Dave Berkman, "You Can't Make Them Learn," *Atlantic Monthly*, 210 (September, 1962), 62–67.

in his mind. For example, the elementary school readers are often so culturally biased that stories in them simply do not make sense to most nonwhite students. Most of these children, and some of their parents, have not been farther from their homes than 25 blocks. Many have not seen a motion picture, eaten in a restaurant, or ridden in a bus; nor have they lived in a situation where a mother and father work together to rear a family. It is little wonder that they find it difficult to identify with the white middle-class "Dicks" and "Janes" in the typical reading books. (Only since the Detroit Public Schools Series in 1962, for example, have Negro characters appeared in first-grade basic readers used in American schools. Within the past few years, several publishers have issued multiracial readers.)

Many college textbooks focus exclusively on the educational problems of Negroes, ignoring Mexican-Americans, Puerto Ricans, and American Indians. Yet, although there are about 22 million Negroes in this country, there also are about 5.5 million Mexican-Americans, 860,000 Puerto Ricans, and 550,000 American Indians. Nearly all of the negative conditions characteristic of Negroes also characterize other minority groups, but there are cultural differences among the groups. We now briefly discuss these minority groups that are too frequently ignored. (The reader is encouraged to take additional courses or do additional reading to gain a better understanding of the problems of these groups.)

Mexican-Americans

Mexican-American students reflect a variety of cultural patterns, including those created by their parental heritage and the length of time their families have been American citizens. Second- and third-generation descendants of early Spanish settlers are usually affluent, but second- and third-generation descendants of agricultural workers tend to be poverty-stricken. There is still a third group: first-generation children of *braceros*—farm workers who have recently migrated from Mexico. The first two groups are likely to be "Americanized"; they have little knowledge of their Spanish heritage and they speak little or no Spanish. Children of migrant workers speak fluent Spanish and hold tightly to Mexican customs and traditions.[18] All groups are discriminated against by the *Anglos*—the white American majority. Indeed, in some communities, Mexican-Americans are the victims of more discrimination and segregation than Negroes.

Mexican-Americans, like American Indians and Puerto Ricans, are truly marginal people. Culturally, they are neither black nor white. Their marginality affects individual searches for identity. In most schools the curriculum does not include material with which the

---

[18]See Luis F. Hernandez, "The Culturally Disadvantaged Mexican-American Student," *Journal of Secondary Education*, 42 (February, 1967), 59–65; (March, 1967), 123–128.

Mexican-American can positively identify. In history classes, for instance, he becomes the villain who massacred the courageous Americans at the Alamo. Most elementary and secondary schools inflict the final blow at the cultural identity of Mexican-American children by forcing them to leave their ancestral language at the schoolhouse door.[19] Many students react to all this by adopting a defense mechanism called "ethnic self-hatred."[20]

Some studies of Mexican-American students in junior and senior high schools conclude that in many instances the negative self-images attributed to Mexican-Americans are *coping devices*. Recent studies also illustrate the detrimental aspects of negative definitions that teachers and administrators hold of the students. Students become aware of the negative views and, in some instances, role-play as people with negative self-images in order to minimize conflicts in school. Submissive acts—"playing dumb"—are ways pupils manage to coexist with the Anglo.

Most of the 2 million or so Mexican-American school children in the Southwest have suffered academic failure because of the unwillingness or inability of schools to build a curriculum around their Spanish-speaking background. Yet as early as the 1920s researchers were aware that Mexican-American students are better able to achieve in reading and other school-related tasks when they are taught first in Spanish. Recently, a few school districts in the Southwest have implemented bilingual classroom instruction. Projects in San Antonio, Tucson, and Albuquerque are proving that *cultural difference does not mean cultural inferiority*.

Puerto Ricans
Like the children of other minority groups, Puerto Rican students are frequently plagued by problems revolving around acculturation, language difficulties, and economic barriers. Furthermore, Puerto Rican parents give little or no parental support to the schools—they are preoccupied with the problems of learning English, finding housing, securing employment, and otherwise trying to survive.[21] When they do turn their attention to the schools, they feel powerless to improve them, controlled as they are by white administrators and teachers. In some communities, Puerto Ricans are joining Negroes in trying to achieve educational and other gains.

Puerto Rican children are taught very early to respect their elders by bowing their heads. In the schools, however, teachers insist that pupils look at them when giving verbal responses. Other illustrations

[19]Frank M. Cordasco, "The Challenge of the Non-English Speaking Child in New York," New York, Board of Education, 1958.
[20]Hernandez, op. cit., 60.
[21]J. Cayce Morrison, "The Puerto Rican Study (1953–1957): A Report on the Education Adjustment of Puerto Rican Pupils in the Public Schools of the City of New York," New York, Board of Education, 1958.

of cultural differences include the Puerto Rican pattern of little physical contact between the adolescent boy and male adults. Thus, in the classroom boys jerk away when male teachers try to touch them. Still other teachers fail to understand that in some families illness in the home requires everyone to remain home until the sick person's health is restored. Ignorance of such differing cultural norms or the inability to understand them results in unjustly labeling students as belligerent or docile or not interested in school. Many teachers not only do not understand cultural differences; they also are insensitive to and often shocked by the accelerated social maturity of slum-dwelling children. Slum children become socially mature at an early age in order to survive.[22] By the time the average slum child is 10 or 12, he has seen too much and done too much. Sex, violence, and crime are all familiar to him.

The more effective teachers and administrators seek to understand their own prejudices and cultural limitations *before* trying to understand and help people from other backgrounds. Much of the turmoil and dissension in recent years in the New York City schools has arisen because too many administrators and teachers have found the concepts "culturally deprived," "disadvantaged," and "different" to be convenient alibis for failing to provide equal educational opportunities.

American Indians

Currently, American Indians are at the bottom of the economic ladder. They have the highest rates of unemployment and school dropouts, live in the poorest housing, and, in some parts of the country, they are accorded the lowest social status.[23] These conditions reflect both what white Americans have done to the Indians and also what the Indians have not been able to do for themselves.

Unable to realize that we do not have an Indian problem but an *American problem,* we have established government-controlled Indian bureaus, reservations, and assistance programs. Each of these shortsighted solutions has contributed to the psychological emasculation of Indian men, the demoralization of Indian women, and the alienation of Indian children. In other words, most government programs have failed to assist Indians in their efforts to maintain individual dignity and cultural identity while achieving success in the larger society. Yet, with missionary zeal, white Anglo-Saxons continue their ill-fated efforts to Americanize the Indians.

Conflicts between white and Indian cultures are found on reservations, in small towns, and in big cities. The strains show up in many ways, including juvenile delinquency, adult crime, and alcoholism. Such social pathologies are but symptoms of man's inhumanity to his fellow

---

[22]See Patricia Cayo Sexton, *Spanish Harlem*, New York, Harper & Row, 1955.

[23]Fred Harris, "American Indians—New Destiny," *Congressional Record—Senate,* April 21, 1966, p. 8311.

man. Historically, non-Indians have "looked at" Indian tribes but have failed to "see" the deplorable social, psychological, and physical deprivations. White teachers in particular tend to think that because an exceptional Indian student has managed to succeed, the others should also.

Of the 150,000 Indian children in schools, one-third are in federally operated institutions. Indian schools range from trailers on Navajo reservations to large off-reservation boarding schools. The dropout rate for Indians is twice the national average, their level of educational attainment is half the national average, and their test scores are far below those of other students. Generally, the longer an Indian child stays in school, the further behind he gets.[24] This *cumulative deficit* partially explains why Indian high school graduates earn 75 percent less than the national average.

The Bureau of Indian Affairs is trying to increase the number of Indians in teaching and administrative positions so that Indian children will have more models to look up to. As school districts improve the quality of education for Indians, they also are teaching that cultural pluralism is not making nonwhite children "white," but, instead, is allowing them to maintain their own cultural identities. The deficiencies in Indian education reinforce the growing need for teachers, administrators, and literature that better reflect a multiethnic society.

SUMMARY

1. More than twice as many white as nonwhite families are poverty-stricken. However, a greater proportion of nonwhite families lives in poverty.
2. There are many criteria of poverty. The absence of funds for minimum subsistence is but one condition; other conditions include low levels of educational and occupational aspirations.
3. As our cities change in composition from middle-class to lower-class residents, social pathologies such as juvenile delinquency, adult crime, and unemployment also increase.
4. Poor people of all racial groups feel alienated. Many of them—because of their life styles—are unable to adjust to middle-class life styles. However, poor Negroes are more socially deprived than poor whites.
5. Teachers who believe that poverty-stricken children are incapable of memorizing facts would be surprised to learn that many of them can remember facts that are important to *them.*
6. The most negative aspect of poverty is that it deprives low-income people of an equal opportunity to enjoy the fruits of our culture.

SELECTED READINGS

Brown, Warren, and Oscar J. Aleks, "Attitudes of White and Non-Whites Toward Each Other," *Sociology and Social Research,* 40 (1956), 310–319. The authors describe attitudes of whites in lower Westchester County, N.Y., toward nonwhites in the Riverton area of New York.

[24]Rosalie H. Wax, "The Warrior Dropouts," *Trans-action,* May, 1967, 40–46.

DeMos, George D., "Attitudes of Mexican-American and Anglo-American Groups Toward Education," *Journal of Social Psychology*, 57 (1962), 249–256. A study of attitudinal differences between Mexican-Americans and Anglo-American groups toward formal education.

Deutsch, Martin P., *Minority Group and Class Status as Related to Social and Personality Factors in Scholastic Achievement*, Ithaca, N.Y., Society for Applied Anthropology, 1960. An investigation of problems unique to minority group education, and their effects upon self-perception, frustration, and rate of learning.

Duhl, Leonard J. (ed.), *The Urban Condition*, New York, Basic Books, 1963. A collection of essays focusing on the problems of urbanization, including slums, racial minority groups, education, and health.

Harrington, Michael, *The Other America*, New York, Macmillian, 1962. A description of poverty in America, especially those who live in it. Harrington discusses the invisible aspects of poverty that go beyond inadequate income.

Landes, Ruth, *Culture in American Education: Anthropological Approaches to Minority and Dominant Groups in the Schools*, New York, Wiley, 1965. An analysis of the effects of different cultural backgkrounds in various school "societies."

Lynd, Staughton, "Urban Renewal—For Whom?" *Commentary*, January, 1961, pp. 34–45. The author suggests possible reasons for the failure of urban renewal to substantially lessen the social pathologies found in urban slums.

Miller, S. M., and Frank Riessman, "The Working Class Subculture: A New View," *Social Problems*, 9 (Summer, 1961), 86–97. A realistic approach to understanding the working class. Many myths about the environments of working-class people are explored.

Simpson, George E., and J. Milton Yinger, *Racial and Cultural Minorities: An Analysis of Prejudice and Discrimination* (3rd ed.), New York, Harper & Row, 1965. One of the most comprehensive and illuminating summaries of minority groups and their interaction with majority groups.

Toby, Jackson, "Orientation to Education as a Factor in the School Maladjustment of Lower-Class Children," *Social Forces*, 35 (March, 1957), 259–266. Examples of ways in which teachers with middle-class values tend to reject and penalize students from the lower classes.

Wax, Murray L., et al., "Formal Education in an American Indian Community," *Social Problems*, 11 (Supplement, 1964), 1–125. This special supplement brings into focus the educational needs of a much neglected minority group, American Indians. A parallel is drawn between disadvantaged Indians on reservations and students in urban slum communities.

Weaver, Robert C., "Non-White Population Movements and Urban Ghetto," *Phylon*, 20 (September, 1959), 235–241. Weaver ponders whether metropolitan areas of tomorrow will have a core of low-income nonwhite families surrounded by middle- and upper-income whites in the suburbs.

Weller, Jack, *Yesterday's People*, Lexington, University of Kentucky Press, 1965. Weller, a renown authority on the Southern Appalachia, describes the hope and despair of poor whites.

Young, Whitney, *To Be Equal*, New York, McGraw-Hill, 1964. Combining statistics and subjective observations, Young describes the environmental forces affecting black Americans.

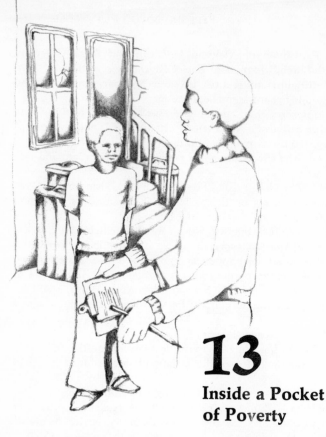

13

Inside a Pocket of Poverty

Past generations of Americans have escaped from the economic insecurity and meanness of ghetto life by bettering their economic circumstances, obtaining for themselves or their children a good education, and moving outside the ghetto. For many reasons, these avenues are closed to most Negroes.*

In his classic *The Protestant Ethic and the Spirit of Capitalism,* Max Weber described the early appearance of the American emphasis on profitable work as a goal in itself. Even though our society has undergone dramatic changes, the work ethic still survives. In recent years, however, Americans have become more *consumption-oriented* than work-oriented. This is not to imply that we devalue work, but that—more than ever—it has a means orientation; work is viewed as being primarily a means to consumer activities and not assurance of one's spiritual salvation. Young children are taught that work is good. All around them people are talking about, seeking, and engaging in work activities. Indeed, a major question that

**A Time To Listen—A Time To Act: Voices from the Ghettos of the Nation's Cities,* Washington, D.C., U.S. Commission on Civil Rights, 1967, p. 41.

American children are continually called on to answer is: "What are you going to be when you grow up?"

Opportunities for upward social mobility through working do sometimes exist for those who are defined as "lower class" (see Chapter 7). Nevertheless, lower-class students are confronted with inconsistent life situations: On the one hand, they are given a work orientation in their elementary and secondary schools; on the other hand, they see chronic unemployment and underemployment in their homes. Even in "good" times, the unemployment and underemployment rates are proportionately higher for their parents. Quite naturally, lower-class children find it almost impossible to believe that a person can ever improve his circumstances by working and saving his pennies. Besides, the social treatment accorded even the most successful nonwhites seems to prove that one needs, in order to be free, something more than a bank account.

In other words, it seems very probable that most lower-class minority-group students do not expect to achieve success within the white society. If this is true, then what is needed to give such lower-class students a sense of belonging—a sense of identity? Certainly it is not enough to add a few passages about minority groups to history books and include pictures of children of different races in other textbooks. We might make some more informed suppositions about what lower-class pupils actually do need if we first examine how they live. To be specific, what is life like inside a pocket of poverty?

A TARGET
AREA

During January and February of 1964, 200 Negro young people living in what later became the core area of the 1967 Detroit riot were interviewed individually in school yards, in schools, and on sidewalks—in short, wherever it was possible to conduct an interview.[1] The respondents, 100 boys and 100 girls, were between 12 and 18 years old. According to the Detroit antipoverty program standards, 150 respondents were poverty-stricken (annual family income less than $3,000) and 50 were middle income (annual family income between $3,000 and $10,000). (Throughout these chapters, the terms "lower class" and "low income" will be used interchangeably to indicate an individual from a family that had an annual income of less than $3,000 and whose main wage-earner was employed in an unskilled or semiskilled capacity.)

Although part of the time was devoted to examining objectively some

[1]This was an exploratory study of the formal education experiences of black and white youths interviewed for a Detroit juvenile delinquency prevention planning project, Community Action for Detroit Youth (CADY). The data presented in this chapter are based on interviews supervised by George Henderson. For a critique of the CADY project, see Michael Schwartz, "The Sociologist in an Unsuccessful Delinquency Prevention Planning Project," in Arthur B. Shostak (ed.), *Sociology in Action: Case Studies in Social Problems and Directed Social Change*, Homewood, Ill., Dorsey Press, 1966, pp. 166–176.

of the environmental factors within the Target Area, the major emphasis was placed on exploring the youths' subjective interpretations of those factors. Partially structured field interviews, each lasting about one hour, were conducted to elicit the respondents' perceptions of their neighborhoods, families, schools, significant other factors, and, finally, their educational and occupational aspirations. Each interview was taped and later subjected to detailed content analysis.

Other studies indicate that under socially strained conditions lower-class youths are extremely adroit in "taking the role of the other." When they do so, they say what they believe to be *socially correct* but not necessarily true. Thus the interviewers tried to avoid seeming to be "typical" well-trained, well-groomed, middle-class outsiders. Instead, they dressed casually and occasionally used local jargon in an effort to gain rapport. Also, because they interviewed only those who volunteered, it is likely that defensiveness was further minimized. Before each interview, the interviewer attempted to convey the feeling that he was aware of and respected the cultural differences of the respondents. Most interviews began this way:

Interviewer: *I'd like to interview you if I may.*
Respondent: *Interview me about what?*
Interviewer: *Oh, about you, your neighborhood, school, and things like that. I'm from Wayne State University and I'm trying to find out what people in this neighborhood think about these things.*
Respondent: *I ain't so sure I can help you.*
Interviewer: *If you can't help me, I guess nobody can. One thing I've learned from going to college is that I can't get to know people by only reading books. I can spend the rest of my life reading books but never really digging people. You know, like a phony, stuck-up cat trying to save the world but not knowing how.*
Respondent: *Yeah, there's lots of cats who think they know it all 'cause they go to college. What they need is for somebody to turn them on.*

The respondents seemed to take great delight in "turning on" the interviewers to a few facts. As one girl said, they were "educating the educators."

An analysis of the data in Table 10 on both the respondents and the total Target Area population reveals that they had very similar characteristics. (The Target Area sample, however, had proportionately higher rates of welfare cases, school dropouts, and broken homes.) The degree of representativeness can be ascribed in part to an earlier pilot study that allowed the interviewers to gain neighborhood exposure and, subsequently, pre-interview acceptance from many respondents. Another reason was the accurate number of "lower-class" and "middle-class" youths recommended for interview by several junior high and senior high school teachers. These recommendations were convenient for the

Table 10
Some Selected Characteristics of Households in the Target Area
Sample and the Total Target Area (in percentages)

| | Target Area | |
| | Sample households[a] | Total households[b] |
Characteristic		
Total nonwhite	100.0	76.2
Population 13–18 years of age	10.2	8.8
Male percent of population		
13–18 years of age	47.9	49.2
Female percent of population		
13–18 years of age	52.1	50.8
Living in owner-occupied housing unit	20.5	22.7
Moved into unit since 1958	53.3	44.2
One or more persons per room	25.0	12.8
Automobile available	31.5	52.2
Adults unemployed		
(heads of households)	24.1	14.9
Welfare, ADC, OAA recipients	18.0	10.3
Male adults employed		
(heads of households)	78.5	83.0
Professional and managerial	6.9	9.2
Clerical, sales, craftsmen, and foremen	20.8	25.0
Operatives, service workers, and laborers	72.3	65.8
Female adults employed		
(heads of households)	82.6	85.1
Professional and managerial	9.9	14.8
Clerical, sales, craftsmen and foremen	29.1	27.4
Operatives, service workers, and laborers	61.0	57.8
Family with annual incomes		
less than $5,000	80.4	14.3
16–18 year old dropout rate	35.6	28.6
Broken homes	26.0	14.3

[a] Based on information taken from interviews.
[b] Based on 1960 Census and social agency reports.

interviewers, but the fact of this kind of classifying presents a problem in itself. We will discuss later the way such labeling by teachers can adversely affect the life chances of lower-class students.

PERCEPTIONS OF
TARGET AREA NEIGHBORHOODS

Most of the youths gave unemotional, terse descriptions of their neighborhoods. Their almost observer-like descriptions created the impression that one was listening to senior anthropologists quite matter-of-factly describing their field experiences. A major reason for their assuming this mannerism was that they did not, as many verbalized it, want to "lose their cool." Losing their cool, getting involved and attached to others, made them more vulnerable to disillusionments. As one boy said:

This a tough life, man . . . ain't nothin' out here but heartache. . . . No sense in losin' your cool, that's where the trouble is. . . . Don't let nobody or nothin' get close to you and you won't get hurt.

Such withholding of affection from others appeared to represent a *survival motif*. If they had not been able to suppress their emotions, many of the youths would have been physically and psychologically overwhelmed by their neighborhoods. This detachment from others showed up in several ways, but basically each effort was an attempt to separate "self" (i.e., poverty-stricken people) from "nonself" (i.e., middle-class people, especially social agency representatives and public school teachers). From the perspective of the lower-class respondents, people were divided into "we" and "they" categories; "we" were the lower class.

Processed (straightened) hair encased in greasy rags, slow, swaggering walks, and near-whispered conversations were extreme examples of a coolness that some low-income youths adopted in order to hide the precarious nature of their poverty-stricken existence.[2] A 15-year-old girl described her neighborhood as follows:

It's . . . kind of big in size. Lots of teenagers around every night. They go out and pick fights with boys. They pick fights and carry knives. . . . At one house party a boy got stabbed in the eye. The police couldn't find him so they just dropped the charges against the boy who gave the party.

The reasons given by the respondents for carrying knives and maintaining menacing expressions were similar to one of the adult rationalizations for nuclear stock-piling: to prevent a war, not to start one. At first glance there did appear to be a lot of fighting, but on closer analysis it was merely the noise and pushing that result wherever large groups of children and youth congregate.

Although the lower-class families in the Target Area had more children than the middle-class families and although they were all compressed into slum neighborhoods, there were far fewer stabbings and fights than *near*-stabbings and *near*-fights. A respondent with a flair for dramatics noted that a constant war of nerves was being waged by two paradoxical opponents, one who was scared and the other who was glad that his rival was scared; thus mortal combat was averted.

Mother-Centered Homes

Over half the youths reported that their fathers were permanently absent from home and that grandparents, especially grandmothers, were

---

[2]The trend to black nationalism (see Chapter 16) has resulted in the abandonment of hair-straightening processes and chemicals by many Negro young people. They now let their hair grow into "naturals" or "Afros." The other behaviors described in this study are very much the same.

present. There was a tendency for stepfathers or other father surrogates to be present. For some children this kind of *extended family* arrangement was psychologically more disconcerting than changing schools each year. The mother was usually perceived as being the "boss" in the family. The importance of the mother was further illustrated by her hierarchical ranking above the father. One youth said: "If you say that my old man [father] is a dirty bastard, I might just laugh. . . . If you say my old lady [mother] is a no good bitch, I'll try to kick your ass. . . . Nobody talk that way about my old lady."

Much of the tension centering on mother-dominated homes was vented in a game called "the dozens." The object of the game is to calmly "talk about" (insult) one's opponent by questioning his parentage, and not to show anger when he offers rebuttal. The youth who "scores" the most points is the winner of the contest. However, the first one who "blows his cool" (resorts to physical aggression or cries) automatically loses, no matter how many points he had scored before blowing his cool. A game of the dozens between two hypothetical youths, "M" and "G," may proceed as follows:

M: *Come here, son.*
G: *I ain't your son, I'm your daddy.*
M: *Oh! You want to play the dozens, huh? Listen, son: I don't play the dozens 'cause the dozens is bad, but I can tell you how many children your mammy had. She didn't have one, she didn't have two, she had 29 bulldogs just like you.*
G: *Now son, is that any way for you to talk to your daddy? If you keep talking like that, I'm gonna tell everybody that your mama wears cast-iron drawers.*

From the interviews it was clear that in subcommunities where there are proportionately more broken homes and illegitimate children than in other sections of the city, derogatory statements about a youth's mother are crushing blows at not only the *most* significant other person in his home but, often, the *only* significant other person in the home.

The Fear

A few respondents talked about their neighborhood in such a way as to suggest that for them it had no meaning whatever. When asked, "Tell me about your neighborhood," several said: "It ain't nothin' to tell." But with a little prodding they described the violence potential. A 13-year-old girl noted the not-too-frequent lulls that broke the noisy routine of her slum life:

Well, it's kinda quiet. The kids get noisy sometimes. It would be a nice neighborhood if it wouldn't be too many fights around there. Kids are fussing, even the grownups and the kids. Then for a while they be quiet again.

Why, we might ask, is it that of all the problems in their neighborhoods that the youths could discuss, aggressive behavior was mentioned most often? One possible answer is that even though few wanted to lose their cool, most were anxious about and fearful of the ever-present violence potential. Other matters were, of course, discussed, but none approached in frequency the topics of violence and near-violence.

Friends

The most immediate answer to the question, "What do you like best about your neighborhood?" was "Nothing." They did not like the dilapidated, roach- and rat-infested buildings. Nor did they like the absence of recreation facilities or the garbage-littered alleys and streets. Positive responses were in terms of people and not surroundings. Only a few respondents mentioned a school, church, or some other community facility as being an aspect of their neighborhood that they liked best. Those who talked about people as an aspect of the community that they liked best seldom referred to teachers, social workers, or other professional persons. Instead they usually talked about nonprofessional area residents, mostly peers. This was the first indication that the "cool" attitude was only a thin veneer.

Even though many of the youths moved from neighborhood to neighborhood, they quickly sought out friends in each new neighborhood. The lower-class respondents verbalized the same kinds of aspirations for companionship as the middle-class youths. The major difference between the two groups was their opportunities for developing and maintaining close social relationships. The higher mobility rate of the lower-class youths decreased their opportunities for interacting with a single set of peers over a prolonged period of time.

Role Models

In response to the question, "What kind of people live in your neighborhood?" the lower-class respondents described unemployed and unskilled and semiskilled employed adults; the middle-class youths described adults employed in higher prestige occupations, such as doctors, lawyers, teachers, and social workers. From the interviews we noted that *the number and the variety of occupations to which the lower-class Target Area youths were exposed on a day-to-day basis were extremely limited.* Most of the youths expressed a desire to engage in occupations that already had a large minority-group representation—social worker, nurse, teacher. Missing were goals that reflected a wide range of occupational choices. Thus the economic effects of racial segregation and discrimination in job opportunities went beyond denying jobs to the poverty-stricken Target Area adults; their children were also denied adult models needed for motivating them to seek a broader range of available occupations. Equally debilitating, most of the low-income youths could not learn behavior patterns from their parents and neighbors that were functional for positive school adjustment.

Illegal Activities

When asked, "Are things going on in your neighborhood that are against the law?" answers ranged from "Definitely yes!" to "Definitely no!" Those who noted illegal activities talked about people making corn whisky, prostitutes standing on corners, pushers selling drugs, youths stealing cars, and friends playing the numbers. For many respondents these were normal activities because, as they stated, there was "some of this going on everywhere." Illegal activities were perceived by the lower-class youths as a "natural" part of their environment. Yet in terms of the total sample, only a small percentage engaged in or expected to engage in such occupations. For most of the respondents, life was a choice between poverty and nothing. A petite 12-year-old girl, dismissing the probability of postitution becoming her occupational adjustment, said: "You can see people taking poison all around you . . . know where to get it, but not take it yourself. Seeing prostitution is the same way. I guess I'll always be poor." She was not aware of the many occupations lying between an illegal activity and poverty. Like several other low-income youths, she was resigned to being poor.

PERCEPTIONS OF
TARGET AREA SCHOOLS

Throughout the Target Area interviews there were indications of a *lack* of communication between teachers and students. It was a lack and not a lag in many instances because most students felt ineffective in their efforts to communicate with their teachers. Teachers and pupils talked "at" each other and not "to" or "with" each other. The language of the lower-class respondents frequently did not correspond to the middle-class language patterns of their teachers. Many words such as "dig," "cool," "hip," and "busted" were not used in accordance with their nonslang dictionary definitions. One student highlighted his inability to communicate: "I told my teacher that she had a crazy dress on and she flipped [got angry] and sent me to the man [principal]. He asked me what I done and I told him. He sent me home until I apologized to the teacher." Neither the teacher nor the principal realized that when the student said it was a "crazy" dress he was paying a compliment in the language of his subculture.

The other side of the communication coin was the inability of the culturally disadvantaged students to understand their teachers. As one confused and embarrassed student complained, his teachers were always cautioning him not to "dangle his participle" or to "split his infinitives." The former warning caused him to check the zipper of his pants to see if it was open; the latter caused him sheepishly to check the seams in the seat of his pants to see if they were split.

Another example of teachers who erroneously assumed that the lower-class Target Area students understood them is taken from an interview with a 16-year-old lower-class boy who was desperately seeking to assert his masculinity. Explaining why he dropped out of a biology course after attending only one class, he said, "That thin, funny-looking cat stood up, smiled, and said that everybody in the class was 'homo sapiens.' " The boy frowned and added, "It was bad enough he was a homo[sexual], but he didn't have to be proud of it." The teacher used a word that was not correctly understood. Still another student said that she couldn't "dig" math courses where pies (pi) were squared because "any fool knows that all pies are round." Finally, the communication problem was most vividly illustrated by the student who accused his English teacher of making derogatory statements about his family. Reconstructing the events leading to the allegation, the student said that the teacher called his relative pronouns "improper." And the student added, "I told her, 'so is your mama.' "

Teachers lament that once lower-class students are outside school, they revert to the language of their contemporaries. Almost all the lower-class students stated that "survival" was the foremost reason they behaved in this manner. The jargon of the lower-class child is functional for his survival in his subcommunity. Those, for example, who speak "proper" English are suspected of becoming "uppity" or "snobs." Target Area respondents who adopted "proper" English often found themselves living as a true marginal people—alienated from the lower-class and not completely accepted by the middle-class.

Favorite Teachers

Many of the lower-class interviewees disliked their school and, particularly, their teachers. Their most frequent answer to the question, "What do you like best about your school?" was "Nothing" (see Table

Table 11
The Most Frequent Reactions to School of Target Area Youth
(in percentages)

Comments	Lower-class students	Middle-class students
What the respondents liked *best:*		
Nothing	25	0
The students	14	10
Don't know	12	2
Going home	8	4
The subjects	5	35
The teachers	4	25
What the respondents liked *least:*		
Everything	20	0
The subjects	16	2
The teachers	12	6
Going to school	10	2

11). The negative feelings of the students were also evident in that the most immediate answer to the question, "What do you like least about your school?" was "Everything." More lower-class than middle-class students talked about being "bored with" or not "hip to" school subjects. When the students talked about teachers they did not like, one could detect feelings of emotional vehemence. A sarcastic witticism expressed by a few students was: "When the last bell rings you'd better clear the halls or you'll be run over by the teachers leaving school. They're the last ones in the building and the first ones out." On the other hand, students with positive feelings about school quickly mentioned favorite teachers who seemed to "care" about them.

A growing community emphasis on black nationalism caused some Target Area students to believe that black teachers "just naturally" had better rapport with lower-class Negro students than white teachers. However, a few students observed that their Negro teachers were very middle-class in their behaviors. These teachers appeared to have a psychological need to reject or repress memories of their less successful past, including students who reminded them of it. A lower-class Negro student described such rejection:

A nigger is a bitch. . . . Them stuck-up colored teachers treat us colored kids like dirt. They won't touch you and don't want you to touch them—scared you'll dirty them up. If I want a break [fair treatment], I go to the patty [white] teachers. . . . Somebody said Mr. —— who acts so high and mighty grew up in this neighborhood.[3]

Probing revealed that in many instances the students were using the teachers as scapegoats to cover up their own inability to pass the courses; several students did, however, cite verified instances of discriminatory treatment.

Adjusting to Failure
More lower-class than middle-class students were under-achieving in school. Several low-achieving, lower-class students felt that they were not participants in the classroom dialogue. In the words of a student:

The teachers give the good kids all the attention. . . . They don't even know I'm in the class. But they know that the good kids are there. . . . They let them ask questions, answer questions, and get away with murder. Me, I just look cross-eyed and I get in trouble. So I wised up and stopped talking. . . .

Unable to succeed in school, most lower-class respondents felt that they had to attend only until they could legally drop out. During this interim

[3]The same is often true for white teachers and lower-class white students. In the CADY project, low-achieving lower-class white students stated that their white teachers were unduly harsh with them, and their Negro teachers tended to be more sympathetic. There is a tendency for some teachers of either race to say, "I made it without special treatment, and so can they [children of my racial group]."

Table 12
Reasons Students Gave for Not Getting Higher Grades (in percentages)

Reasons	Lower class (N = 127)	Middle class (N = 46)	Total (N = 173)
Working at capacity	11.8	28.2	19.1
Not working at capacity	7.3	32.6	12.7
Can't concentrate	16.5	4.4	13.3
Teachers don't like me	15.0	8.8	13.3
Acting out in class	11.9	2.2	9.3
Don't want to do better	8.7	12.2	9.8
Other students cheat	5.5	0.0	4.1
Can't think of a reason	3.9	0.0	2.9
Other reasons	19.4	10.6	15.5
Total	100.0	100.0	100.0

Note: N signifies number of respondents.

period school was perceived by many of them as having positive attractions: It was warmer than home, it was the place where they could meet their friends, and it was cleaner than home. Nevertheless, although teachers could have provided the most immediate and direct assistance in connection with certain problems (e.g., difficulty with school subjects and knowledge of occupations), the lower-class students were likely to turn to less-qualified sources (e.g., parents and friends).

As Table 12 shows, the reasons given by the lower-class Target Area students for not getting better grades differed from the reasons given by the middle-class students who had the same grade-point averages. The low-achieving lower-class students tended to blame *others* (particularly their teachers and high-achieving classmates) for their own difficulties; the low-achieving, middle-class students tended to blame *themselves*. As a whole, the lower-class students seemed to lack self-confidence when competing for school success symbols. The competition literally horrified most of the lower-class students in the study. One disgruntled youth said:

Sometimes I think that I know my lesson real well, but when I get to class I can't remember nothing. Lots of times I'd like to ask for help, but I don't want to look stupid in the eyes of the class. The [middle-class] kids from LaSalle Street are always ready. It's the same in all classes. They get the good grades and I get what's left.

Only a few of the lower-class students responded to failure by vowing to do better, whereas almost all of the middle-class students predicted that they would get better grades. The major difference between the lower- and the middle-class students was their realistic expectations, not their desire for "good" grades. Most lower-class respondents verbalized the desire but did not expect to succeed in classroom competition; most middle-class respondents wanted and *expected* to succeed.

PERCEPTIONS
OF JOBS

There are basically two types of aspirations, *ideal* and *real* (expected). The ideal aspiration reflects what a person would most like to achieve, whereas the real aspiration reflects what he believes he actually will achieve. The middle-class youths projected considerably less difference between ideal and real aspirations. On the other hand, there was a noticeable discrepancy between the lower-class respondents' ideal and real levels of occupational aspirations. The majority of both the lower-class (78 percent) and the middle-class (82 percent) youths ideally aspired to professional and managerial occupations. This may have indicated either that they wanted to conform to the dominant society's educational push toward high-prestige jobs or that they sought to give "socially correct" ideal aspirations. Whatever the reason, the ideal aspirations of both groups indicated some internalization of the "American Dream."

As for real aspirations, however, 72 percent of the middle-class youths expected to achieve professional and managerial jobs, but only 13 percent of the lower-class youths had such expectations. The great discrepancies between the lower-class youths' ideal and real occupational aspirations may have been caused by a "settling-down" effect; the lower-class students, in the face of their school performances and other negative environmental factors, found their aspirations settling down to a lower reality level (see Table 13). The following portion of an interview illustrates such a lowering of aspirations:

Interviewer: *If you could be anything in the world and nothing was stopping you, what would you be?*

Respondent: *(without hesitating) If I could be anything in the world, I'd be a nurse.*

Interviewer: *Why do you want to be a nurse?*

Respondent: *It's a high profession and I've always wanted to be one. I could help people and earn a decent living.*

Interviewer: *What do you think you actually will be?*

Respondent: *(hesitating) I don't know. . . . Maybe I'll just work the streets or get married.*

Interviewer: *Why do you change from wanting to be a nurse to expecting to work the streets?*

Respondent: *Working the streets is easier than going to nursing school. Besides I can earn more money.*

Only a small percentage of the Negro youths either ideally (1.5 percent) or realistically (4.5 percent) aspired to skilled trades occupations. Considering the large number of available skilled jobs, it appeared that

Table 13
Ideal and Real Levels of Occupational Aspirations of Target Area Youths (in percentages)

Occupational aspiration	Ideal			Real (expected)		
	Aspiration					
	Lower class (N = 150)	Middle class (N = 50)	Total (N = 200)	Lower class (N = 150)	Middle class (N = 50)	Total (N = 200)
I. Professional and managerial	78.0	82.0	79.0	13.3	72.0	28.0
II. Clerical and sales	13.3	16.0	14.0	44.7	20.0	39.5
III. Skilled	1.3	2.0	1.5	3.3	8.0	4.5
IV. Semiskilled	6.6	0.0	5.0	31.3	0.0	23.5
V. Unskilled	0.8	0.0	0.5	7.4	0.0	5.5
Total	100.0	100.0	100.0	100.0	100.0	100.0

Note: N signifies number of respondents.

neither the middle-class nor the lower-class Negro youths were aware of or motivated to seek skilled occupations.

Job Information

On intensive probing it became evident that most of the lower-class youths could not describe the training they would need in order to achieve either their ideal or real occupational aspirations (see Table 14). It was almost as if most of them expected to go to sleep and wait until their fairy godmothers came, waved magic wands over them, and—presto!—they would become occupational successes. One student all but said as much:

It don't take a lot of brains and studying to get a good job. All it takes is a little luck and you'll get it. If you ain't got no luck, you'll never get a job. Worrying about it ain't gonna change your luck.

Exceptions to this were the few lower-class respondents who expressed real aspirations to socially deviant occupations. These youths could describe in much detail the training that was required to be gamblers, pimps, prostitutes, and other types of hustlers.

As noted earlier, the adults in the families of the lower-class respondents did not, as a rule, work in occupations above the semiskilled category. When the lower-class youths aspired to middle-class occupations, they frequently sounded as misinformed as one teenager living in the Target Area:

Interviewer: *What does a stenographer do?*

Respondent: *She does plenty of things. Like she types letters and answers the phone. Most of the time she doesn't have nothing to do, that's why I wants to be one. The pay is high, and the work is easy.*

Interviewer: *What kind of training would you need to be a stenographer?*

Respondent: *Typing and I guess that's all except good clothes. Of course, quite naturally you need to know how to answer the phone.*

Interviewer: *If you could not be a stenographer, what would be a suitable related job?*

Respondent: *I guess a switchboard operator if it is a real big office. If it is a little office ain't nothing else to do.*

More middle-class than lower-class youths could name occupations that were closely related to their ideal and real occupational aspirations (see Table 14). None of the middle-class youths aspired to semiskilled or unskilled occupations. Although there was no comparison of their knowledge of these occupations, it is probable that the lower-class youths were more knowledgeable about them (see Table 15).

Unless there is a great change in their readiness to plan, to work, and to succeed, it is probable that most of the lower-class Target Area respondents will ultimately engage in semiskilled and unskilled work. It follows that as employment trends continue to move away from

Table 14
Target Area Youths' Detailed Knowledge of Skills Needed in Their Occupational Aspirations (in percentages)

| | Knowledge of needed skills | | | | | |
| | Ideal aspiration | | | Real aspiration | | |
Occupational aspiration	Lower class (N = 150)	Middle class (N = 50)	Total (N = 200)	Lower class (N = 150)	Middle class (N = 50)	Total (N = 200)
I. Professional and managerial	7.8	48.8	25.9	40.0	66.7	57.1
II. Clerical and sales	25.0	50.0	32.2	29.9	66.7	32.5
III. Skilled	50.0	100.0	40.0	40.0	50.0	33.3
IV. Semiskilled	40.0	0.0	40.0	53.2	0.0	53.2
V. Unskilled	100.0	0.0	100.0	63.6	0.0	63.6

Note: N signifies number of respondents.

Table 15
Target Area Youths' Knowledge of Occupations Closely Related to Their Aspirations (in percentages)

| | Knowledge of closely related occupations | | | | | |
| | Ideal aspiration | | | Real aspiration | | |
Occupational aspiration	Lower class (N = 150)	Middle class (N = 50)	Total (N = 200)	Lower class (N = 150)	Middle class (N = 50)	Total (N = 200)
I. Professional and managerial	12.8	39.8	19.6	30.0	58.4	47.1
II. Clerical	15.0	50.0	25.0	22.4	40.0	24.7
III. Skilled	0.0	100.0	33.3	40.0	50.0	44.4
IV. Semiskilled	30.0	0.0	30.0	38.3	0.0	38.3
V. Unskilled	100.0	0.0	100.0	45.5	0.0	45.5

Note: N signifies number of respondents.

Table 16
Comparison of Ideal and Real Aspirations, by Attitude of Parents Toward Choice (in percentages)

Parents' attitude	Ideal aspiration			Real aspiration		
	Lower class (N = 150)	Middle class (N = 50)	Total (N = 200)	Lower class (N = 150)	Middle class (N = 50)	Total (N = 200)
Parents approve	66.7	82.0	70.1	63.3	78.0	67.0
Parents indifferent	26.7	16.0	24.0	27.3	12.0	23.5
Parents disapprove	6.6	2.0	5.9	9.4	10.0	9.5
Total	100.0	100.0	100.0	100.0	100.0	100.0

Note: N signifies number of respondents.

semiskilled and unskilled occupations toward skilled or higher occupations, the youths appear destined to perpetuate their culture of poverty.[4]

Parental Pressures

Many researchers state that lower-class children do not realistically aspire to middle-class goals because of a lack of encouragement from their parents. This was *not* true of the Target Area youths interviewed. As Table 16 shows, their parents did attempt to motivate them toward middle-class goals; in almost the same breath they also tried to prepare them for what appeared to be probable failure. The youths described such conditioning as follows:

My mama is always bugging me 'bout finishin' school. "Chile," she say, "ain't no sense in you growin' up like me. Better git yourself a good education so you won't be no domestic like me. . . . Colored people got to be better educated then white folks just to get a job workin' for white folks."

. . .

My old man tell me to go to school and learn. Ain't nobody hiring muscles these days unless they be between your ears. . . . Need a high school diploma before they let you fill out a application for a job. . . . Like my old man says, "It's bad enough to be black. No sense in being black and stupid."

In summary, most of the lower-class parents—conditioned by their own failures—sought to prevent their children from absorbing undue disappointments. As a result, most of the lower-class interviewees were conditioned to expect failure when performing middle-class tasks. Even so, they ideally aspired to occupations that were socially higher in prestige than their parents'. Although out of the mainstream of the dominant culture, the lower-class parents passed on high occupational aspirations to their children.

IMPLICATIONS
OF THE STUDY

The aspirations of the youths living in the Target Area were directly related to easily discernible factors such as race, income, and education. They also were related to less discernible factors of subjective definitions of environmental situations. W. I. Thomas wrote that if men define situations as being real, they *are* real in their consequences.[5] This

---

[4]As reported in an August 5, 1967, *Business Week* article, "For Negroes, the Pie Cuts Too Thin": "For the long haul, better education is probably the answer. But unless Negroes speed up their penetration into higher-skilled, white collar jobs where employment is growing, the future looks grim. At current rates of penetration, the Labor Department estimates, Negroes in 1975 will still suffer from twice the jobless rates of whites, and Negroes will still be over-represented in the less-skilled jobs." See George Henderson, "Occupational Aspirations of Poverty-Stricken Negro Students," *Vocational Guidance Quarterly*, 15 (September, 1966), 41–45.

[5]For an extensive discussion of Thomas' theorem, see Robert K. Merton, *Social Theory and Social Structure*, Glencoe, Ill.: Free Press, 1957, chap. 11. See also

theorem also applies to children and youth. As behavioral scientists gain more insight into cognitions, motivations, and attitudes, it becomes clear that in many instances false definitions of social conditions are as important as real definitions. For example, the concerned Target Area student who falsely believed that he had failed an examination in history was not less anxiety-ridden than the concerned student who correctly believed that he had failed the examination. Wattenberg, commenting on levels of aspirations of school children, concluded:

The ideal situation for normal children is for their level of aspiration to be just high enough so that they have to put forth effort to reach it, and yet, low enough for them to achieve success. In school, at least in the beginning for any subject, children tend to accept the teacher's expectation and standards as their level of aspiration. Therefore, we can influence this level quite effectively. Now, when the level favors success with effort, a number of fine things happen.

The situation itself is satisfying. The child will want to return to the type of task. So to speak now he is motivated, shows interest, and puts out effort. Moreover, unless he is emotionally disturbed, he will begin to raise his sights. After each success he will set himself a somewhat higher level of aspiration. . . .

If the task at hand is clearly beyond his ability, he fails. What does failure do? Not only does it rob the task of interest, but it can have a depressant effect on his future level of aspiration. His ambition for himself will curve sharply downward. . . . He sets himself a level considerably below his true ability.[6]

We could compare the level of aspiration to a furnace thermostat—it protects us against cold, demoralizing, progress-slowing failures; it also keeps us to the comfortable warmth of safe, morale-building successes. When the mechanism of the level of aspiration is thrown out of balance, it fails to perform its protective function. Aspirations may then be maintained consistently *above* achievement; that is, the individual then experiences continual failure. On the other hand, aspirations may be maintained consistently *below* achievement, reflecting lack of ambition, broken morale, exaggerated caution, and cynicism.

Conflicting Data

Aspiration theories are symbolic constructs that allow us partially to account for and predict human behavior. When studied in this perspective, each theory has some potential for adding to our knowledge of human behavior. The importance of not forgetting or repressing this fact is shown by a recent college graduate who, though armed with many fine and complex theories, was much confused by the behavior

George Henderson, "Rags to Rags: A Probable Effect of Poverty," *Teachers College Journal*, 38 (December, 1966), 105–109.

[6]William W. Wattenberg, "Levels of Aspiration," *Michigan Education Journal*, 37 (November, 1959), 231.

of the students in his classes when he began teaching. His problem was not to acquaint the students with the relevant theories and thereby cause them to behave "correctly" but, instead, to expand his theories to account for their behavior. This situation has been vividly described as follows:

Miss B. has accepted an assignment to teach in a new school which will enroll Negroes and whites for the first time in a West Coast community. Miss B. is thrilled with her assignment. She is filled with a missionary zeal to do good for the down-trodden; she visualizes the Negroes as poor, meek children upon whom she will confer dignity and status.

Miss B. is completely unprepared for the brash, impudent, and aggressive conduct of some of her Negro (as well as white) pupils. Gone forever, after a week, is her mental picture of herself as the kindly benefactress who will help the colored children feel at ease in their new surroundings. She had visualized the victims of prejudice as being submissive; it was shocking to her middle-class mores to have them "sass" a teacher, fight, and swear. She does not realize that what she is seeing is lower-class behavior, regardless of color. She begins to think, "Give these Negroes an inch and they'll take a mile." She takes over with a firm hand and . . . is kept busy dealing with incidents which arise.[7]

Most of the Target Area respondents were in the lower socioeconomic class and this, by middle-class standards, placed them in socially and economically undesirable positions. Interestingly, there are arguments both for and against the proposition that the American tradition of wanting to get ahead is shared by poverty-stricken people. The results of some research studies suggest that middle-class parents place greater emphasis on the maintenance of high levels of school and vocational success than lower-class parents; other studies conclude that the reverse is true.[8] Such studies, however conflict only if we are looking for a single type of aspiration that can be attributed to a particular social class. There is less discrepancy if we view members of all social classes as having approximately the same aspirations, but also as having the option to choose consciously the aspirations attributed to other social classes. This would partially account for the high aspirations that the lower-class Target Area parents held for their children.

Probably, most lower-class youths do not acquire real aspirations to high-status middle-class occupations. There are enough college-graduate handymen to discourage such conditioning. Of course, there are examples of lower-class people who have managed to "make it" by legitimate means, but the mere fact that children see such adults does not mean that they will identify with them. Most lower-class Negroes, for example, believe that the Marian Andersons, Jackie

[7]Celia Burns Stendler and William E. Martin, *Intergroup Education in Kindergarten-Primary Grades*, New York, Macmillan, 1953, pp. 32–33.

[8]See Max Weiner and Walter Murray, "Another Look at the Culturally Deprived," *Journal of Educational Sociology*, 36 (March, 1963), 319–321.

Robinsons, Ralph Bunches, Robert Weavers, and Thurgood Marshalls would have made it if they had been polka-dotted; they are the exceptional, the gifted. (Besides, there are few white youths who expect to achieve the goals reached by these undeniably talented Negroes.)

False Assumptions
There were instances when teachers in the Target Area erroneously assumed that the poverty-stricken children could not and would not learn to master their school tasks. What seemed to be an inability on the part of lower-class students to learn their school assignments was frequently their teachers' inability to present the material so that it could be understood.

This was illustrated by a 13-year-old who had failed three courses in mathematics but who could explain the operation of the "numbers" (gambling):

You can play any amount you wants to from a penny on up. . . . For every penny you hit [select the winning three-number combination] you get five dollars back. . . . Like if I play for a dollar and hit, I get 500 dollars back. . . . You can box numbers [play all possible combinations of three numbers] but each way cost money. That is, like I think 245 is a good number and wants to play all the ways it can fall [be a winner], then I play it six ways: 245, 254, 425, 452, 542, and 524. It cost, say a dollar each. That's six dollars to box it. With two races [times numbers are selected] a day at six dollars a race to box it, I need 12 dollars a day. . . . So you got to have a whole lot of money to box numbers.

Although this boy was unable to figure out how long it would take five men to build a house if it took one man 200 hours, he could explain the very complex system of checking the daily newspapers to determine the winning numbers. There was no perceived pay-off for him in solving the house-building problem. He had never heard the people who were important to him talk about building a house, nor had he ever seen a house being built. All around him, however, people were talking about and playing numbers. This was an example of a latent ability that was not developed because of nonmotivating curriculum material. School assignments did not appeal to his interests, allow him to identify with some of the characters or scenes, or psychologically motivate him.

Bridging the Gap Between Theory and Practice
As a bit of academic hindsight, it seems easier for a researcher to criticize an existing educational institution than to criticize it and then, if needed, offer practical alternatives for achieving more effectiveness. The latter task is psychologically disconcerting; it highlights the gaps between social theory and social practice and, equally important, it reminds the researcher of his own inadequacies. Yet, of all the social practitioners, action researchers or social engineers have built the sturdiest bridges between theory and practice.

Bridging the gap between educational theories and practices requires a knowledge of the *past*, an appreciation of the *present*, and an eye to the *future*. To state merely that our schools should change is not as meaningful as to suggest some directions for change.

Although not illustrative of all poverty areas, the Target Area sheds much light on low-income youths living elsewhere. The major purposes of the following chapters will be to elaborate on some of the variables that negatively affect the low-income child's school achievement and to suggest techniques and programs for diminishing or even eliminating them.

SUMMARY

1. Lower-class youths frequently are confronted with inconsistent life situations. On the one hand, they are taught that education is good; on the other hand, they see unemployed youths with high school diplomas.
2. The Target Area youths tried to "keep their cool." That is, they hesitated to become friendly with and dependent on middle-class people.
3. There were far fewer actual incidents of aggression in the Target Area than near-incidents. Slums and poverty are prime conditions for breeding violent people.
4. In most instances, the mother not only was the most significant other person in the lower-class youths' homes but also was the *only* significant other person.
5. The lower-class respondents did not like their dilapidated buildings, inadequate recreation facilities, and overcrowded schools.
6. The Target Area teachers and students generally talked "at" each other and rarely "with" each other. The language patterns of lower-class and middle-class people can create serious communication problems.
7. Few lower-class students liked their school experiences, but those who did ascribed their attitude to a few teachers who "cared" about them.
8. Although there were no major differences between the ideal occupational aspirations of lower-class and middle-class students, the lower-class youths verbalized lower real (expected) aspirations. The lower-class respondents did not have adequate role models or motivation to acquire real aspirations for middle-class jobs.
9. Contrary to popular opinion, the lower-class parents did encourage their children to seek middle-class goals.
10. Students of human behavior should remember that their theories are at best guides to understanding students. They should expand the theories to include all human behavior and should not be preoccupied with constricting human behavior to fit the theories.

SELECTED READINGS

Cohn, Werner, "On the Language of Lower Class Children," *School Review*, 67 (Winter, 1959), 435–440. This article regards lower-class language as a separate dialect related to, but distinct from, "standard" English.

Frost, Joe L., and Glen R. Hawkes (eds.), *The Disadvantaged Child*, Boston, Houghton Mifflin, 1966. A compilation of articles related to the characteristics and education of children from culturally disadvantaged homes. In addition to theory, the book analyzes sound educational programs and practices.

Galler, Enid H., "Influence of Social Class on Children's Choices of Occupations," *Elementary School Journal*, 51 (April, 1951), 439–445. An investigation of the influence of social class on the occupational choices of children from lower, middle, and upper classes. The author considers social class as a variable independent of chronological age.

Harlem Youth Opportunities Unlimited, Inc., *Youth in the Ghetto: A Study of the Consequences of Powerlessness and a Blueprint for Change*, New York, 1964. Extensive interview data pertaining to life in Central Harlem. Chapters 6 and 12 are especially related to schools and educational problems.

Kardiner, Abram, and Lionel Ovesey, *The Mark of Oppression*, New York, Norton, 1951. A study of Negroes and their sociocultural climates. This book clearly illustrates that the overt responses of Negroes are expressions of the social pressures to which they are subjected.

Krugman, Judith I., "Cultural Deprivation and Child Development," *High Points*, 38 (November, 1956), 5–20. Stresses the importance of understanding the influence of culture on the personalities of children.

Miller, Daniel B., et al., *Inner Conflict and Defense*, New York, Holt, 1960. An empirical study of the relationship between social class and resolution of inner conflicts.

Pettigrew, Thomas F., *A Profile of the Negro American*, Princeton, N.J., Van Nostrand, 1964. Presents clinical data on the psychological damage to the Negro personality resulting from racial segregation and discrimination.

Sears, Pauline S., "Levels of Aspiration in Academically Successful and Unsuccessful Children," *Journal of Abnormal and Social Psychology*, 35 (October, 1940), 498–536. A now classical study that illustrates that differences in past experiences influence a child's anticipation of future consequences in a familiar task.

Street, David, and John C. Leggett, "Economic Deprivation and Extremism: A Study of Unemployed Negroes," *American Journal of Sociology*, 67 (July, 1961), 53–57. Readers of this article will better understand conditions under which violence becomes a way of life. The primary settings of this study were depressed segments of two predominantly Negro neighborhoods in Detroit.

Zimmer, Basil G., "The Adjustment of Negroes in a Northern Industrial Community," *Social Forces*, 9 (Spring, 1962), 378–386. This article describes in detail some problems of adjustment when Negroes migrate to northern communities.

14

Opportunity and Alienation

In a general social order in which most persons confront the danger of alienation, the American lower class and particularly the Negro lower-class person faces his own peculiar and magnified estrangement, a counterpoint to that of the society of which he is a part and yet not a part.*

The perennial problems of neglected and maladjusted children, the aging and aged, the sick and disabled, the unemployed and underemployed, and majority and minority groups become accentuated in large urban areas. The impersonality of a city compounds these problems and breeds despair among many of its people. The paradox of a city is that although it houses many people, it is also a place of intense loneliness.

Lured by the dream of a better life, rural people with extremely limited educational and occupational experiences migrate to cities in search of better economic opportunities. More often than not, they find that they lack the prerequisites for adjustment to urban life, which is too demanding and

*Harry L. Miller and Marjorie B. Smiley, *Education in the Metropolis*, New York, The Free Press, 1967, pp. 125–126.

too unpredictable. In their confusion and discouragement, they cling to their familiar rural life styles. These life styles are noticeably different from urban life styles in such things as speech patterns, housekeeping habits, and child-rearing practices. Each deviation from urban patterns adds to the social visibility and the social difficulties of southern migrants; these difficulties are so intractable that most of the migrants are labeled "culturally deprived" or "disadvantaged" by researchers. Whichever term is used, a substantial number of children growing up under these conditions become school failures.

Reviewing the literature, we learn that the behavior of these children has been described in a variety of ways, ranging from the wholly nonscientific to the scientific. Some hypotheses have stood the test of empirical investigation; others have not. Theories of *opportunity* and *alienation* seem to be most relevant for understanding and altering the behaviors of culturally disadvantaged students. "Opportunity" refers to an appropriate time or occasion to function as an integral part of the dominant society; "alienation" refers to acts of withdrawal or estrangement from the dominant society.

OPPORTUNITY

Deviant or asocial behaviors grow out of a lack of opportunity to carry out conforming social behaviors. Restricted opportunities to conform are a problem even if they are only imagined. This theoretical position is based on the belief not only that an individual must have an opportunity to conform to the dominant societal demands but also that he must be *aware* of such an opportunity, aside from the problem of whether or not he is capable of the necessary conformity. Inherent in this view is the belief that, with few exceptions, urban residents desire to participate in the dominant community and to be rewarded in it. The same is true of the children from low-income families who comprise most of the school failures. Studies have shown that middle- and low-income children do not differ in their aspirations to achievement; what they do differ in is their readiness to plan, work, and win rewards.

Range of Opportunities

Deviant styles of life are usually initiated in response to a series of persistently thwarting experiences, not because of a single instance of denial of opportunity. The family is found to be the primary source of such frustrating experiences, but minority-group status, inadequate schools, and other exploitative environmental conditions also produce them.[1] It seems plausible that the main reason for permitting access to a "legitimate" opportunity structure is to enhance an individual's

[1]James H. S. Bossard and Eleanor Stoker Boll, *The Sociology of Child Development* (3rd ed.), New York, Harper & Row, 1960, chap. 13.

feelings of self-worth with respect to the prevailing system of cultural expectations. Opportunity, as used in this context, leads to the entire range of behaviors that are defined as being legitimate in the dominant community. Along with the opportunity to succeed, however, comes the reverse condition—failure. Advocates of equal opportunity tend to overlook the failure potential inherent in open competition. Nevertheless, when the competition *is* open, it is at least "democratic." Thus school failures that solely reflect a student's abilities are more "democratic" than those resulting from nonability factors such as family income or race.

Learning Appropriate Roles

Reckless has concluded that a positive self-concept based on the dominant culture norms is the best insulator against deviant behaviors in minority groups.[2] Minority-group children must be permitted and encouraged to learn a set of socially acceptable roles, since it is only by performing such roles that they can develop feelings of positive self-worth. For example, boys must have opportunities to engage in activities that will permit them to be successful in playing male roles. The lack of such opportunities for Negro males has been amply documented. At the same time, girls also need opportunities to carry out conforming behaviors. Most illegitimate births to lower-class girls, for instance, can be traced to restrictions in opportunities to develop and maintain stable monogamous families. Their problem is not that they become unwed mothers, but rather that their opportunities for becoming wed mothers are greatly limited.

A Case of Illegal Opportunities

One of the respondents in the Target Area study described in the last chapter was an 18-year-old Negro prostitute, Toni. The youngest of five children, Toni was born and grew up in a section of Detroit's lower East Side. The adult and juvenile crime rates in her neighborhood were among the highest in Detroit. Numbers men, dope-pushers, gamblers, pimps, and prostitutes were the most "successful" adult role models in her neighborhood. Her parents separated shortly after she was born and her adult male contacts were mainly with a constantly changing group of "uncles." In addition, her "home" consisted of one inexpensive rooming house after another in neighborhoods where the schools were old, understaffed, and overcrowded.

Toni dropped out of school at 14, before completing the tenth grade, to give birth to her illegitimate child. After the baby was born, determined not to live with her mother or on Aid to Dependent Children (ADC), she secured a variety of unskilled jobs, including waiting on tables and cleaning the homes of wealthy white families. From none of

[2]Walter C. Reckless, et al., "Self-Concept as an Insulator Against Delinquency," *American Sociological Review*, 21 (December, 1956), 744–746.

these jobs was she able to earn enough money to support both herself and the baby adequately.

On the block.   When she was 16, Toni met a pimp who convinced her that he could help her earn a decent "salary" and not have to resort to welfare. Following a brief on-the-job training period, she began working the streets. We could discuss the prostitute-pimp relationship as being *functional* and *reciprocal*. That is, for teaching her the "profession," paying her rent, buying her clothes, and providing her with bail when she was arrested, the pimp received the major share of Toni's earnings. Many relationships in cultures of poverty embrace patterns of adjustment that differ from middle-class patterns but that nevertheless are quite functional for survival. Toni explained her socialization as follows:

Interviewer: *Toni, tell me something about the streetwalker. Is there a certain technique to this business and what are the hazards?*
Toni: *Before I started working the corner, I was really a country hick, not knowing anything. My pimp taught me how to walk, talk, dress, and how to examine men for v.d. [venereal diseases]. The prostitute on the corner is always in constant danger of being busted [arrested] by the man [police] or being hurt by a john [customer]. You never really know who you're dealing with and what that person might do to you.*

The possibilities of being arrested, contracting a venereal disease, and being beaten by chiseling customers are normal risks a prostitute assumes. Despite the hazards, prostitution seemed to be less of a risk to Toni than trying to finish school. On the block, Toni said, the rules were clear, but in school they were always changing.

Often the system of prostitution (and other illegal occupations) is perpetuated by unofficial, cordial police-prostitute relationships. Little things, such as being on a first-name basis and teasing, act to reinforce instead of discourage prostitution. Children observing this type of interaction in their neighborhoods find it difficult to equate prostitution with "bad" behavior. Instead, it sometimes assumes heights of dissorted altruism. Toni, for example, with tongue in cheek, referred to herself as a "lay analyst."

The pay-off.   Toni's response to a question about her satisfaction with her work clearly illustrated her perception of legitimate opportunity structures:

Interviewer: *How do you feel about this business? Do you enjoy your work?*
Toni: *It's not bad. It's good work. . . . Sometimes I don't like it, but there ain't many jobs where a high school dropout like me can earn 300 to 400 dollars a week. . . . I thought about applying for one of those poverty program jobs, but I just couldn't make it on 50 or 60 dollars a week.*

Prostitution may not have been the ideal occupation for Toni, but it was the only occupation she had. Equally important was her question: "What can you offer me instead?" Although Toni's condition did not begin with prostitution, it may end there. Furthermore, as she worked the streets, she became a role model for other girls in her neighborhood. Thus the cycle is self-renewing.

ALIENATION

Seeman, Blauner, McGee, and others have described four broad characteristics of alienation—feelings of "powerlessness," "meaninglessness," "normlessness," and "isolation."[3]

1. *Powerlessness. "The expectancy or probability held by the individual that his own behavior cannot determine the outcome he seeks."[4] The powerless person is an "object controlled and manipulated by other persons or by an impersonal system (such as technology) and . . . he cannot assert himself as a subject to change or modify this domination."[5]*

2. *Meaninglessness. Exists in a person whose "individual acts seem to have no relation to a broader life program. . . . When individual roles are not seen as fitting into the total system of goals of the organization but have become severed from any organic connection with the whole."[6] The individual has a "lack of understanding of the events in which he is submerged, . . . he is unclear as to what he ought to believe because his minimal standards for clarity in decision-making are not met."[7]*

3. *Normlessness. "The high expectancy that socially unapproved behavior is necessary to achieve given goals. . . . The social rules regulating individual conduct have broken down or are no longer effective as rules for behavior."[8]*

4. *Isolation. "The feeling of being in, but not of, society, a sense of remoteness from the larger social order, and absence of loyalties to intermediate collectivities."[9] The assignment by the individual of "low reward values to goals or beliefs that are typically highly valued in the given society."[10]*

The individual who experiences success is productive and is likely to feel that he can control at least some of his destiny. Unproductive experiences, on the other hand, are perceived as failures. A dispropor-

[3]Melvin Seeman "On the Meaning of Alienation," *American Sociological Review,* 24 (December, 1959), 783–791. See also George Henderson, "Opportunity and Alienation in Public Schools," *Teachers College Record,* 69 (November, 1967), 151–156; Robert Blauner, *Alienation and Freedom: The Factory Worker and His Industry,* Chicago, The University of Chicago Press, 1964, chap. 11; Reece McGee, *Social Disorganization,* San Francisco, Chandler, 1962, pp. 69–77.

[4]McGee, op. cit., p. 70.
[5]Blauner, op. cit., p. 32.
[6]Ibid.
[7]McGee, loc. cit.
[8]Seeman, loc. cit.
[9]Blauner, loc. cit.
[10]Seeman, op. cit., 787.

tionate number of children in poverty areas are familiar with failure, as shown by the large number who accumulate low school achievement records or who become school dropouts or unemployed high school graduates. These negative factors are reinforced by racial discrimination and adult underemployment and unemployment. There are many aspects of living in poverty that combine to hide the personal identity of both adults and children.[11] Rebelling against the ego disintegration that comes from being a nobody, many youngsters are striving to be heard, to be "something," even if delinquency seems to provide the only way.

Building in Alienation

There is ample evidence to support the contention that *most public schools are instruments of the dominant society*. There is very little evidence to support the contention that they take the initiative in effecting social change. In other words, they reflect the existing dominant social order. As a matter of fact, although the schools of this country vary widely in location, type, organization, and other characteristics, their basic educational premises are remarkably uniform. One authority describes them as follows:

1. *Native intelligence in children is measurable.*
2. *Our devices used for measuring children's intelligence are sufficiently accurate to be relied upon.*
3. *Only certain children are capable of completing an academic program in depth.*
4. *Children capable of completing an academic program can be identified in the early years of their elementary education.*
5. *Program tracks other than academic, such as vocational and clerical, should be provided for children incapable of completing an academic curriculum.*
6. *The school must help each student to adjust realistically to his abilities and potentialities as determined primarily by intelligence and achievement measuring devices.[12]*

Adding to such conditions that lead to alienation, most elementary and secondary schools demand that students (1) use "decent" language as opposed to "vulgar" language; (2) use grammatically correct language; (3) exhibit "clean" attitudes toward sex, drinking, etc.; and (4) talk over their problems instead of resorting to physically aggressive behaviors. There is little acceptance of lower-class coping techniques in classrooms, which frequently seem to be a world of "no" and "quiet."

In terms of low-achieving students, alienation can be redefined as

[11]See, for instance, William C. Kvaraceus, "Some Cultural Aspects of Delinquency," *Federal Probation*, 23 (March, 1959), 8–12.

[12]Nathaniel Hickerson, *Education for Alienation*, Englewood Cliffs, N. J., Prentice-Hall, 1966, p. 23.

follows: It is a general syndrome made up of a number of different objective conditions and subjective feeling states that emerge from certain relationships between students and the school setting. It exists when students are unable to control their immediate educative processes, to develop a sense of purpose and function that connects their education to the over-all organization of society, or to belong to integrated educational communities; and when they fail to become involved in the activity of education as a mode of personal self-expression.[13]

Student Reactions

There are many ways to adjust to feelings of alienation (see Table 17). Some students *retreat*—withdrawing and refusing to play the middle-class game of hard work and striving. Dropping out of school or getting "hooked" on drugs are symptoms of retreating. Other techniques include "tuning out" teachers by day-dreaming.

Some students become dissatisfied with their deviant behaviors and seek to *conform* to the standards of the dominant culture. This is playing the middle-class game with an expectation of winning. Conformists attend remedial or retraining courses. As a group, they are highly receptive to innovative programs that seem to offer a way to school success.

In other instances, students become moderately dissatisfied with "the system" of opportunities. When this happens, they substitute new means to achieve the goals of the dominant culture. Cheating on examinations or "shaking down" high-achieving students to get the answers are examples of ways students *innovate* to acquire passing grades.

Table 17
Modes of Individual Adaptation to Alienation

Modes of adaptation	Dominant culture goals	Dominant culture institutionalized means
Conformity	+	+
Innovation	+	−
Ritualism	−	+
Retreatism	−	−
Rebellion	±	±

+ = acceptance; − = rejection; and ± = rejection of prevailing values and substitution of new values.

Source: Reprinted with permission of the Macmillan Company from *Social Theory and Social Structure* by Robert K. Merton. Copyright © 1957 by The Free Press.

[13]This redefinition of alienation follows many of the thoughts of Blauner, op. cit., pp. 2–34.

Severe dissatisfaction with the existing dominant social system causes a few students to *rebel* in noncriminal, but nevertheless variant, ways (e.g., becoming hippies or black nationalists). These students have no illusion that they can succeed in the existing system, so they substitute new ones that seem to offer more hope of success.

There is also the possibility that when norms disappear or lose their holding power, a student may lose the ability to evaluate himself, to know what he is or even who he is. In *The Lonely Crowd*, David Riesman discussed alienated people who are "other-directed."[14] Even though such alienated individuals seem to follow the rules and regulations of the school, these lower-class students actually are playing the middle-class game of life just for the sake of playing it—believing that success is beyond their grasp. Life becomes a *ritual* in which they take pride in being "low achievers, but honest." These students receive low grades in academic subjects and high grades in citizenship.

A student's success or failure in school is not confined to academic achievement in itself. In one study, students who failed reading tests were observed to have symptoms of nervous tension such as restlessness, nail-biting, and insomnia; they physically or psychologically withdrew from school; they resorted to loudness and defiance; they became cruel to other children; they were generally inattentive.[15] In a similar experiment, pupils failing in reading and arithmetic tasks were studied. As a result of experiencing failure, some of these students appeared to be so afraid of additional failures that they set goals below past achievement, thereby protecting themselves from the possibility of further failure. Others were so demoralized that they set goals that were too high to be realistic, causing them to fail repeatedly.[16]

The child who fails in school tasks usually sets up some type of *defense mechanism* to protect himself (see Table 18). If, for example, he believes that he will fail, he may deny the reality of school and not study at all. In this way he can tell himself and others that he could have succeeded if he had wanted to. The emphasis on "good" grades increases anxiety and tension levels in students. Furthermore, oral recitations in the classroom add to these feelings, since incorrect answers are embarrassing, causing students to "look stupid" to the rest of the class. In this type of environment there may develop a comradeship between low-achieving students who have the ability to do better and those who lack such ability. Students in the former group may altruistically refuse to achieve at a higher level so as not to embarrass their friends in public.

[14]David Riesman, *The Lonely Crowd*, New York, Doubleday, 1955.
[15]Adolph A. Sandlin, "Social and Emotional Adjustments of Regularly Promoted and Non-Promoted Pupils," *Columbia University Monograph*, No. 32, 1932.
[16]Ernest R. Hilgard, "Success in Relation to Level of Aspiration," *School and Society*, 55 (April, 1942), 423–428.

Table 18
Summary Chart of Ego-Defense Mechanisms

Denial of reality	Protecting self from unpleasant reality by refusal to perceive or face it, often by escapist activities like getting "sick" or being preoccupied with other things.
Fantasy	Gratifying frustrated desires in imaginary achievements.
Rationalization	Attempting to prove that one's behavior is "rational" and justifiable and thus worthy of self- and social approval.
Projection	Placing blame for difficulties upon others or attributing one's own unethical desires to others.
Repression	Preventing painful or dangerous thoughts from entering consciousness.
Reaction formation	Preventing dangerous desires from being expressed by exaggerating opposed attitudes and types of behavior and using them as "barriers."
Undoing	Atoning for and thus counteracting immoral desires or acts.
Regression	Retreating to earlier developmental level involving less mature responses and usually a lower level of aspiration.
Identification	Increasing feelings of worth by identifying self with person or institution of illustrious standing.
Introjection	Incorporating external values and standards into ego structure so that individual is not at their mercy as external threats.
Compensation	Covering up weakness by emphasizing desirable trait or making up for frustration in one area by overgratification in another.
Displacement	Discharging pent-up feelings, usually of hostility, on objects less dangerous than those that initially aroused the emotions.
Emotional insulation	Reducing ego involvement and withdrawing into passivity to protect self from hurt.
Intellectualization	Cutting off affective charge from hurtful situations or separating incompatible attitudes by logic-tight compartments.
Sublimation	Gratifying or working off frustrated sexual desires in nonsexual activities.
Sympathism	Striving to gain sympathy from others thus bolstering feelings of self-worth despite failures.
Acting out	Reducing the anxiety aroused by forbidden desires by permitting their expression.

Source: From *Abnormal Psychology and Modern Life* by James C. Coleman. Copyright © 1964 by Scott, Foresman and Company and reproduced with their permission.

RELATED
THEORIES
Several theories that emphasize that adult behaviors can cause or prevent juvenile delinquency have relevancy to teacher-pupil interactions. We will briefly mention a few that seem apropos.

Parent Rejection
Nye concluded that rejection by parents is directly related to delinquent behaviors.[17] Indifferent or hostile parents are not likely to give their children sympathetic and constructive supervision; they often give no supervision at all. Only when they are embarrassed by the actions of their children will such parents attempt to maintain some or closer supervision. Even then, the parental supervision is not likely to be sympathetic and constructive. This type of adult response generates negative feelings in children toward their parents. Scott surmised that inconsistent patterns of indulgence and rejection also lead to delinquency.[18] Capricious variances of this nature tend to produce psychologically anxious children who are unhappy at home and unhappy when they are away from home. The general pattern of adjustment for such children is either withdrawal from contact with their parents and all adults or the seeking out of substitute parents who can offset the parental deficit in the home. We may further note that the outward mannerism of this type of child is often described as being "overbearing"—projecting a false picture of confidence. Teacher rejection, like parent rejection, not only has adverse effects on the child's adjustment while he is in school, but also has negative effects on his perceptions of other adults, impairing his ability to identify with middle-class role models.

Punishment
Short, Faris, and Nye have commented on the relationship between punishment and delinquency. Short hypothesized that love-oriented techniques of discipline are associated with strong superego formation and high guilt, whereas techniques of punishment not threatening loss of love are associated with normal superego formation and low guilt. Faris opposed punishment on the assumption that it is unnecessary if positive family relationships are present. Nye further stated that if discipline is extremely restrictive it may prevent the child from being able to participate effectively in family and peer-group activities. Yet, if discipline is absent or inadequate, the child not only will lack external control over his behavior but also will lack a set of clear-cut parental expectations. Finally, if discipline is unfair, it may prevent

[17] F. Ivan Nye, *Family Relationships and Delinquent Behavior*, New York, Wiley, 1948, p. 73.
[18] D. H. Scott, "Diagnosing Family Situations," *Social Work*, 11 (July, 1954), 940–953.

the parents from serving as positive role models to be imitated by the child.[19]

In a study of family management and delinquency, Slocum and Stone concluded that "democratic" management of the family is inversely associated with delinquent behavior. Teenagers in "democratic" families are more likely than those in "undemocratic" families to be social conformists. It is important to note that nagging and love withdrawal are present in most homes, democratic or undemocratic. The frequency of these conditions distinguishes the two types of families. Children accept and adjust better to discipline that is not punitive in nature.[20] Other studies imply that as long as there is an affectional relationship with parents or teachers, the child is least likely to rebel when discipline becomes a bit punitive.

Environmental Factors

Most juvenile delinquents live in environments conducive to perpetuating their behaviors. Inadequate recreation facilities, overcrowded and slum housing, adult crime, and unemployment are but a few of the environmental forces associated with juvenile delinquency. However, the fact that there are middle- and upper-income delinquents shows that the problem of delinquency is too complex to be attributed to a single variable such as income or a slum environment. The complexity of the problem is further shown by the fact that many boys and girls in low-income areas are able to insulate themselves against delinquency; nevertheless, it is difficult for schools to provide this insulation if they too reflect negative environmental conditions—overcrowded classrooms, dilapidated and inadequate physical plants, and underpaid personnel.

NEEDS OF STUDENTS

There are 43,000,000 children in the public elementary and secondary schools of America.

They attend classes in 110,000 buildings operated by 23,000 districts and staffed by 1,800,000 teachers, two-thirds of them women.

Their education costs about $28 billion a year, of which roughly 60 percent is raised through local taxes.

They have many things in common. But in many more they are as different as suburbia and Appalachia, Nob Hill and Harlem, poverty and wealth, ambition and apathy.

The schools they attend are as different as the communities that created those schools and operate them.[21]

[19]James F. Short, *Group Work and Gang Delinquency*, Chicago: The University of Chicago Press, 1965; Robert L. Faris, *Social Disorganization*, New York, Ronald, 1955, pp. 391–402; Nye, op. cit., p. 96.

[20]Walter L. Slocum and Carol L. Stone, "Family Culture Patterns and Delinquent-Type Behavior," *Marriage and Family Living*, 25 (February, 1963), 206.

[21]Adapted from Peter Schrag, *Voices in the Classroom: Public Schools and Public Attitudes*, Boston, Beacon, 1965, p. 1.

Much of the plight of middle-class teachers (white and nonwhite) assigned to teach students who live in depressed areas stems from their inability to understand the educational needs of culturally disadvantaged students. Many teachers erroneously think that culturally disadvantaged students are alien people, having needs unlike those of "normal" students. A closer analysis of the behavior of such children shows that *it is not the classroom adjustment patterns of low-income students that are "abnormal" but their opportunities to behave as "normal" students.*

The Deprived-Student Syndrome

Recent studies indicate that culturally disadvantaged students do not need misplaced kindness; instead, they need empathetic—but fair— guidance. Often teachers attempt to "make up" for cultural differences. That is, with so much emphasis being placed on understanding and assisting culturally disadvantaged students, some teachers fall victim to the urge to engage in overcompensatory actions. No matter how well intended, however, social promotions, watered-down curricula, and unearned rewards cause additional problems. They may, in fact, lead to the *deprived-student syndrome.*

The deprived-student syndrome refers to the process by which students use their deprivations to "beat" the system. "When I want to get out of doing my school work," a Target Area high school student confided, "I just tell my teachers that I couldn't do it because my old man was drunk or the light company turned off the lights." This is beating the system—getting by without doing the required work. Using their cultural differences as a crutch, they hobble through school, manipulating their perceived manipulators (school personnel). Another student, sharing a trade secret, said: "If I wants to sack in late and miss my first class, I don't worry about it. My principal says it's a miracle that I come to school at all with all the hardships that I have to put up with." Few students in this category are seeking success in school. They only seek to minimize the complications during their stay in school.

To the student who knows that he is not putting forth the required effort but receives positive sanctions, success in school is meaningless. Yet, in a way following the maxim that the shortest distance between two points is a straight line, many students are content to "slide by" with a minimum of effort. In the study cited in Chapter 12, most of the respondents who had slid by wished that their teachers had caught them. Commenting on her school efforts, a high school graduate said: "I got through with no sweat, but it didn't learn me anything. . . . If I had to do it over again, I'd study harder. Now, the only thing that I can do is day work or something else that don't call for school work." School under these conditions becomes a game in which, if one wins, he still loses. Making it "easy" for disadvantaged students to succeed in school also makes it easy for them to fail in the world of work.

Negative Sanctions

Other studies indicate that the less effective teachers assume that if a child comes from a poverty-stricken home he is also of low intelligence. Along with this assumption goes the belief that low-income students do not know the difference between properly executed and improperly executed school tasks. These teachers capriciously parcel out rewards and punishments. Unlike those who love them to their academic deaths, teachers using this technique are thwarting the student's desire to compete for middle-class success symbols.

"Why bother?" a resigned Target Area student frowned. "When they feel like giving you a good grade, they will. Johnny and I turned in the same book report. I copied his. He got a 'C' and I got a 'B.'" Negatively conditioned for school life, most low-income students desperately need positive sanctions to keep them in school. This does not mean that they should be given high grades for low achievement but, instead, recognition for effort and improvement. The positive sanctions should fit the achievements. Such sanctions can range from smiles and words of encouragement to superior rating and scholarships.

Psychologically, it is less difficult for students to adjust to consistent teachers than whimsical ones. For example, the teacher who consistently marks low is better appreciated than the teacher who is a low marker on some days and a high marker on others. "I don't mind him giving me a 'D,'" a puzzled junior high student said, "but he gave me a 'B' for the same score last week." Confused and powerless, many low-achieving students simply give up and sink deeper into the mire of mediocrity. Teachers who ignore individual needs for fair evaluation are given noncomplimentary titles. Both bad work *and* good work become synonymous with wasted work. If enough teachers act this way, students do not drop out—they are pushed out!

Desired Qualities

Culturally disadvantaged students need more teachers who will touch them, smile at them, yes, smell them. Teachers who view them as being a group of highly contagious disease germs either consciously or subconsciously seek to avoid contact with them. "These teachers are as phony as a three-dollar bill," a Target Area student remarked. He was specifically referring to a teacher who habitually poured disinfectant around the classroom and wiped all books and pencils with tissues before accepting them from students.

The methods used by the more effective teachers to gain the confidence of culturally disadvantaged students usually do not include human relations lectures but, instead, human relations *actions*. The teacher who routinely schedules an "I understand your problems" lecture is suspected of being a phony. In fact, the students frequently test this pretense of comradeship by contriving a "moment of truth." Many teachers fail these human relations moment-of-truth tests, as did the one who jumped back violently when a shabbily dressed Target Area girl rushed up to receive the warmth that had just been promised in the lecture.

Studies indicate that low-income students are more likely to conform to middle-income standards of cleanliness if they believe that conformity is for *their* benefit and not a squeamish teacher's. Sometimes the antagonism shown by low-income students is an attempt to gain recognition. The classroom cut-up illustrates this point. Unable to gain recognition under calmer conditions, a student acting up in class goads a reluctant teacher into at least touching and smelling him.

Advantaged or disadvantaged, all students need (1) teachers who are honest in evaluating their work, (2) teachers who tell them where they are in their current skill development and what they need to achieve in order to improve, and (3) teachers who assist them in their efforts to improve.

PROGRAMS TO
COMBAT ALIENATION

To put it bluntly, more and more students in our public schools are not learning the basic skills. It is obvious that alienation, with all its unfortunate concomitants, is both a cause and a result. Some stark conclusions can be drawn from these facts: The successful programs that do exist must be increased in number and scope merely to "hold the line," to prevent the creation of an even larger proportion of alienated people. Furthermore, basic changes and modifications must be made in many of our social institutions if the development of alienation is to be prevented in the future. Such basic changes require the basic reorientation of much of our social philosophy. Then the reorientation must be translated into social action on a broad scale. (There has been a beginning, of course, although only a beginning. The federal antipoverty programs are an example.)

We now consider, specifically, programs to combat the pernicious effects of alienation in the schools. There are those, both professional and nonprofessional, who advocate punishment, strict discipline, or psychiatric clinic referral as treatments for alienated students. The studies cited earlier show that these methods are almost never required; furthermore, they are rarely effective. Educators who believe that punishment stops deviant behaviors should heed criminologists who state that punishment per se has never proved an effective deterrent to crime. Nor is strict discipline a good solution. After all, many studies show that alienated children come from a variety of home discipline situations, including those in which parents are overly strict, indifferent, lax, or inconsistent in administering discipline. Reasonable guidance and understanding between the younger and the older generations are more likely to produce conformity. As for referral to psychiatric clinics, this is not a cure-all. For instance, two investigators who evaluated the methods and results of one clinic concluded that it did not prevent most youths referred to it from becoming adult criminal offenders.[22] It thus appears that solutions to student alienation must go beyond punishment, strict discipline, and psychiatric clinics.

The major emphasis, therefore, should be on *organizational changes*, particularly in removing blocks to learning, broadening opportunities for work or leisure-time activities, and otherwise making education a more meaningful experience for all students. The aim of any school-community program undertaken to improve student opportunities and reduce alienation must reward socially acceptable behaviors in order to enhance the self-concepts of students. A wide variety of programs, based on specific needs, should be available. Personality disturbances are best ameliorated through individual treatment. On the other hand, intergroup conflict suggests the need for community organization programs; diminishing antisocial group behaviors usually requires group work programs.

The establishment of meaningful criteria for the development of comprehensive action programs is a difficult task. In the case of alienation, any action program must "pay off" in terms of a measurable reduction in alienation. This is best done through a *multidiscipline* approach. Social practitioners generally agree that a multidiscipline program should not only consist of lectures, sermons, or films. It should rather include a great amount of student involvement. Along with this change should go rewards that are realistically meaningful to the students. For example, initially, a trip to a jazz workshop may be far more meaningful to low-income students than a visit to a concert. (Later, the concert may be a suitable reward.)

Programs in which students are the actors are better than those in which they are acted upon. Some school officials realize that inner-city students feel powerless and that action programs therefore must provide them with opportunities to control and manipulate their school experiences successfully by using procedures acceptable to their teachers. Programs designed primarily for the institutionalization and containment of students are inferior to those that permit individual growth and development. Any program that is capable of helping alienated students to succeed or fail on the basis of their abilities is vastly superior to one in which they must passively await the capricious or paternalistic decisions of their teachers.

[22]LeMay Adamson and H. Warren Dunham, "Clinical Treatment of Male Delinquents: A Case Study in Effort and Results," *American Sociological Review*, 21 (June, 1956), 312–320.

Successful Programs

The following are only some of the activities conducted by schools that have been successful in curtailing student alienation:

1. Existing educational opportunities are expanded and new opportunities created. This requires adjusting the school program to meet the needs of the students. Teachers attempt to plan systematic, concrete, and meaningful experiences *with* students.

2. Remedial programs are provided to prepare unqualified youths to utilize existing opportunities and be prepared for future opportunities.

3. Counseling programs are provided to raise the educational and occupational aspirations of students to a sufficiently high level to channel them out of cultures of poverty—and keep them there.

4. Provisions for rewarding approved behaviors are built into the school program. Such rewards include letters of commendation, scholarships, camperships, promotions, contest prizes, and public recognition.

5. "Successful" student and adult role models are provided, not only from the middle class, but from all social classes. Teachers attempt to make it psychologically comfortable for students to aspire to any occupation that is functional for survival in the dominant culture. Where possible, teenagers and adults living in the local communities are used as role models.

6. Local community organizations are encouraged to initiate and/or expand school-community projects.

7. Special programs for leisure-time activities, including those encouraging self-direction, are expanded.

8. Periodic surveys are made to evaluate the effectiveness of existing services and also to point out gaps in total services. Frequently, "outside" evaluators are used.

Conditions of alienation exist in all schools, but they are more pronounced in urban schools. The specific programs each school enacts are better when they are based on research findings significant for the specific students concerned. That is, school programs should take into account who the students are, the nature of their world, and their particular needs. By working cooperatively with other agencies, schools can avoid needless duplication of research or program efforts. Strategies for intervention to achieve or influence change in the lives of "deprived" and "alienated" students require a number of techniques. Because school programs are "helping" or "enabling" programs, their major focus should be on activities that assist students to achieve success within the dominant society.

SUMMARY

1. Deviant behaviors often reflect a lack of opportunity to carry out conforming behaviors. Students who are unable to succeed in school become *alienated*.

2. The four dimensions of alienation are powerlessness, meaninglessness, normlessness, and isolation. Because most public schools are instruments of the dominant society, they are likely to be alien places for lower-class children.
3. There are many student modes of adjustment to alienation: Some retreat, others innovate, a few rebel, and some become ritualists, but most seek to conform to teachers' expectations.
4. Teacher rejection has adverse effects not only on a pupil's school adjustment but also on his ability to identify with middle-class adults.
5. It is not the classroom adjustment patterns of low-income students that are "abnormal" but their opportunities to behave as "normal" students. Culturally disadvantaged students need teachers who will be honest in evaluating their work, tell them where they are in their current skill development, and assist them when they want to improve.
6. The best programs for combating students' alienation allow the student to conform voluntarily to the norms of the school. Lectures, sermons, or films alone are not adequate; the students must be involved in the change process.

SELECTED READINGS

Bereiter, Carl, and Siegfried Englemann, *Language Learning Activities for the Disadvantaged Child,* New York, Anti-Defamation League of B'nai B'rith, n.d. Suggestions of ways to make learning fun for culturally disadvantaged children. Program guides include those under the broad headings of "language fundamentals," "reading readiness activities," "counting," "singing," and "hints for conducting language learning activities."

Bernstein, Basil, "Language and Social Class," *British Journal of Psychology,* 11 (September, 1960), 271–276. An analysis of differences in speech and language patterns between social classes, and also analysis of performance on intelligence tests.

Crow, Lester D., et al., *Educating the Culturally Disadvantaged Child,* New York, McKay, 1966. The purpose of this book is to assist the classroom teacher in understanding problems of lower-class children.

Davis, Allison, *Social Class Influences Upon Learning,* Cambridge, Mass., Harvard University Press, 1948. A brief summary of middle- and lower-class subcultures and their relationship to basic learning patterns.

Kirman, Joseph M., "Teacher Survival in Difficult Schools," *High Points,* 46 (April, 1964), 69–70. Believing that middle-class discipline techniques are ineffective with lower-class children, Kirman offers alternative techniques for controlling slum school classes.

Klineberg, Otto, "Life is Fun in a Smiling Fair-Skinned World," *Saturday Review,* February 16, 1963, 75 ff. This article examines widely used readers for children in elementary schools and questions their relevancy for non-whites.

Merton, Robert K., "Social Structure and Anomie," *American Sociological Review,* 3 (October, 1938), 672–682. A sociological approach to understanding alienation and the various modes of adjustment.

Miller, Harry L., and Marjorie B. Smiley, *Education in the Metropolis,* New York, The Free Press, 1967. The special focus is on analyzing conditions of alienation in urban schools.

Noar, Gertrude, *Teaching and Learning the Democratic Way,* Englewood Cliffs,

N.J., Prentice-Hall, 1963. This book offers (1) a perspective of the classroom from the vantage point of "slow learners" and (2) gives practical suggestions for bridging the cultural gap between school and lower-class values.

Riessman, Frank, *The Culturally Deprived Child,* New York, Harper & Row, 1962. Riessman challenges the schools to broaden their curriculums to provide a better education for culturally deprived children. This book complements John M. Beck, et al., *Teaching the Culturally Disadvantaged Pupil,* Springfield, Ill., Charles C Thomas, 1965; Robert D. Strom, *Teaching in the Slum School,* Columbus, Ohio, Merrill, 1963.

Smith, Herbert A., and Lawrence L. Penny, "Educational Opportunity as a Function of Socio-Economic Status," *School and Society,* 87 (September, 1959), 342–344. A discussion of educational opportunities as a foremost requisite for quality education.

Smuts, Robert W., "The Negro Community and the Development of Negro Potential," *Journal of Negro Education,* 26 (Fall, 1957), 456–465. The author considers both the utilization and development of the Negro population. He also examines the willingness of whites to grant Negroes greater opportunities.

15

Attitudes Reconsidered

There are, I suppose, all kinds of prejudice and discrimination, and not all of it is either obvious or overtly brutal. There is also a kind of prejudice that is swaddled around with appearances of benevolence and of compassion and the kind that is expressed commonly not as an explicit hostility to Negroes so much as an affectionate preference for a "different type of child." *

Dilapidated buildings, inadequate facilities, and racially segregated schools are part of a pattern found in cities throughout America. The slums of the inner-cities, limited access to legitimate opportunities for minority groups, and the competition inherent in the existence of differing socioeconomic classes—all are interconnected. Building new schools, improving facilities, and racially integrating classrooms help somewhat, of course; the foremost problem in American education, however, is to adjust the curricula to meet the needs of culturally disadvantaged students.

The challenge to those professionally involved in public education is to find a way to bridge the culture gap between school personnel and core-city students. If we cannot bridge the gap, more and

*Jonathan Kozol, *Death at an Early Age*, New York, Bantam Books, 1967, p. 149.

more schools will become merely custodial settings, sterile, cold, dedicated primarily to the maintenance of discipline; while possible educational innovations are ignored, even resisted. Quality education requires a top-quality school staff. *A top-quality staff does not spring into existence as soon as black and white bodies are placed together within the same school.* Nor is length of time in the teaching profession an adequate indication of quality. College courses and in-service training programs aimed at improving staff knowledge of culturally disadvantaged students are vitally important, of course. But what about the many teachers who, in spite of such training, cling to the belief that disadvantaged children are innately inferior? This basic question can be answered only by exploring the causes and effects of a basic aspect of our existence—social attitudes.

SIGNIFICANCE OF SOCIAL ATTITUDES

It has long been known that there is a general relationship between the conditions of social and economic status and attitudinal development. Attitudes are, in a sense, the causes of one's psychosocial effectiveness or ineffectiveness. What are attitudes? How are they formed?

Attitudes pertain to the way a person feels, thinks, and behaves in a definite situation. They are the results of feeling tones associated with every human experience. An individual responds with approval or disapproval when stimulated by a person, situation, idea, or activity. This response of acceptance or rejection is established by the person's past experiences. If most of these previous experiences have taken place in a negative stimulating environment, his attitudes are likely to be negative. Positive or negative attitudes become engrained in the personality. When an individual accumulates too many undesirable feeling tones, he develops negative attitudes toward himself, others, school, and society in general.

For our purposes, *a social attitude is a mental and neural readiness to behave in a given manner toward an object or a situation.* Broadly, it defines an individual's position for or against an object, situation, person, or group. Although not directly observable, attitudes can be inferred from overt behaviors. Whether or not attitudes can actually be measured is the subject of conflicting opinions among scholars. The great educational psychologist Edward Thorndike believed that everything that exists, including attitudes, can be measured.[1] On the other hand, many behavioral scientists consider attitudes too intangible to be measured accurately. In any case, although numerous attitude-measurement tests and scales have been developed, their validity is debated among experts. This lack of confidence in the ability of scales to

[1]See, for instance, Edward L. Thorndike, "Nature, Purposes, and General Methods of Measurement of Educational Products," *Yearbook of National Social Studies Education*, 17 (1918), 16–24.

measure attitudes is the major obstacle to wider acceptance of attitude study findings. Whatever the difficulties of measurement, educators have been warned over the years, even as early as 1929, that many negative attitudes toward racial minority groups are developed in elementary and secondary schools and, specifically, that *teachers* and *textbooks* are often responsible for fostering prejudice in children.[2]

The following propositions about attitudes are now quite generally accepted:

1. Attitudes are learned.
2. Attitudes are learned mainly from other people.
3. Attitudes are learned mainly from other people who have high or low prestige for us.
4. Once attitudes have been learned, they are reinforced by a variety of motives.

In other words, social attitudes represent the residue of an individual's past experiences.

Some Determinants of Attitudes

A person seldom has a single clear-cut attitude on any given issue. It is likely, for example, that inner-city teachers are both for and against raising the academic standards within their schools. Nor are all attitudes on a given issue equally well recognized by the individual. For instance, when, as is all too frequent, a teacher rejects low-achieving students of another race, such behavior is not merely a consequence of the teacher's attitude toward the students in question, but also toward his normative reference groups and toward himself.

Most people seek to maximize the rewards in their external environment and to minimize the punishments. They also seek to minimize internal discomforts. Because they serve as judgmental standards, many of our attitudes are defenses of our self-images. We usually have psychological balance when most of the others in our groups have the same attitudes as we have. Festinger vividly illustrated this:

It is not necessary for a Ku Klux Klanner that some northern liberal agree with him in his attitude toward Negroes, but it is eminently necessary that there be other people who also are Ku Klux Klanners and who agree with him. The person who does not agree with him is seen as different from him and not an adequate referent for his opinion.[3]

Even though we cannot always accurately predict an individual's overt behaviors from his known attitudes, it is probable that an attitude results in overt behavior directly proportional to rewards and indi-

[2]For two early examples, see Bruno Lasker, *Race Attitudes in Children,* New York, Holt, 1929; *Can You Name Them?* New York, American Committee for Democratic and Intellectual Freedom, 1939.

[3]Leon Festinger, "Informed Social Communication," *Psychological Review,* 57 (Summer, 1950), 273.

rectly proportionate to punishments. It further is likely that insofar as people maintain attitudes, they hold or relinquish them depending on the social context and their relationship to it.

The Persistency of Attitudes

Some attitudes are maintained *in spite of* evidence to the contrary, especially when the evidence contradicts an individual's established habits of thought. An example of this might be a high school counselor who refused to assign a high-achieving inner-city student to the college preparatory curriculum because most of the relevant studies conclude that inner-city students fare poorly in college preparatory courses.

Many attitudes are maintained *in the absence of* evidence. For example, when in doubt about the abilities of low-income students, some teachers assume that they are incapable of achieving at the same level as affluent students. These teachers believe it is sufficient to offer work at "the level" of the students, not providing them with opportunities to achieve at a higher level.

Still other attitudes are maintained *on account of* evidence. People who think this way generally cite evidence (e.g., inner-city parents do not attend PTA meetings) that supports their beliefs (e.g., inner-city parents are not interested in their children's education). Implicit in this method of attitude formation is the assumption that what has been true in the past will be true in the future.

Finally, some attitudes are maintained *on the basis of objective* evidence. Not many such attitudes, however, are based on minimally biased, scientific data. Instead, most are the results of less objective "common sense," "faith," and "intuitive" methods of inquiry.[4]

EFFECTS OF NEGATIVE ATTITUDES

Weaknesses in the validity of attitude measurements are not adequate reasons for failing to seek ways to diminish negative student self-concepts that, in turn, impede their ability to succeed in school. *It is likely that until culturally disadvantaged students feel good about themselves, as a reflection of their perceptions of the "educational climate," they will have great difficulty learning academic concepts presented in the classroom.* This premise is consistent with Jersild's view that if the perceptions of self in the educational climate are mainly derogatory, then the growing child's general attitudes toward himself are mainly derogatory. The child toward whom the predominant attitude of significant persons has been one of hostility, disapproval, and dissatisfaction tends to view the world in similar terms. He has difficulty

[4]For a critique of the basic methods of attitude formation as related to philosophical inquiry, see John H. Randall, Jr., and Jestus Buchler, *Philosophy: An Introduction*, New York, Barnes & Noble, 1961, pp. 44–73.

in seeing or learning anything better, and, although he may not openly express self-depreciatory attitudes, he has a depreciatory attitude toward others and toward himself.[5]

Students' attitudes toward school can be measured by the extent to which they think about their school experience in favorable or unfavorable terms. Their opinions, of course, reflect how much at ease and how welcome they feel in the school. And these feelings in turn reflect the extent to which administrators and teachers encourage or discourage their participation in both academic and extracurricular activities. When a student believes that there is no opportunity to voice his particular concerns or complaints and that there will be no opportunity for fair and full consideration of them by the school personnel, he becomes frustrated and critical, refusing to cooperate with or support them.

Administrators

School administrators are called upon to play a myriad of social roles, including being able to judge standards, coordinate programs, write reports, and bridge the culture gap between the school and home and community. They are placed in the unenviable position of *ombudsmen* who must cut through the system's rules and regulations without being offensive to anyone. Above all, they must be able to work well with community residents, even though many do not desire a cooperative relationship.

Warner's "Jonesville" study shows clearly that school administrators come into pre-existing sociocultural complexes where "what to do" and "what not to do" are determined by local values, beliefs, prejudices, and ground rules. Not only must they immediately adjust to and become an integral part of these preexisting social systems, but they must also organize school activities to meet the demands of people outside the community who are in power positions.[6] Hollingshead's "Elmtown" study points out that administrators must respond to the pressures from both outside and inside the system, as well as to the pressures imposed by their own professional standards. The role expectations emanating from these three sources often lead to conflict.[7]

Because inner-city administrators (and teachers) typically do not serve in schools of their own neighborhoods, they are thought of as "strangers." Furthermore, because of their high turnover rate, administrators usually do not remain in one community long enough to become a part of it. To a great extent, they are professional "gypsies." Except for superintendents, urban school administrators are almost totally inbred and they tend to organize into formal and informal

---

[5]Arthur J. Jersild, *In Search of Self*, New York, Teachers College, 1960, p. 13.
[6]W. Lloyd Warner, et al., *Social Class in America*, Chicago, Science Research Associates, 1949, p. 86.
[7]August B. Hollingshead, *Elmtown's Youth*, New York, Wiley, 1949, pp. 128–132.

associations that protect the status quo. In the case of large-city superintendents, many grew up and first taught in small towns and gained their major administrative experience in rural or suburban schools; thus they are likely to be conservative in their approaches to educational changes.

Lacking intimate knowledge of their school neighborhoods, many administrators seek to compensate by becoming *regulations specialists*, committing to memory school rules and regulations. When performing as regulations specialists, they also become *defensive specialists*, reacting to community problems but seldom acting *before* problems erupt. This type of fire-fighting activity creates additional problems for other administrators who earnestly desire to be the education leaders in their school-communities but, instead, find themselves forced to be inept followers.

The principal has the key role in determining the educational climate within his building. He makes the major difference between a school that holds competent teachers who can get a fair amount of work done and a school that has a high turnover of demoralized, dissatisfied teachers. Indeed, no one person has greater influence on every phase of school life than the principal. Although limited somewhat by external controls, each principal can initiate new school programs. This initiatory power takes on added importance in inner cities where many slum school students and their parents feel that the school is a closed system and that they are outsiders. Such attitudes create an atmosphere in which students feel like recalcitrant prison inmates who are "serving time" while anxiously seeking an opportunity to escape.

The administrative problems in an inner-city school are only partially reflected in concrete factors such as student dropout and teacher turnover rates. Other problems are related to the maintenance of self-esteem. In an only slightly exaggerated illustration, a vicious *administrative self-esteem circle* can operate as follows: department heads do not want the assistant principal to know that they have problems; the assistant principal does not want the principal to know that the department heads have problems; the principal does not want the assistant superintendents to know that he has problems in his school; the assistant superintendents do not want the superintendent to know that they have problems within their districts; the superintendent does not want the board of education to know that he has problems within his system; the members of the board of education do not want the voters to know that there are any school problems.

Some other factors that may negatively affect the attitude of an inner-city school administrator are: students who frequently are as much as three years behind the achievement level of non-inner-city students, high absenteeism and yearly turnover, teachers who are unprepared to teach culturally disadvantaged students, and parents who have hostile attitudes toward the school. When a principal believes that the maintenance of discipline is his chief function, he is likely to behave in a manner that fosters negative staff attitudes toward the students, parents, and school-community. In these instances, a principal gives support to the myth that lower-class students are uneducable. On the other hand, when a principal views his job as being the community's education leader and the one to bridge the culture gaps between students, parents, and school personnel, he is likely to foster a positive school climate.

Most studies suggest that a principal should approach his school's problems with an adequate degree of sensitivity to the needs, motivations and aspirations of the staff, the students, and the community. This involves giving recognition and support to staff members who believe that most inner-city students have both the ability to learn and the capacity to acquire the motivation necessary to achieve at a higher level than current data indicate. This also involves developing and maintaining an atmosphere in which the staff, students, and parents participate in a common effort to improve the quality of education within the school. Although changes in physical facilities and lowering of class sizes are important to this endeavor, no such limited effort can compensate for the lack of administrative sensitivity.

Teachers

A considerable part of the socializing task performed by parents in earlier times has now been given to teachers. Teachers supervise meals and recreation; give training in hygiene; inculcate ideals of fair play; and give lectures about sex, public safety, and moral obligations. The importance of teachers' successfully playing their roles is underscored by the fact that they can promote or fail students, reward or punish them, encourage or discourage them, clarify or confuse assignments. What the teacher does with this power is of much significance to the quality of education afforded students.

Role expectations for teachers, like those for administrators, are varied and conflicting. A few of the roles a teacher is expected to perform are:

Judges achievement
Conveys knowledge
Keeps discipline
Gives advice, receives confidences
Establishes a moral atmosphere
Is a member of an institution
Is a model for the young
Participates in community affairs
Is a public servant
Is a member of a profession
Keeps records[8]

[8]Jean D. Grambs, "The Role of the Teacher," quoted in Lindley Stiles (ed.), *The Teacher's Role in American Society*, New York, Harper & Row, 1957, pp. 73–93.

Of these and the many other roles that could be listed, two main categories emerge. One category refers to the teacher as a *director of learning*. The other category refers to the teacher as a *mediator between the cultures of the school and the community*. Although the more effective teachers are able to perform most roles without conflict, the specific attributes of a "good" teacher are difficult to describe.

As more schools become community-oriented, the role of the teacher is pushed and pulled into greater vagueness. Contradictory demands from community leaders result in teachers being called on to be permissive but strict, helpful but nondirective, masters of subject areas willing to accept evaluation from parents, and participants in community affairs not able to vote on vital school-community issues (teachers are seldom members of school boards). Somehow they must maintain discipline, "proper" social distance, and respect, while simultaneously overcoming student resistance to learning.

Vagueness in teacher roles is further reflected in definitions of "correct" and "incorrect" student behaviors. There is considerable variation even within a school, although in general the climate or tone is fairly consistent within a given school. This climate is set by the principal and passed on to the teachers through educational "osmosis." In judging student behavior, many teachers think in terms of specific factors such as the following:

Teachers seem very ego-involved in what they consider to be "correct" standards of behavior, and the student who violates these standards is in for a difficult time, even though the violation has little connection with the intellectual tasks of the classroom. These standards involve cleanliness, dress, speech, and control of aggression. They often override academic factors in selecting those who will be educationally mobile.[9]

It is obvious that *the key figure in the entire educational process is the teacher*. Teacher attitudes have the most significant impact on pupil achievements, including intelligence test scores. In short, a teacher's attitude can determine the failure or success of his students.

If a teacher believes that a child is incapable of being educated, it is likely that this belief will in some way be communicated to the student in one or more of the many forms of pupil-teacher interactions and that the belief will then be proved to be true. This is the self-fulfilling prophecy. Conversely, there is impressive evidence that shows that if a teacher believes a child is capable of being educated, he often *becomes* capable. Thus, the self-fulfilling prophecy also can work in a good way.

The whole area of teacher attitudes and behavior and their effect on children has been the subject of an increasing amount of research in recent years. For instance, Robert Rosenthal, professor of social relations at Harvard, and Lenore Jacobson, principal of a San Francisco school and a former teacher, have reported on their study of teacher

[9]Harold L. Hodgkinson, *Education in Social and Cultural Perspectives*, Englewood Cliffs, N. J., Prentice-Hall, 1962, p. 88.

attitudes in a thought-provoking book, *Pygmalion in the Classroom.* At a public elementary school in a lower-class community, they led the teachers to believe that the results of a test showed that certain pupils would "spurt" in achievement. Actually, the designated children were picked at random. Later testing showed that these children had improved in their school work to a significant degree, whereas those not designated as "spurters" had made far smaller gains. Some of the achievements of minority-group children who had been designated as "spurters" were particularly dramatic.

Nothing was done directly for the disadvantaged children at the school—no crash programs, no tutoring, no museum trips. There was only the teachers' belief that certain children had competencies that would become apparent. Rosenthal and Jacobson speculate that the teachers who brought about intellectual competence simply by expecting it must have treated those children in a more pleasant, friendly, and encouraging way. In other words, they must have indirectly communicated their expectations to the children. Such behavior is known to improve intellectual performance, probably because it increases motivation. They speculate further that additional research might show exactly *how* teachers can effect dramatic improvement in their pupils' competence without changing their teaching methods. Then other teachers might be taught to do the same. They eloquently conclude:

As teacher-training institutions begin to teach the possibility that teachers' expectations of their pupils' performance may serve as self-fulfilling prophecies, there may be a new expectancy created. The new expectancy may be that children can learn more than had been believed possible. . . . The new expectancy, at the very least, will make it more difficult when they encounter the educationally disadvantaged for teachers to think, "Well, after all, what can you expect?" The man on the street may be permitted his opinions and prophecies of the unkempt children loitering in a dreary schoolyard. The teacher in the schoolroom may need to learn that those same prophecies within her may be fulfilled; she is no casual passer-by. Perhaps Pygmalion in the classroom is more her role.[10]

Teachers' attitudes present a long-term problem; the solution to it may well revolutionize the teaching in our public schools. Meanwhile, there are many other obvious and more immediate problems connected with the role of teachers in American education today. As many critics of the public schools have pointed out, most of the teachers who are teaching the disadvantaged are not able to do the job properly; many of them are not able to do it at all.

It is extremely difficult to recruit competent teachers for inner-city schools. Experienced teachers are reluctant to accept positions in these schools for several reasons, including fear of having to maintain discipline, teach apathetic students, and counsel hostile parents. Teacher-preparation institutions unfortunately do little to explode the erroneous

[10]Robert Rosenthal and Lenore Jacobson, *Pygmalion in the Classroom: Teacher Expectation and Pupils' Intellectual Development*, New York, Holt, 1968, pp. 181–182. (The book describes the authors' procedures, careful scientific methods of analysis, results, and conclusions in detail.)

myths about slum schools or, where needed, give neophytes adequate coping techniques. Some of the characteristics of slum-area schools and those who *are* teaching in them make depressing reading. For one thing, the teachers are more likely to feel that other teachers regard their school as inferior.[11] As a researcher put it, "The common thought is that you must be dumb or flunked basket-weaving in college to get in a school like this."[12] In another illustration of a negative attitude, a teacher in a New York City school that was 85 percent Negro said, "Most of the teachers here are rejects from the other schools in the system, and the principal only wants a quiet school."[13] One observer wrote, "Just walk the halls in many of the inner-city schools and one can hear more evidences of vehement scolding and admonishing than evidences of lessons being taught and learned."[14] It is not surprising that slum schools have the highest teacher turnover rates.

It also seems to be true that teachers in slum schools are more likely to have low verbal abilities, to have a more limited understanding of the cultural differences of their students, and to be less knowledgeable about their subjects than other teachers.[15] Many inner-city teachers have a low level of irritability, causing them to be fearful of and anxious about student misbehavior. The typically restless slum child quickly becomes a "trouble-maker" and a target of unrelenting discipline. At the other extreme, teachers become overly permissive and encourage play skills instead of academic achievement. The former type of teacher does not want his students to make any noise and the latter type does not want them to be quiet.

The child brings to school the "enculturated" patterns and disorders of home. Usually these are classified by teachers' anxious assumptions into stereotypes about "poor-whites," Negroes, Mexicans, Japanese, Indians, and others. Some stereotypes are more precise than others. In California, Negroes are considered "aggressive" (the old South would say "impudent"); Mexicans are considered to be of two classes, one "aristocratic," the other undesirably common; American Indians are at the bottom of the minorities' heap, the Japanese are close to the top; "poor-whites" are alarmingly "uncooperative." Struggling to impart middle-class goals, the teachers actually deal with the responses of pupils to their social horizons. . . . These teachers call such pupils "retarded . . . apathetic . . . underachieving . . . truant."[16]

In many cases, teachers who do have positive attitudes toward inner-city students are themselves the subjects of ridicule and cynicism from

[11]U.S. Commission on Civil Rights, *Racial Isolation in the Public Schools*, Washington, D.C., U.S. Government Printing Office, 1967, p. 105.

[12]A. B. Cheyney, "Teachers of the Culturally Deprived," *Exceptional Children*, 32 (October, 1966), 83.

[13]Carol LeFevre, "Inner-City School: As the Children See It," *Elementary School Journal*, 67 (October, 1966), 10.

[14]Nancy L. Arnez, "The Effect of Teachers' Attitudes Upon the Culturally Different," *School and Society*, 94 (March, 1966), 151.

[15]U.S. Commission on Civil Rights, op. cit., p. 203.

[16]Ruth Landes, *Culture in American Education: Anthropological Approaches to Minority and Dominate Groups in the Schools*, New York, Wiley, 1965, pp. 47–48.

other teachers (although they often are well liked by their students). The ridiculing teachers frequently are trying to escape the guilt associated with their own lack of achievement. If nonconforming behaviors persist, the norm-violating teachers may even be ostracized. The actual reasons for ostracism are usually hidden by ostensible ones, failing to contribute to the school social fund, refusing to eat lunch with the "in-crowd," or being too "open" in staff meetings. To put it bluntly, such teachers who try to improve the quality of education in slum schools are thought of, in labor union terms, as "scabs" who seek to increase the work output above the usually low standards.

Despite all the uncertainties in their roles, some teachers are able to accomplish a great amount of work. Perhaps what is needed are more studies of *successful* teaching practices. Young teachers are rarely supervised by experienced teachers who have been able successfully to motivate and teach culturally disadvantaged students. They are seldom shown how they too may be able to teach the erroneously labeled "unteachables" (see Chapter 13). The environmental pulls and pushes not only affect the role performances of teachers but also the academic achievements of their students. Those who feel at ease in their job tend to create a classroom atmosphere that is conducive to learning; those who do not, make their classrooms a repressive place for themselves and their students.

Pupils

Pupil-teacher relationships are best when they are *reciprocal*. That is, by means of supportive guidance the pupil learns to develop academic skills through successive experiences; in turn, the teacher also matures through the interaction. As a pupil grows in proportion to the fulfilled expectations and respect a teacher has for him, his self-concept, attitudes, and aspirations grow accordingly. Failure in this type of educational climate becomes not a way of life, but a challenge to be overcome. A teacher's understanding of a child's cultural and environmental background better enables him to accept the child, whatever his failings.

A large number of slum-school children desperately want to accept and believe their teachers, but because of a lack of believable experiences, the prodding of the teachers often falls on selectively deaf ears, trained to "tune out" the "fairy tales" of middle-class success. Most of those who initially believe in middle-classness become bitter, marginal people unable to achieve the great dream; their bitterness is intensified by the chiding of their equally disenchanted peers who say "I told you so." Teachers and administrators, more often than not, are perceived by students as being *remote adults*. The students' relationships with school personnel are typified by mutually resistant, hostile, and suspicious attitudes. They come to believe that school personnel are adults who do not understand them or want to talk with them or take time to listen to them.

School expectations for cleanliness, punctuality, orderliness, and other middle-class behaviors are initially unrealistic for most lower-class students. Few allowances are made for students who have not learned these behaviors before attending school. Instead, most teachers assume that rapidly reading the school rules once or twice is sufficient indoctrination. Other problems center on classroom behavior. Overtly aggressive behavior, for example, is a masculine characteristic that is not condoned in the classroom. In addition to being a threat to the superordination role of teachers and administrators, it disrupts the sterile decorum of the classroom. Nevertheless, this denial of a role characteristic prevents boys from trying to overcome the negative psychological conditioning associated with female dominance. Even though inner-city teachers are encouraged to "take the lower-class child from where he is" to middle-classness, most behave as though these children are capable of conforming to school rules with a minimum of difficulty.

The achievement role is the most difficult for lower-class students to perform. Sometimes they are able to pretend to high job aspirations and identity with nonlower-class characters in textbooks. But their luck runs out when they are taking examinations and aptitude tests. The frustrations that many inner-city students feel because they are unable to succeed in school cause them to devalue the role of "scholar." Yet, like automatons, they come back time and time again for an enormous dosage of negative reinforcement. Low-achieving students often learn demeaning role behaviors—frequently becoming overly accommodating and obsequious—in hopes of at least gaining non-academic teacher acceptance.

Students with low academic records find nonacademic activities closed to them. This decision is usually made by administrators and teachers on the ground that they should not "overextend" themselves. The result is that such activities become luxuries that low-achieving students are rarely given an opportunity to experience. Their inability to achieve either academic or nonacademic success earns most slum-school students the depreciatory labels "slow learners" and "un-educable." As a result, when placed in one of the low-ability groups, they learn to play the appropriate roles of school failures.

Community Leaders

Inner-city school educators are becoming increasingly community-conscious. Many are thus striving to eradicate the negative attitudes of parents and community leaders toward the schools. Negative parental attitudes of course affect the achievement and attitudes of students. Every school-community has within it the source and power to engender positive attitudes. The need for more educators to assume leadership roles has been explained by Kenneth Clark:

A default in leadership by professional educators can only reduce their total influence in the community at large. . . . If leaders do not lead when the need is urgent, what is the nature of their leadership? If the educators respond merely to pressure, whether it is against integration, like the Parent's and Tax Payer's groups, or for it, as in the case of civil rights boycotts, they have abdicated their right to decision on the basis of their knowledge and insight as educators, and submitted to force for the sake of peace at almost any price. This is a passive rather than dynamic, socially responsible role. They must respond rather to need, for the poor and neglected are generally too intimidated by authority, too fearful of rejection and humiliation, to press their own cause. It is the responsibility of strong leadership to represent the common good—not only because it is right, but because the despair of the weak in the end threatens the stability of the whole.[17]

There are three prerequisites to working with local leadership: (1) educational leaders must identify community leaders who are outside the formal institutions and agencies of local government; (2) they must educate the informal leaders to the needs of the schools; and (3) they must show their educational leadership through professional competence and participation in community programs. All this requires leadership that is wise in the sense that school representatives can communicate with all members of the community; that they have a thorough knowledge of their community's social-cultural structure; and that they are aware that there should be no special segment of the community bearing the entire responsibility for decisions on the education of the young. Thus the school must be "of" and "in" the community, not an isolated agency claiming to serve it.

The more effective school-community programs encourage and support indigenous leadership. With the assistance of specialized personnel (i.e., community agents and school social workers), community leadership is both identified and allowed to develop. This approach to school-community leadership does not support the status quo, not even a benevolent one. In any case, there are relatively few successful "neighborhood schools" or "community schools" in the inner-cities. Too often, school personnel discourage neighborhood or community resident participation. This is reflected in the small number of schools that operate evening programs or reach out to bring neighborhood residents into their decision-making processes. It is also reflected in professional resistance to bringing volunteer and paid paraprofessionals into the schools as teachers aides.

CHANGING
ATTITUDES
It is easier to detect negative attitudes than to change them. Three general techniques for changing attitudes are: offer new information, threaten punishment, or promise a reward.[18] None of these techniques

[17]Kenneth B. Clark, *Dark Ghetto*, New York, Harper & Row, 1965, p. 152.

[18]Daniel Katz, "The Functional Approach to the Study of Attitudes," *Public Opinion Quarterly*, 24 (Summer, 1960), 165–204.

works well, however, in modifying ego-defensive attitudes. When attitudes are based on defense of ego, additional techniques are required —removal of the threat, catharsis or the opportunity for ventilation of feelings, and acquisition of understanding by the individual of the reasons for his attitudes.

Very important in any practical attempt to change attitudes is group influence or pressure.[19] The group serves two basic purposes in relation to attitude change: It can be a medium of change and it can be a target of change. Furthermore, the greater the sense of belonging an individual has, the greater will be the influence of the group on him; and the greater the prestige he has in the group, the greater will be the influence he can exert on others.

As a rule, *attitudinal change is more likely to occur when there is free expression within the group without fear of reprisal and when the group members are allowed full participation in important group decisions.* The lecture method by itself has practically no influence on attitudes.

Within the Classroom
Teachers can change students' attitudes toward learning by uncritically accepting questions and ideas (while at first ignoring mistakes in speech) and by helping them develop sophisticated skills of inquiry—especially how to sustain, refine, and test a hypothesis. This approach is related to numerous suggestions that teachers orient their techniques to the students' backgrounds, needs, and abilities. Pupils learn better in classes where they feel wanted and respected. Therefore, the classroom climate must take account of students' feelings; it should not be focused only on learning subject matter. Pupils must first accept themselves as worthy beings before they can comfortably venture forth into ego-threatening classroom learning situations. The characteristics of school programs that assist in the formation of positive attitudes in children toward themselves and others have been outlined as follows:

1. *That program is most desirable which accepts the child as he is and provides recognition of accepting behavior on the part of each child toward every other child. The teacher herself must be the first and primary exponent of such a policy. . . .*

2. *That program is most desirable which leads to an understanding on the part of children of the reasons why different people live as they do. Children ought to have an opportunity to learn that there are reasons for the way in which any people live. . . .*

3. *That program is most desirable which fosters interaction among representatives of different groups, with each representative being given equal status. Every child in every classroom group ought to have an equal opportunity, within the limits of his ability, to undertake any task. . . .*

[19]Dorwin Cartwright, "Achieving Change in People: Some Applications of Group Dynamics Theory," *Human Relations*, 4 (1951), 381–392.

4. That program is most desirable which makes it possible for each child to achieve but not at the expense of others. Too often our schoolroom programs are such that in order for one person to feel successful, it must be apparent that he is first or second rather than last or next to last. . . .[20]

Many educators conclude that teachers can combat antiintellectualism by appealing to the interest of the child and by consciously working toward "higher levels" of intellectual appreciation. However, they question the soundness of seeking unilateral conformity to middle-class standards. Instead, they urge that the disadvantaged child be given an opportunity to assist in making changes in school procedures.

Within the School

Attempts to bring about attitudinal changes can result in a wide variety of individual behaviors that result from resistance to the changes. For example, a person who is the target of efforts to make him change may become angry or silent, blush, change the subject, or withdraw. Alvin Zander outlined a number of factors related to such resistance:

1. Resistance can be expected if the nature of the change is not clear to the people who are going to be influenced by the change. . . . There is some evidence to support the hypothesis that those persons who dislike their jobs will most dislike ambiguity in a proposed change. They want to know exactly what they must do in order to be sure to avoid the unpleasant aspect of their jobs. . . .

2. Different people will see different meanings in the proposed change. . . . We tend to see in our world the things that we expect to see. Complete information can just as readily be distorted as incomplete information, especially so if the workers have found discomfort and threats in their past work situation.

3. Resistance can be expected when those influenced are caught in a jam between strong forces pushing them to make the change and strong forces deterring them against making the change.

4. Resistance may be expected to the degree that the persons influenced by the change have pressure put upon them to make it, and will be decreased to the degree that these same persons are able to have some "say" in the nature or direction of the change. . . .

5. Resistance may be expected if the change is made on personal grounds rather than impersonal requirements or sanctions. . . . Many administrators can expect trouble in establishing a change if it is requested in terms of what "I think is necessary" rather than making the request in light of "our objectives," the rules, the present state of affairs, or some other impersonal requirement.

6. Resistance may be expected if change ignores the already established institutions in the group. Every work situation develops certain customs in doing the work or in the relations among the workers. The administrator who ignores institutionalized patterns of work and abruptly attempts to

[20]Celia Burns Stendler and William E. Martin, *Intergroup Education in Kindergarten-Primary Grades*, New York, Macmillan, 1953, pp. 22–27.

create a new state of affairs which demands that these customs be abolished without further consideration will surely run into resistance.[21]

Resistance to change is minimized to the degree that the change agent helps the subject to understand the *need* for the change and gives the subject an opportunity to exert an influence on the change process. Only after reasonable efforts to change negative attitudes have failed does it seem advisable that malfunctioning personnel be relieved of their administrative or teaching assignments. Those who would quibble over what is "reasonable" should remember that if professional educators cannot decide on its limits, less experienced, nonprofessional groups will do so by default.

Within the Community

Inner-city school personnel make a serious mistake if they sit quietly back and assume that their pupils will automatically become "ambassadors" creating positive public opinion. More often than not, slum-community residents are familiar only with negative school characteristics, especially low-achievement and high dropout rates. If a school is to become truly a *community* school, its staff must do the following: (1) meet with citizens face-to-face to discuss such things as school needs, new programs, boundary changes, and complaint procedures; (2) seek ways to improve two-way communication between school and community, with special attention given to reaching residents who do not normally attend school meetings; and (3) clearly indicate that they want community residents to participate in school affairs and that they want their opinions. Finally, *the more effective school is a place of innovation and constant evaluation*, and this fact, too, must be communicated to the larger community.

SUMMARY

1. Children learn many of their negative attitudes toward racial minority groups in elementary and secondary schools.
2. It is likely that until culturally disadvantaged students feel good about themselves, as a reflection of their perception of the "educational climate," they will have great difficulty learning basic subjects.
3. The principal plays the key role in setting the educational climate within his building. He has influence over *every* phase of school life. If a principal has a negative attitude toward his school-community, he is likely to communicate this feeling to his staff.
4. Teachers are the single most influential force on the student. Their attitudes have impact on pupil achievements. If a teacher believes that a student is uneducable, the student is given this message in one or more of the many forms of pupil-teacher interactions.

[21]Alfred Zander, "Resistance to Change—Its Analysis and Prevention," *Advanced Management*, January, 1950, 10.

5. Pupil-teacher relationships are best when they are reciprocal; both pupils and teachers should "grow" as a result of the interactions.

6. Attitudinal changes are likely to occur when there is free expression without fear of reprisal and when the person with the attitudes to be changed is involved in the change process.

7. A student's negative attitudes toward learning generally change when teachers first uncritically accept his questions and ideas and later help him to develop sophisticated skills of inquiry.

8. Teachers' and administrators' negative attitudes generally change when they realize the *need* for change and are given an opportunity to influence the change process.

9. Community residents' negative attitudes change when school personnel show that they want and will accept community participation in school affairs. Community schools should be places of innovation and constant evaluation.

SELECTED READINGS

Association for Supervision and Curriculum Development, *Leadership for Improving Instruction*, Washington, D.C., National Education Association, 1960. This book can be of great use in workshops and courses aimed at changing attitudes by working with formal and informal group leaders.

Becker, Howard S., "Social Class Variations in the Teacher-Pupil Relationship," *Journal of Educational Sociology*, 25 (April, 1952), 451–465. An objective study of ways in which teachers observe, classify, and react to social class differences in the behavior of their students.

Clark, Kenneth B., *Prejudice and Your Child*, Boston, Beacon, 1955. This book provides a lucid analysis of factors that contribute to prejudice in children. Along with the causes, the author suggests cures and methods of prevention.

Dahlke, H. Otto, *Values in Culture and Classroom*, New York, Harper & Row, 1958. A presentation of relationships between teacher values and classroom behaviors.Teacher-pupil and school-community relationships are the main areas of concern.

Davidson, Helen H., and Gerhard Lang, "Children's Perception of the Teachers' Feelings Toward Them Related to Self-Perception, School Achievement and Behavior," *Journal of Experimental Education*, 29 (December, 1960), 107–118. The authors corroborate earlier studies that emphasize the importance of teacher attitudes upon pupil performances.

Duryer, Robert J., "Reactions of White Teachers in Desegregated Schools," *Sociology and Social Research*, 44 (May–June, 1960), 348–351. A description of the attitudes of white teachers toward minority group children. Implicit in this short article are other problems of desegregation.

Kozol, Jonathan, *Death at an Early Age*, New York, Bantam Books, 1967. An excellent study of the effects of teacher attitudes on pupil performances. A more scientific analysis is found in Robert Rosenthal and Lenore Jacobson, *Pgymalion in the Classroom: Teacher Expectation and Pupils' Intellectual Development*, New York, Holt, 1968.

Loretan, Joseph O., and Shelley Ulmans, *Teaching the Disadvantaged*, New York, Teachers College, 1966. This book is based on the rationale that children from lower-class homes have intellectual capacities far greater than standardized tests indicate. Programs and guidelines are offered for better developing the capacities of disadvantaged children.

Stiles, Lindley J. (ed.), *The Teacher's Role in American Society*, New York, Harper & Row, 1957. Analysis of the wide range of social backgrounds from which teachers come and implications of this diversity for the attitude of administrators, teachers, and students.

Yoshino, I. Roger, "Children, Teachers and Ethnic Discrimination," *Journal of Educational Sociology*, 34 (May, 1961), 391–397. A descriptive study of the ethnic attitudes of young children and their teacher's influence in shaping these attitudes.

16

Role Models for Middle-Classness

Malcolm, one of life's first needs is for us to be realistic. Don't misunderstand me, now. We all here like you, you know that. But you've got to be realistic about being a nigger. You need to think about something you can be. You're good with your hands —making things. Everybody admires your carpentry shop work. Why don't you plan on carpentry?*

WITHIN THE
DOMINANT SOCIETY
In earlier chapters we have drawn many generalizations that serve as bases for this chapter. Some of them are:

1. Opportunity should accompany raised aspirations (Chapter 14). If we raise the aspirations of students without offering corresponding opportunities for their realization, we may cause *more* psychological damage than if we left the low aspirations unchallenged. Initially, low-aspiring students think only that they cannot succeed in school. They often believe at the same time that they will somehow succeed in "real life." But if we raise their aspirations without providing opportunities to

---

*Malcolm X, *The Autobiography of Malcolm X*, New York, Grove, 1964, p. 37.

match the new expectations, we doom them to complete self-depreciation —to the realization that they cannot succeed at *anything*.

2. Pedagogical abilities and attitudes are more important than racial characteristics where teachers are concerned (Chapter 15). Ignoring individual teaching abilities and attitudes merely to integrate a school staff certainly assures the students of multiracial teachers, but it assures them of little else; indeed, it may actually mean that most of their teachers are ineffective.

3. Schools alone are seldom able to raise the educational and occupational aspirations of students significantly (Chapter 13); there are too many other influences in their lives. Nevertheless, teachers and administrators can set the change process in motion. If school personnel are limited in their effectiveness as change agents, they should at least be aware of the extent of their limitations. It might be better to acknowledge that educating the "whole child" is hardly ever a real possibility.

We have also considered at some length ways to assist lower-class youths in their efforts to fit rigid middle-class molds. At this point, we should again ask: What's so good about being middle class? And we should again answer the question: Children of lower-class, poverty-stricken homes statistically are least likely to succeed, either in education or occupation. This is a demonstrated fact that we must recognize. When we do recognize it, we have taken a first important step: we enter the social-action arena realistically aware of the effects of poverty.

Facing a problem realistically equips us to evolve a solution realistically. It is obvious that if we are to prepare poverty-stricken children to compete equally in the larger society, we must enlist the full cooperation of all three important factors in children's lives—the home, the school, and the community.

We must then evaluate the solution realistically. This kind of total cooperation is difficult to achieve, and even when it is achieved, the task is formidable. For instance, social practitioners often use the culture gap as an excuse for the low quality of education in inner cities; it is actually more a cause. In other words, the culture gap impedes attempts to coordinate community efforts; the lack of community efforts impedes attempts to improve the schools; the poor schools impede attempts to diminish the culture gap. It is a classic *vicious circle*. But it must—and can—be broken. Meanwhile, while trying to organize total community cooperation, each community organization must do its best to help poverty-stricken people to become socially and financially secure citizens. After all, the fact remains that *no matter how many, if any, related community forces assist in the educational process, lower-class students will be thrown into competition with middle-class students for most of the dominant society's success goals.* It is therefore up to the school to help the lower-class students to survive by learning middle-class roles; for if they reject them, they resign themselves to a life of lower-class roles.

It is important to note that middle-classness is *not* a panacea for solving social problems. Changing one's life style is equivalent to substituting one set of social problems for another. The better adjusted students are able to select the best aspects of many subcultures.

Types of Models

The concept of *role models* is not new to the social sciences, but systematic attempts to analyze the concept in terms of "role theory" and "occupational identification" are fairly recent. One sociologist concluded that the selective character of identification should be emphasized. In "identifying" with his father, for example, a boy does not *become* his father (even in imagination); he wants to be *like* his father (and his older male siblings) in the *sex role*.[1]

Inner-city children most frequently are socialized in an environment conspicuous for families that lack high-status occupational role models. It is true that within the school setting, there are many role models for students to emulate, most of which are fairly high status: superintendent, principal, assistant principal, teacher, counselor, secretary, custodian. But it is well known that the influence of the family is more important. In any case, social scientists and educators generally agree that it is not the lack of high-status occupational role models alone that is debilitating, but this lack combined with the psychological effects of being poverty-stricken. Foremost among these effects are a poor self-image and a correspondingly low level of educational and vocational aspirations. Few low-income students, for example, realistically project themselves into professional or top-level white collar jobs; few realistically expect to attend a college or technical school after graduation from high school. One study of the post-high school plans of Detroit high school seniors found that most of the inner-city respondents did not plan to enter any type of school after graduation, nor did they have a prospect of a job.[2] In most cases, they foresaw entering a period of "nothingness," drifting from place to place, seeking vocational direction. In guidance terms, individuals under these conditions are still developing preferences for types of occupations.

Vocational development can, however, be a descending movement as well as an ascending movement. It is not true that most inner-city youth are already at the bottom of their occupational development and can only go "up." Repeated failures may cause them to give up and stop trying entirely. There is an urgent need for educators and community leaders to help lower-class students gain better insight into the broad range of occupations and to assist them in acquiring the educational preparation necessary for achieving these goals. In addition,

[1]Harry M. Johnson, *Sociology: A Systematic Introduction*, New York, Harcourt, Brace & World, 1960, p. 104.
[2]Ernest T. Marshall, "Post-School Plans of Detroit Public School Seniors," Detroit, Detroit Public Schools, 1964 and 1965.

there is a need to improve their self-images. None of these needs is being adequately met by the school, home, or any other social agency. It is hardly surprising, therefore, that the disadvantaged are the least effective producers in our society.[3] Graduates of inner-city schools have an unemployment rate several times that of their more fortunate contemporaries. Even when they do secure employment, it is generally of the semiskilled, unskilled, or service categories.

Social Class Identification

A person is said to identify with a *social role* when he internalizes it, adopts it as his own, and strives to learn the necessary behaviors for conformity. He is said to identify with a *social group* when he internalizes the role system of the group and considers himself a member of it. An individual's false judgment of his ability to achieve a social role is as important as a true judgment. For example, a potentially brilliant student who falsely believes that he cannot become class valedictorian because his parents are lower class is not less discouraged than a student who correctly holds this belief because he has little aptitude for school subjects. Most aspiration theories do not take into account variations of aspirations that may be caused by social class identification and the strength of the drive for success. In other words, although members of a given social class are holders of the same general aspirations, they can and sometimes do acquire aspirations attributed to other social classes. The following assumptions about lower-class youths and middle-class roles seem valid:

1. Individuals who try to function only as members of their own cultural groups are less likely to experience severe adjustment problems. On the other hand, those who seek to function as members of groups other than their own are more likely to experience severe adjustment problems. It is extremely difficult, but it is not impossible, for lower-class youths to identify with middle-class role models.

2. The degree of success that an individual has in switching social roles depends to some extent on the strength of his desire to achieve the feat. Thus, in trying to predict the success an individual is likely to have in switching, we refer to a *high-motivated* or a *low-motivated* person.

3. There are no rigid lines of behavior based solely on income. Middle-class-oriented students identify closely with their teachers and other middle-class adults; lower-class-oriented students do not. Inner-city schools have low-income, middle-class-oriented students, as well as middle-income lower-class-oriented students.

[3]Educational Policies Commission, *Education and the Disadvantaged American,* Washington, D.C., National Education Association, 1962.

Focal Concerns

The lower-class community has been described in terms of six "focal concerns"—trouble, toughness, smartness, excitement, fate, and autonomy.[4] These concerns are not unique to the lower-class community, but they seem to be accentuated there. Because lower-class boys have more school adjustment problems than girls, the following comments relate the concerns mainly to boys.

Trouble is the dominant focal concern of lower-class boys. Needless to say, their neighborhoods have ample built-in trouble factors: high crime rate, hazardous buildings, overcrowded schools, and a disproportionate amount of unemployment and underemployment. Nevertheless, although they live in what may be called "marginal communities," most youths are not marginal people; they manage to adjust to these conditions. Indeed, when they cannot adjust, they are overwhelmed, psychologically and physically, by their neighborhoods. Sometimes, of course, this happens.

A boy's status usually is based on his ability to risk trouble but to escape its consequences, thus maintaining a positive peer-group self-concept. Teachers, police, social workers, and other adults who demand law-abiding behaviors merely add to the challenge to engage in law-violating behaviors. If a youth's peer group condones low school achievement, he will actively seek to conform to this norm. In fact, below-average school performance is a kind of initiation rite necessary for acceptance into some lower-class groups. Teachers may have good intentions when they state that low-achieving lower-class students have negative self-concepts. But, as can be the case even with a theory that has compassionate origins, this one is only partially true. Teachers should not forget that, although the students' self-concepts may seem to be negative, low achievement in school can actually be a source of *positive* self-concepts in the minds of such students.

It is likely that middle-class adults who adopt an attitude of "cultural relativism" will be accepted as role models. According to this view, that which is good or bad is only so by *cultural* definition; thus law-violating behaviors of youths are neither praised nor condemned, but are understood within their cultural framework. Change from law-violating to law-abiding behavior comes as a result of exemplary adult role performance rather than moralistic preachings by teachers. Lower-class youths tend to identify with middle-class adults when they believe that middle-classness is not only a more meaningful alternative but also a possible one.

Toughness includes physical prowess, athletic abilities, and proclaimed scorn for "cultural" things like art and literature. Much of the emphasis on toughness in lower-class subcultures appears to be related to mother-centered homes; boys continually seek to establish their masculine

[4]Walter B. Miller, "Lower Class Culture as a Generating Milieu of Gang Delinquency," *Journal of Social Issues*, 14 (1958), 5–19.

identity. In the dominant culture, masculinity is closely tied to physical toughness but limited to formally sanctioned games such as football, basketball, and hockey. On the other hand, lower-class youths develop a physical toughness that is not directly related to formal games. For them, it is a means of neighborhood survival. Thus, lower-class boys enter school culturally conditioned to disrupt orderly classroom decorum.

The boy who cannot defend himself in a fight or who does not have other things "going for" him becomes an easy mark for shakedowns, pranks, and other ego-deflating activities. "Other things" include being able to run faster than most boys, having tougher siblings or friends, or being physically handicapped. Effeminate male teachers are seldom considered role models. Although they may be highly competent in their jobs, the boys tend to reject them because of their lack of masculinity. Such teachers are jokingly referred to as "queers," "fairies," or "homos." Adult role models need not be athletes, but it would be to their advantage to be able to talk about sports. Usually they should not talk about art or literature (unless it is their occupational field) until they have convinced the youths that they are men who understand physically aggressive boys.

Smartness is the ability to outsmart someone else without being outsmarted or "conned" yourself. The hustlers on the block are considered to be smart because they work with their brains and not their backs. The list of smart people ranges from numbers men to pimps, many of whom have big cars, lots of money, and pretty women as proof of their abilities. Middle-class adults who make derogatory statements about such smart people usually do not score (rate) high with lower-class youths. Such remarks not only give a "sour grapes" impression, but also focus unneeded attention on deviant occupations. A better tactic seems to be for middle-class adults to let the lower-class youths know that they too are aware of the youths' usual range of occupational choices and then to show them the advantages of a wider range that includes middle-class occupations.

Rarely is income a good selling point when middle-class adults are competing for a lower-class youth's acceptance with lower-class adults engaging in deviant occupations. After all, a successful pimp or card shark earns considerably more than a successful school teacher. The real appeal of middle-classness is its conformity to the dominant cultural norms. Thus, such seemingly obvious attributes of middle-class occupations as "acceptance," "honesty," "legitimacy," and "prestige" should be emphasized, for they can become part of the lure for lower-class boys who seek middle-classness.

Excitement is found in activities that flirt with trouble. Drinking, playing the "dozens" (see Chapter 13), and being sexually promiscuous are some of the most usual of these activities. Excitement, of course, is closely related to toughness. Middle-class adult role models should provide lower-class youths with new types of activities that are exciting but do not lead to trouble. Scouting trips, roller-skating, ball games, wrestling matches, and jazz concerts are examples. Sometimes a quiet milk-shake in a local drug store is excitement enough for a boy. There are many activities middle-class boys find boring and "old hat" that are new and exciting for lower-class boys.

Fate, most lower-class people believe, is the controlling factor over their lives. Believing that they are powerless to control their own lives, many lower-class youths easily become discouraged. The world of middle-classness is a chess game in which they are pawns but rarely kings, knights, or rooks. To black youths it is the white man's world. And most black youths are alienated from the white man's world.

Lower-class youths' preoccupation with fate makes them vulnerable to "get-rich-quick" schemes. Gambling is imagined to be the quickest and easiest way to "luck out." Although few lower-class people do "luck out," the hope of doing so provides excitement in an otherwise psychologically hopeless existence. Adults trying to motivate lower-class youths to seek middle-class occupations must convince them that they *can* control a portion of their lives. This is done by demonstrating the positive relationship between school success and job opportunities. Adult role models who have emerged from a background similar to that of the youths appear to have an edge in being able to make this comparison effectively.

Field trips to business establishments should include opportunities for the students to talk with employees who had once lived in neighborhoods comparable to the students'. In all instances, the students should be given an honest appraisal of their chances to get "good" jobs if they meet employment requirements. Finally, where possible, job requirements should be explained.

Autonomy, the absence of external positive group controls, is a basic obstacle to lower-class adjustment to middle-class norms. Feeling that they cannot achieve equal status, many lower-class people simply withdraw from middle-class competition. Ironically, when they set up new norms, these norms can lead to lower-class group conformity. The resulting behavior, which by middle-class standards is called "social disorganization," more correctly is "different cultural organization." Lower-class disdain for those who give information about neighbors to the police, teachers, and social workers illustrates behavior that rejects the patterns of a smoothly functioning middle-class society. This type of behavior is regulated by what might be called from a middle-class perspective "external negative group controls"—a form of autonomy. Such autonomy is exhibited by lower-class youths when they are late for appointments, when they conceal either happiness or unhappiness, or when they openly challenge middle-class authority. These displays of detachment and rebellion usually hide a cautious desire to be accepted by middle-class adults. Failure to understand this condition has caused many teachers prematurely to give up trying to motivate lower-class youths.

ROLE MODELS
FOR NEGRO BOYS

Because most lower-class Negro students identify with lower-class Negro adults, their occupational aspirations generally are not substantially middle-class. Instead, they stretch middle-class values *down* to their level of attainability. Lower-class adults, unlike middle-class adults, are mainly concerned with survival rather than status; thus they tend to have low aspiration levels.[5] Very seldom can adults other than parents, without parental assistance, alter a child's occupational aspirations. Thus, determining the social class *orientation* or *identification* of the parents is often far more illuminating than merely determining their race and income in assessing their influence and the probable level of the child's aspirations. Some lower-class children are able to identify with middle-class adults.

Much has been written about ways in which lower-class Negro students can be motivated to seek middle-class goals. Supplying role models for these students is a technique frequently recommended but seldom discussed analytically. There is a growing body of literature recommending that guidance personnel recruit "successful" Negro adults to serve as occupational role models for lower-class Negro students. Nevertheless, this frequent procedure—providing only Negro adult role models for Negro children—*may inadvertently impede the movement of lower-class Negroes into the mainstream of the dominant American culture.* There are three primary reasons for this:

1. Identification with a role model in every detail does not usually occur. Seldom do we accept the "whole" of another person. Rather, we attempt to incorporate only those features to which we attach positive meanings. For example, small boys watching television programs generally identify with the heroes or, in some instances, the "socially acceptable" villains. This identification is primarily focused on non-racial characteristics. A cowboy with a fast draw, to continue the illustration, is admired for his fast draw and rarely for his racial designation in itself. However, the novelty of a Negro cowboy in a plot might cause some children initially to focus on his racial characteristics.

2. As a civil rights strategy, the concern for expanding job opportunities for minorities is well founded. Negro adults should be able to engage in *all* occupational activities. However, past and present conditions of racial discrimination have limited the kinds of jobs available to black Americans. Projects centering on providing Negro role models are attempts to expose lower-class black children to a broader range of occupational choices. A second disadvantage to providing only Negro role models, therefore, is that although they help in improving the self-concepts of lower-class Negro children, they do not demonstrate the total range of occupational alternatives. Along purely racial lines,

[5]Orville R. Gursslin and Jack L. Roach, "The Lower Class, Status Frustration and Social Disorganization," *Social Forces*, 43 (May, 1965), 501–510.

lower-class white students with only middle-class white role models are exposed to considerably more occupational choices than are lower-class Negro students with only middle-class Negro role models. Studies of racially integrated school staffs provide clear evidence that teachers whom the students like and seek to imitate represent all races.

3. Providing only Negro role models for Negro students implies an importance to "race," overshadowing occupational competency. It is ironic that a democratic society's concern for improving the self-image of a long neglected minority group is adding to the philosophical basis of "black separatist" doctrines. For example, some Negro students complain about white teachers who offer courses in Afro-American or Negro history. A typical remark is: "We need black people to teach black history. This will give us pride in being black. No white man can tell me about my past." A logical extension of this type of argument is that only Negroes can adequately teach and motivate Negroes.

Most lower-class Negro students *do* need to have their self-concepts improved. However, we should not confuse elements of programs that seek to enhance self-concepts with those that seek to expose students to the broad range of available occupations. These two aims must sometimes be accomplished in two different ways. Job competency, empathy with students, and masculinity are as important as race. Ideally, every male teacher should be a role model for lower-class Negro boys. Furthermore, no white teacher of either sex should feel that his race alone prevents him from being an adequate role model for his Negro students of the same sex. The widespread belief that this is the case is a false one.

BLACK NATIONALISM

Should American Negroes intentionally preserve the present caste-like social environment? That is, should they abandon all attempts to enter the dominant society on an equal basis with whites? As the black nationalists express it, should American Negroes think "black," buy "black"—live as "blacks" first and as Americans only incidentally? These are the stark questions raised by the current black nationalist movements in America.

Types of Nationalism

First, what is black nationalism? There are two basic types of black nationalist movements in this country today, *religious* and *political-economic*. Timothy Drew (1886–1929) was the first nationally recognized American Negro advocate of a religious movement (Moorish Nation of Islam), and Marcus Garvey (1887–1940) is the best-known American Negro advocate of a political-economic movement (Universal

Negro Improvement Association).[6] Both movements began in the 1900s. The two groups have some points in common (such as stressing personal cleanliness), but they also differ in many ways.

Religious black nationalism is primarily concerned with establishing racial identity through Oriental religious thought; it stresses "Asiatic" identity based on combined Moslem-Christian rituals. Members of these movements oppose secular entertainments and the use of alcohol, cosmetics, and tobacco. They also stress—as long as they are physically present—obedience and loyalty to the United States.

On the other hand, political-economic black nationalism ranges from establishing "African" identification to seeking separate black communities in the United States. The formation of a national state is the most immediate goal. Other major goals of these movements center on achieving black political and economic independence from white communities.

In addition to these two distinct types of movements, there are some black nationalist groups, such as the Black Muslims, that incorporate elements of both the religious and the political-economic philosophies. This fusion results in religious groups that seek political and economic independence within the United States.

Psychological Bases

To understand black nationalism fully, we must go beyond emotionalism and think through some of the social and psychological conditions that may lead Negroes to support a black nationalist movement. Things are not merely happening to Negroes; they are also being made to happen by them. The view that our past and current race problems in America are only a Negro (or white) problem is an oversimplification of the principles of social interaction; in fact, it is an erroneous oversimplification. The black racial bigot is no less a result of racial strife than the white racial bigot. Both are causes and effects of the same social phenomena.

According to Carl Jung, all men, regardless of their racial designation, strive for psychological unity, equilibrium, and stability.[7] Alfred Adler coined the term *creative self* to describe an individual's unique processes of interpreting and making meaningful experiences aimed at achieving psychological balance.[8] In other words, members of a group make no single response to psychological disequilibrium. Some become hostile, others clown, others assume proud mannerisms, still others withdraw. The type of adjustment will depend to a great extent on the sociocultural modes of reaction that have been inculcated.

[6]C. Eric Lincoln, *The Black Muslims in America*, Boston, Beacon, 1963, pp. 13 ff. See also George Henderson, "Black Nationalism and the Schools," *National Elementary Principal*, 57 (September, 1967), 15–20.

[7]Carl G. Jung, *The Integration of the Personality*, New York, Farrar and Rinehart, 1939.

[8]Alfred Adler, "The Fundamental Views of Individual Psychology," *Journal of Individual Psychology*, 1 (1935), 5–8.

Evaluating his experiences, Andras Angyal argued convincingly that the image that an individual has of himself may not be appropriate to his real needs.[9] Applying this analysis to Negroes, we can say that their negative self-concepts are causing many of them to project an unreasonably low estimate of their own worth. Before the late 1960s researchers observed that few Negroes had race pride. The present emphasis on teaching Negro or Afro-American history in elementary and secondary schools is one of many attempts to instill race pride in black children. Other efforts include providing racially integrated employment and showing Negroes regularly in the mass media—for instance, in magazine and television advertisements.

A Negro self-concept that is negative emerged out of unique group experiences. It emerged out of prolonged conditions of racial segregation and discrimination. The self-concepts of Negroes in America have been contaminated by a color-caste complex. Continuous second-class citizenship has dulled the aspirations of most Negroes. History is replete with illustrations of the failures of those who have actively sought to overcome racial inequalities. Failure, not success, is the norm. When considered as a group whose members have had many individual experiences, Negroes have a tradition of frustration when seeking racial equality.

It is a somewhat chilling thought, but it is true, nevertheless, that Negro reactions to group frustration are quite similar to the behavior of the Jews in Nazi Germany. These reactions appear in various ways:

1. *Resignation and defeat.* These reactions are characterized by feelings of depression and bitter consciousness of being submissive.
2. *Heightened in-group feelings.* Such emotions are expressed in a strengthening of family, religious, and racial group ties.
3. *Adoption of temporary frames of security.* The frames include those minority-group activities, such as jobs and organizations, that appear to offer a "way out."
4. *Shifts in levels of aspiration.* Diminishing aspirations are most notable in the areas of occupational and community status.
5. *Regression and fantasy.* These may range from mild neurotic reactions to severe psychotic diseases.
6. *Conformity to the majority-group norms and expectations.* Conformity to such norms evolves out of a need to avoid punishment.
7. *Changes in philosophy of life.* In contrast to the conformity reactions, changes in philosophy of life are closely related to resignation and defeat reactions and reflect the group's dominant preexisting philosophical tendency, which is usually fatalistic in outlook.
8. *Direct action.* Direct action resulting from ingenious, adaptive, and realistic planning is the basis of most organized nonviolent group activities.

[9]Andras Angyal, *Foundations for a Science of Personality,* New York, Commonwealth Fund, 1941, p. 121.

9. *Aggression and displaced aggression.*   Aggression against the majority group tends to be spontaneous but least likely to occur. When direct aggression does occur, it often takes the form of a riot. Until recently, the usual pattern was for minority-group people to displace their aggression to other minority-group targets.

The comparison between Negroes in America and Jews in Nazi Germany is particularly relevant in illustrating the fact that aggression is only one of many possible reactions to the social pressures of discrimination and frustration. Furthermore, this comparison appears to be more valid than one between Negroes and any other minority group in America. Jews were and Negroes still are the primary objects of hostile discriminatory practices; in both cases, much of the aggression of the dominant group was or is therefore diverted from other equally accessible minority groups. (By comparing a religious group with a racial group, we emphasize "human," instead of religious or racial, group reactions to extreme conditions of aggression.)

Of the reactions listed, resignation and defeat, diminishing aspirations, regression and fantasy, conformity to majority-group norms and expectations, and aggression are the behaviors most likely to be expressed in negative self-concepts. Clearly, no single set of reactions automatically causes people to adopt negative self-concepts. Most Negroes, however, seem to be prevented from acquiring positive social self-concepts as a result of their inability to achieve assimilation in the "dominant" white society.

Normative Reference Groups
Enthnocentrism is an outstanding characteristic of members of dominant cultures; they possess an exaggeratedly low opinion of minority groups and tend to judge them by the standards of their own culture.[10] Moreover, the self-concepts of persons who do not think highly of themselves appear to be determined largely by the responses of others, especially members of a dominant culture. Because ethnocentrism has not been an important characteristic of American Negroes, they have been receptive to ideologies of the white majority.

From birth to death, the Negro is handled, distorted and violated by the symbols and tentacles of white power, tentacles that worm their way into his neurons and invade the gray cells of his cortex. As he grows up, he makes a tentative adjustment to white power. At puberty, if he survives and if he remains outside prisons or insane asylums, he makes a separate peace—a peace of accommodation or protest. The price of this peace is high, fantastically high. The price, quite simply, is emasculation. The Negro not only dons a mask; he becomes, in many instances, the mask he dons.[11]

[10]Ross Stagner, "Personality Dynamics and Social Conflict," *Journal of Social Issues,* 17, No. 3 (1961), 28–44.
[11]Lerone Bennett, Jr., *The Negro Mood,* Chicago, Johnson, 1964, p. 9.

The concept of *anticipatory socialization*—taking on the views of a nonmembership group to which one aspires to belong—has added importance for this analysis. In the past, the amorphous, nonmembership "white middle-class" was the *normative reference* group to which almost all Negroes aspired. Even today, it probably is true that the definitions of the dominant white culture supersede contradictory Negro group definitions. The American Negro's dilemma has been summarized thus:

The Negro cannot choose both the dominant white culture and his own subculture. This sense of suspension between two societies and of dual membership presents enormous impediments to the process of adjustment. Negroes are involved, subconsciously though it may be, in assertion of membership in one [society] and the denial of membership in the other, or in the feeble assertion of both, or in the denial of the affinity with both.[12]

Given the historical and continuing relative deprivation of Negroes in America, it is surprising that we have not seen more incidences of Negro mob violence, psychiatric maladjustment, and other social pathologies. Perhaps the main reason why we have not is the desire of most Negroes to be members of the dominant culture. However, they react to social deprivation in many ways, and support for black nationalist movements is one such reaction.

A New Dream

Social rejection has caused some Negroes to abandon the American Dream of equality and substitute a new dream, black nationalism. As one psychologist has pointed out, we should not attribute a single reason to all individuals who join a group:

The real point to be stressed is that both organized and spontaneous social movements and processes are possible not because all individuals participating in them are identically (and sociologically) motivated, but because a variety of authentically subjective motives may seek and find an ego syntonic outlet in the same type of collective activity.[13]

Marginal Negro businessmen may view black nationalism as an escape from competition with white businessmen; aspiring black politicians may view it as a way to offset the effect of powerful white political machines; the unemployed may see it as an opportunity to get a job. In short, black nationalism attracts many people whose needs are by no means identical.

Black nationalist groups take lower- and middle-class black people out of the social arena that has white role models for emulation. At first glance this displacement of white role models appears to be a

[12]E. U. Essein-Udom, *Black Nationalism: A Search for an Identity in America*, Chicago, The University of Chicago Press, 1962, p. 24.

[13]George Devereux, in Neil J. Smelser and William T. Smelser (eds.), *Personality and Social Systems*, New York, Wiley, 1963, p. 29.

negative adjustment. It is negative *only* when acceptance by whites is a reality. Otherwise, the devaluation of white role models is both bearable and desirable. For those who feel that they can never achieve maximum success in the white man's society, black nationalism offers a black society, a new hope. John Howard wrote that Black Muslims, for example, believe that the Negro is lost in ignorance, that he must seek out his true *black identity,* that racial integration is a plot of the white race to forestall its own demise, that the time of white dominance is drawing near its end, and that the American black man must gain control over his own economic fortunes by setting up his own businesses.[14] Finally, according to Black Muslim philosophy, the black man should seek his own land within the continental United States.

Modern black nationalists are less attracted to the religious oriented Muslims and more drawn to the politically and economically oriented organizations that idolize the memory and writings of Malcolm X. They find direction in "black power," with its three basic components: black *pride,* black *self-determination,* and black *self-defense.* Elements of this doctrine form the basis for the thousands of Afro-American societies that have been organized in public schools and colleges throughout the nation. Black youths have "demanded" and in many instances received black studies programs and more black school personnel. Because of the growth of black nationalism in our schools, the once rigid system of public education is undergoing rapid changes.

Like certain aspects of psychotherapy, black nationalist organizations have therapeutic value, in the strict sense of removing symptoms of racial inferiority. The therapy results from changing the Negro's view of himself in a positive direction (black is good) and altering his view of white people and his relation to them (the black man is superior). Public school teachers would do well to analyze the effective teaching techniques and curriculum materials in Black Muslim schools. When based on a rigid code of conduct (such as cleanliness, well-mannered behavior, and abstention from alcholic beverages and narcotics), black nationalism contributes to an orderly society. However, when it is based on overt aggressive behavior called "self-defense," it is a threat to the white society. Contrary to many opinions, violence is not the black nationalist's *raison d'être,* although in any group process *de-individuation*—a reduction of inner restraints in individual members—makes violence possible.

Teachers and administrators represent the society that black nationalists have been taught to reject. This rejection tends to be based on exposure to teachers and administrators who consciously or subconsciously thwart the aspirations of students and parents. By using proper intervention techniques, educators can cause some black nationalists to change their negative views.

[14]John R. Howard, "The Making of a Black Muslim," *Transaction,* 4 (December, 1966), 15–21.

Counteracting Negative
Parental Attitudes
What are the techniques that educators can use to counteract negative attitudes of black nationalists toward public schools? In some instances the answer is "there are none"; feelings are too polarized and organizational structures are too rigid to allow either party to modify its behavior. In other instances, we can take our guidelines from the group dynamic principles.

Sense of Belonging.   Black nationalists must be given a sense of belonging to the school-community. This is best done by inviting them to participate in school programs and to serve on school committees. They should be given an opportunity to express *their* views. Until recently, parents living in economically disadvantaged communities were described as being "dormant," "nonparticipating," and otherwise "indifferent" to the operation of the schools. This lack of minimum level of community involvement provided some teachers with rationalizations for not giving low-income students a better education. "We can't reach them because their parents don't care" or "We do the best we can, but the home situation negates our efforts" are two of many reasons still bantered about at educational conferences. Underlying such rationalizations is a failure to understand negative attitudes toward the school and toward society in general.

Children who experience success in school are likely to find it easier to go to a school and participate as parents when they become adults. They hold a positive image of the school. Most low-income black adults, however, have negative images of their early school experiences. They, more than middle-income black parents, were the dropouts or the pushed-outs. This negative image of the school is likely to be reinforced when they return in later years as parents; their visits are likely to be only to discuss their children's failures. Thus, when low-income adults do join committees or causes aimed at improving school conditions, they bring along "chips" or "grudges."

The civil rights struggle and the advent of President Johnson's "Great Society" programs, especially the "war on poverty," have accelerated the involvement of alienated adults in school matters. Although they have been advocating this type of involvement for years, few school personnel are prepared to accept it when it actually happens. As a matter of fact, school people recently have begun to complain: "There's too much participation in school affairs by nonprofessionals." It is hard to avoid the conclusion that the type of parental involvement school people actually wanted was a rather submissive type. School personnel must now learn to work with community residents who are often anything but submissive; sometimes, in fact, they are militant.

Empathetic personnel.   School-community relationships take on a positive tone only after school staffs demonstrate that they empathize with the community residents and that they have enough professional competence to provide a top-quality education. The staff must adopt an attitude that conveys, in effect, "We are here to receive you, to understand your cultural conditions, so that we can provide you with the best possible education." To do this, school personnel need not feel *like* neighborhood residents, but they do need to feel *with* them.

As alienated community residents come into contact with understanding and helpful school personnel, their initial hostility gives way to friendly alliances. Many schools are administered so rigidly that school personnel are unable to break down hostile community barriers. Communication in these instances is a one-way process going from school to the community, with few channels open for the school to receive information or suggestions from nonschool sources. A common technique used by teachers and administrators in schools where low-income parents are considered "antagonists" rather than "protagonists" is "fancy academic footwork." It goes as follows: A visiting parent is first paralyzed by a series of unfamiliar four-syllable words; then the children's test scores are recited rapidly without explanation; then the teacher asks the parent why she cannot do a better job in helping her children adjust to school. The last question is a verbal "karate blow," aimed at humbling and embarrassing the already psychologically weakened parent. Relationships in such schools are, like the community residents, poor.

Parent organizations.   Parent organizations can provide a broad base of community participation in school activities. Parents should be recruited from the ranks of those who are sympathetic to the school administration, as well as from those who are not. Diversity, not consensus, should be the guide. When this happens, school personnel receive a wider range of feedback and are not likely to be in the position of the big-city school staff that, when confronted with a picket line around the school, suddenly realized that many community residents had complaints about the school. Parent-teacher meetings should serve as open forums for discussing problems *and* possible solutions.

Counteracting Negative
Student Attitudes
Curriculum.   Students should be encouraged to discuss controversial issues, including black separatism. Courses that place black people in proper historical perspective should be given priority over those that take them out of historical context and treat them as separate and unrelated Americans. Textbooks and other materials that present a realistic picture of Afro-American heritage should be used. Although historians now generally agree that life for black Americans did not begin with their slavery, some school textbooks have yet to concede this fact.

Black nationalist students must be shown that there is a "pay-off" in going to school. Schools in suburban and near-suburban neighbor-hoods generally turn out a statistically better product; the reading, writing, and arithmetic scores of their students tend to be higher than those of inner-city students. As inner-city residents become aware of these differences, their rhetorical questions become: Education for what? Dropping out of school? Getting a factory job? Or filling out forms for welfare assistance? Positive answers are likely to come if school systems employ black Americans in *all* roles, ranging from custodians to superintendents.

The attraction of schools.   The primary attraction that public schools have for black nationalists is their occupational preparation and not their social pronouncements. Educators who use class time in trying to change the philosophy of black nationalists are neglecting their aca-demic offerings, thereby minimizing the attraction of the school and certainly also minimizing their own effectiveness. Changes in philosophy are more likely to come about indirectly as all black children experience success in classroom situations. Teachers who are successful in chang-ing the attitudes of black nationalists are equally successful in creating marginal people, those who are neither black nationalists nor members of the dominant white society. Unless educators are willing to accept *completely* students when they do really want to enter the mainstream, it is better not to try to motivate them to change. Half of the task consists of bringing about an acceptance of a biracial society. The other half of the task consists of maintaining this acceptance.

Theory and practice.   Educational theorists periodically advise teachers to teach the "whole" child, but actually, of course, no teacher or any other person can ever know the whole of another individual. The major reasons for this gap between theory and practice lie in the unknown dimensions of each personality and also in the continual restructuring of its recognizable portions. Teachers should define clearly in their own minds what portions of the child they *can* educate and concentrate their efforts in those directions. This is not to say that teachers should seek only academic information about their students. Each student is a whole unit at any given moment of his school activities. He operates as a social, psychological, and physical entity, in terms of both his school successes and his failures. Furthermore, his school behaviors are inter-related with his other social and physical environments, his past ex-periences, and his own feelings about these aspects of his life.

In many instances, school systems must provide in-service training programs to acquaint their teachers with the social, economic, and philosophical reasons for majority-minority group differences. Teachers who are the most successful in teaching all children are those who understand and respect their students, whatever their backgrounds. This understanding comes from many sources—from experience, from study, from training, and from the teacher's own innate characteristics. When school personnel are involved in community life and when persons from the community are actively involved in school activities, school-community relationships are at their best, and still another way is provided for teachers to gain in understanding of and empathy with their students. These teachers are not trying to make black students over into whites, but, instead, to accept and educate all students.

The exact nature of a student's educational and occupational aspirations is determined largely by how well teachers help him to fit into the cultural environment of his school. The results of many studies unfortunately force us to the conclusion that most schools perpetuate, rather than ameliorate, cultural differences. Education, often described as being "the great social class equalizer," usually is anything but an equalizer in neighborhoods populated with a large percentage of alienated black residents. This fact naturally increases the disillusionment felt by black separatist adults who no longer perceive an opportunity to succeed within the dominant community's established channels of social mobility. If educators assume that the children of these adults are not worth teaching, then we shall see further growth of black separatism. As they experience failure and rejection by representatives of the white middle-class society, Negro children are pushed further into separatist philosophies. *The best way to educate black-nationalist-oriented students is basically the same as the best way to educate all students—provide them with the best possible quality of education.*

SUMMARY

1. In our middle-class-oriented society it is no longer debatable whether lower-class children must compete in such a society. To become social and economic successes outside their depressed neighborhoods, they must compete. Thus schools should provide all children with the *opportunities* to compete successfully for middle-class success goals.
2. Lower-class children need middle-class adult role models with whom they can identify. Black students need both black and white role models for emulation.
3. Environmental forces in slum communities that impede acceptance of middle-class life styles include those that accentuate trouble, toughness, smartness, excitement, fate, and autonomy. Lower-class youths tend to identify with middle-class adults when they perceive that middle-classness is both meaningful and possible for them.
4. The emergence of black nationalist ideologies complicates the task of school personnel who are attempting to teach black students. Black nationalist-oriented students reject administrators and teachers as being undesirable and insignificant role models. Schools can counteract separatist philosophies by becoming dynamic institutions that build in racial pride and use materials and techniques with which the students can identify.
5. Educators must not only accept cultural differences of students but also emphasize the positive aspects of different cultures. This involves planning school programs *with* and *for* community residents.

SELECTED READINGS

Baldwin, James, *The Fire Next Time*, New York, Dial, 1963. Baldwin describes the attraction of black nationalism for Negroes who feel unable to enter the mainstream of American life.

Carmichael, Stokely, and Charles V. Hamilton, *Black Power: The Politics of Liberation in America*, New York, Random House, 1967. The three major aspects of black power—self-pride, self-determination, and self-defense—are explained.

Havighurst, Robert J., "Knowledge of Class Status Can Make A Difference," *Progressive Education*, 27 (Fall, 1950), 100–105. Havighurst offers advice to teachers who are attempting to assist lower-class students in becoming middle-class.

Kell, Leone, and Esther Herr, "Reaching Low Income Students in a Home Economics Class," *Marriage and Family Living*, 25 (May, 1963), 214–218. A study of 45 low-income ninth-graders' perceptions of their family background and aspirations. The subjects are Mexican, Negro, and "Anglo" girls.

Kimball, Solon T., "Cultural Influences Shaping the Role of the Child," in George D. Spindler (ed.), *Education and Culture*, New York, Holt, 1963, pp. 268–283. An analysis of the role of children in American society and the pressures upon them to become adults.

Lincoln, C. Eric, *The Black Muslims in America*, Boston, Beacon, 1961. A widely quoted study of the Black Muslim movement as a religious and social institution.

Malcolm X, *The Autobiography of Malcolm X*, New York, Grove, 1964. An excellent illustration of the social conditions which turned a black integrationist into a black separatist.

Schrieber, Daniel, "Identifying and Developing Able Students from Less Privileged Groups," *High Points*, 40 (December, 1958), 5–23. A description of a program aimed at early identification and stimulation of able students from low socioeconomic homes to graduate from high school.

Stendler, Celia Burns, "Class Biases in the Teaching of Values," *Progressive Education*, 27 (Fall, 1950), 123–126. The author attempts to answer the question "What happens when teachers attempt to teach values which conflict with the values the child acquires from his social class?"

Voss, Elsa, "On Making the Image 3-Dimensional," *High Points*, 46, (January, 1964), 59–63. Examples of ways teachers can raise the self-image of disadvantaged children in order to elevate their educational aspirations.

Wrightstone, Jacob W., "Demonstration Guidance Project in New York City," *Harvard Educational Review*, 30 (Summer, 1960), 235–251. Analysis of a guidance program designed to identify and stimulate academically able lower-class students to reach higher educational and vocational goals.

Part V
THE PROMISE OF AMERICAN EDUCATION

Prospects for the Future   Chapter 17 is both a summary and a forecast. It documents the thesis that the most serious threats to the future of mankind are power, population, prejudice, and pollution. But the fabulous future that is unfolding before us is also examined. Changes in school facilities and programs that seem both imminent and desirable are discussed.

17

Prospects for the Future

We shall spend our lives in the midst of change. We shall do well —indeed, we shall survive— in proportion as we can understand what is going on in our civilization, can in some measure adjust ourselves to it, and can in some measure shape it.*

This chapter must be both a summary and a forecast. The post-modern era in which we have been living since 1945 belongs more to the future than it does to the past. We have tried to describe recent trends in schools and society clearly and accurately in the preceding chapters; it follows that the reader already has at least a general idea about the shape of things to come. There remains only the task of pulling the threads together and of making some general predictions about what lies ahead for future generations.

The role of the prophet has always been a hazardous one. People generally prefer to be told that all is right with the world than to be told that catastrophic changes are taking place that

*The Rockefeller Panel Reports, *Prospects for America*, Garden City, N.Y., Doubleday, 1958, p. 5.

will require drastic changes in conventional ways of thinking, planning, and acting. Predicting some of the conditions that are likely to exist tomorrow, however, does not require the abilities of a soothsayer. The nature of the life of the foreseeable future can be forecast simply by examining trends that are easily observed in the life of today.

During World War I, Blasco Ibáñez wrote the famous novel, *The Four Horsemen of the Apocalypse,* taking his title from the four horsemen described in the last book of the Bible, *Revelation,* which is also called *The Apocalypse.* The four horsemen identified by Blasco Ibáñez as the eternal curses of mankind were: war, famine, pestilence, and death.[1] A great deal of progress has been made since World War I, but though the cataclysmic effects of these scourges have been reduced, they are still with us.

The four horsemen that might be called even greater threats to the hopes of mankind today are power, population, prejudice, and pollution. Man has become so powerful as the result of releasing the forces of nature that it is conceivable that he will totally destroy civilization unless this power is directed toward constructive goals. The population of the underdeveloped nations is increasing so rapidly that it is not possible for them to feed their people adequately, much less accumulate the savings on which a productive economy is based. Prejudice stands as the principal barrier to achieving equality of educational opportunity and to improving the life chances of minority groups in our society. Air and water pollution threaten the health of the citizens in every big city in the land.

GLIMPSES OF THE FUTURE

Children now enrolled in the elementary schools will live much of their lives in the twenty-first century. It is not possible to predict with any degree of accuracy the details of the society in which they will be living or the schools their children and grandchildren will be attending. Yet, unless we assume that certain conditions are likely to exist in the society of tomorrow, there can be no intelligent planning of school programs for the future.

A careful look at current trends in school and society indicates that science and technology will continue to produce changes at a constantly accelerated rate; that new sources of energy can be used constructively to produce an age of abundance and increased leisure to an extent never before imagined; and that the right amount and kind of education can release the potentials of children and adults and act as a lever to lift a nation from poverty, ignorance, and superstition to abundance, enlightenment, and cultural attainments. In brief, if men of intelligence

---

[1]Vicente Blasco Ibáñez, *The Four Horsemen of the Apocalypse* (translation by Charlotte B. Johnson), New York, E. P. Dutton, 1919, pp. 479–480.

and goodwill can cultivate the science of human relationships, if they can find a way to avoid the cataclysm of a nuclear war, the world in which people will be living ten, twenty, or a hundred years from now will indeed be a fascinating one.

The Challenge of Increased Power

The word *power*, of course, has many shades of meaning. It is used here in the sense of man's increasing control over energy—the development of other sources of energy to do the work that once depended on the muscle strength of men and domestic animals. One writer calls attention to the increased tempo of technical change as follows:

It took man roughly 475,000 years to arrive at the Agricultural Revolution. It required another 25,000 years to come to the Industrial Revolution. We have arrived at the "Space Age" in a hundred and fifty years—and while we do not know where we go from here, we can be sure that we shall go there fast.[2]

Promises and threats.   Woodrow Wilson once said that the colleges should give to the nation men and women who can distinguish between promises and threats. When the invention of the printing press made it possible to provide textbooks for every pupil, the development was regarded by many as a threat to the teaching profession; textbooks, however, were instrumental in making it possible for every child, instead of a favored few, to have educational opportunities. When automobiles appeared on the scene, they were regarded as a threat to those whose livelihood depended on horse-shoeing and harness-making; instead, the event provided opportunities for employment in much more rewarding and exciting jobs. When man finally succeeded in releasing the energy stored in the atom and created devices for using this energy as a source of power, the destruction that followed convinced many that this would mean the end of civilization; scientists now believe that atomic power provides the only way to produce enough food for the rapidly increasing population of the world. There is no longer any valid reason for half the people of the world to go to bed hungry every night; there is no longer any valid reason for forty million Americans to live at the bare subsistence level.

One technological development that has produced a great deal of uncertainty is automation. Will it provide fewer jobs or more jobs? Is it a threat to the masses? Or does it promise a richer and fuller life for all mankind? Here are some facts that support those who regard automation as a threat:

1. During recent years, 200,000 production jobs have been eliminated in the aircraft industry alone because of technological change.

---

[2]Charles Frankel, "Third Great Revolution of Mankind," in August Kerber and Wilfred Smith, *Educational Issues in a Changing Society* (rev. ed.), Detroit, Wayne State University Press, 1964, p. 14.

2. Since World War II, output per man-hour in the soft coal industry has risen 90 percent, but employment has fallen by 262,000
3. Steel production in 1960 was almost the same as in 1950, but employment had declined by 14 percent.
4. In the chemical industry, the number of production jobs has fallen 3 percent since 1956, but output has increased 27 percent.
5. Production in the meat industry has increased 3 percent since 1956, yet 28,000 workers have lost their jobs.

Those who see in automation the promise of more jobs and a richer life for all offer the following arguments:

1. Although machines are now doing 94 percent of the work, there are more jobs available per 1000 population than there were in the 1850s, when machines did but 6 percent of the work.
2. Scholars who have studied the trends intensively foresee the time when one-fourth of the nation's labor force will be employed in semi-professional and technical jobs that did not exist in 1930.
3. With automation taking over jobs in agriculture and material production, our society will have the potential to expand education, health, welfare, and recreation functions, as well as creative efforts, including planning and research.
4. The government will surely take up the slack in jobs for urban renewal, social welfare, beautification, and so on.[3]

The unprecedented rate at which energy has been released since 1945 has confronted our people with the necessity to make adjustments to new conditions, learn new habits and skills, and change social institutions so that they will more nearly serve the needs of a new and different age. The impact of this "Third Great Revolution of Mankind" has created new problems for labor leaders and industrial managers; for families and schools; and for city, state, and national governments. This is why we have emphasized throughout this text that drastic reforms in education are demanded by the realities of the age in which we are living. As a management expert, Peter Drucker, has pointed out,

Because we can now organize men of high skill and knowledge for joint work through the exercise of responsible judgment, the highly educated man has become the central resource of today's society, the supply of such men the true measure of its economic, its military, and even its political potential.[4]

Problems of Population Growth

Population growth and mobility can, of course, present either promises or threats. This text has discussed the population explosion in the

[3]Adapted from Clyde M. Campbell, "The World of Work," *The Community School and Its Administration*, Midland, Michigan, Ford, 1967.
[4]Peter F. Drucker, *Landmarks of Tomorrow*, New York, Harper & Row, 1957, p. 114.

United States, the rural-urban migration, and the relation of the population explosion to the problem of developing a productive, industrialized economy in the underdeveloped countries of the world. Particular attention has been given to the consequences of failure to provide adequate educational opportunities for disadvantaged children in the cities.

The population of the world was 1.6 billion in 1900, 2.5 billion in 1950, and 3.3 billion in 1965. The estimate for the year 2000 is 7.4 billion. The implications of the estimated increase in the world's population have been described as follows:

The prospect is frightening. In the span of 35 years the world population is expected to increase by 124 percent, but the underdeveloped parts will grow 151 percent. In contrast, the regions with an advanced economy will increase only 53 percent. To put it another way, the underdeveloped countries, which now constitute 73 percent of the world population, will in the year 2000 comprise 81 percent of a more than twice as numerous world population.[5]

Since World War II, 48 new nations have come into existence. Most of these countries lack the stable government, the educational system, and the investment capital necessary to develop an industrialized economy which requires technically trained workers and capable managers. This situation poses both challenges and threats for the underdeveloped countries and for the human community as a whole. The Rockefeller Panel stated the situation concisely:

This panel believes that the United States has an objective that needs to be defined in new terms, broader than the old concept of "national interest." This objective is to foster the development of a world order in which all peoples can live in security and realize their fullest potentialities.[6]

This text has, therefore, emphasized the need for understanding the revolutionary age in which we are living, for education for world citizenship, and for greater emphasis on our heritage of human freedom.

The Problem of Prejudice
Prejudice is now recognized as one of our nation's most dangerous threats. It can be defined in terms of attitudes or in terms of behavior. As a social problem, it can best be defined as human behavior motivated by the desire to exclude certain racial, religious, and ethnic groups from the attainment of equality of opportunity or status. The persons and groups that exhibit prejudiced behavior do not recognize the characteristics of an individual; rather, they treat individuals as indistinguishable parts of a stereotyped group.

Prejudiced behavior, together with rising aspirations on the part of Negroes, has brought this country to the brink of an armed conflict

[5]Jan O. M. Broek and John W. Webb, *A Geography of Mankind,* New York, McGraw-Hill, 1968, p. 446.
[6]The Rockefeller Panel Reports, op. cit., p. 21.

between black people and white people. The most serious phases of prejudiced behavior relate to housing restrictions, discrimination in employment practices, and educational opportunities. This situation represents a serious violation of our democratic ideals; it also represents a serious waste of human resources. The situation has been very well described thus:

The opportunity for every man to develop his capacities is no longer just an abstract ethical precept that attaches to democracy. It is a practical condition of a modern industrial society. Such a society can function efficiently only if opportunity for full development and participation is not arbitrarily removed from large groups of its population.[7]

The same authors described encouraging progress that has been made in desegregating the armed forces, public housing, and industries receiving contracts from the government. They also pointed out, in their section on "The Prejudiced Community," that patterns of community practices are more influential than prejudiced attitudes on the part of individuals in maintaining polarization as opposed to integration in our society; that, in communities where this polarization has been broken down, prejudiced behavior has been reduced; and that it is the social situation in which an individual lives that largely determines his prejudiced behavior and his prejudiced attitudes.

This text has, therefore, provided information relating to the gap that exists in our society between the life chances of the majority of Americans and those of minority groups; explained how the urban crisis has developed in recent years; examined the programs that have been initiated to remedy the situation; and presented estimates of the cost of a program that is needed to deal effectively with the problem. It has also suggested steps that need.to be taken to provide adequate educational opportunities for culturally-disadvantaged children and youth as well as programs in intercultural education for all American children and youth.

The Problem of Air and Water Pollution

The cultural and economic advantages of living in an American city; the steady increase in the gross national product; and the rapid progress that has been made in the development of supersonic airplanes and space vehicles are widely recognized as achievements of American inventive genius and management skill. But these accomplishments have brought with them serious threats to the health of the increasing numbers of our people who live in the cities. As more people move to the cities the demand for water increases. The industrial use of water has increased 11 times since 1900, and the demand for water for recreational purposes has also increased rapidly as people have had more time for leisure. The hazard of water pollution has been summarized as follows:

[7]Earl Raab and Seymour M. Lipset, *Prejudice and Society*, New York, Anti-Defamation League of B'nai B'rith, 1963, p. 9.

At the same time that our use of water is increasing, the wastes that we dump into our water are also increasing; miles of streams are being lost each year to fishing and millions of fish are being killed because of waste products being dumped into streams; both the Gulf coast and the Atlantic coast have had epidemics of hepatitis because of polluted water; and water pollution continues to grow as more complex waste products are finding their way into our water supplies.[8]

The health hazard of air pollution continues to grow as industrial production increases, as more people move to the cities, and as more automobiles are used. The problem of providing pure air to breathe is no longer confined to Los Angeles; it has become a problem for every large, industrialized city in the land. It is not suggested that school children can solve the problem of water and air pollution; they can, however, recognize the problem as one of the social realities existing in our nation and they can become familiar with the measures being taken to combat it.

The Fabulous Future

Despite the problems that plague us, a future bright with promise is already unfolding before our eyes. We are living in an age of revolutions. The biological revolution, which has been relatively overlooked in the shadows of the atomic revolution, the computer revolution, and the aerospace revolution, is perhaps more crucial than any of the others; indeed, it has been largely responsible for all of them. Computers, for example, are products of the biological revolution; they represent extensions of the human brain. The biological revolution has enabled man to increase his numbers, to manipulate his environment, and to gain a better understanding of himself.

The virtual elimination of communicable disease, the transplanting of human organs, and new cures for mental illness are already in sight. As a by-product of atomic weapon research conducted at the Oak Ridge National Laboratory, a machine has been developed for the production of a safer and more effective vaccine for influenza, other respiratory diseases, and virus-caused diseases. Scientists predict that control of some genetic characteristics, such as the sex of our offspring, may sometime be feasible; that farming of the sea will be commonplace; and that there will be a great reduction in the use of domestic food animals because plants can convert solar energy into food much more efficiently.[9]

There is no doubt that the future will glow with many devices and products that will revolutionize life in the home. The following quotation mentions only a few of these:

[8]William B. Ragan, *Modern Elementary Curriculum* (3rd ed.), New York, Holt, 1966, pp. 402-403.
[9]Paul R. Ehrlich, "The Biological Revolution," *Stanford Review* (September-October, 1965).

A new electroluminescent glass panel will heat and cool a room instantly, and the color of the wall will vary in response to the movement of a dial to the color desired. It will be possible to have cold packaged anywhere in the house, eliminating the need for a refrigerator. Clothes will be cleaned by ultrasonic waves while they hang in the closet overnight, and radio and television will be built into the wall to be tapped on and off like a wall switch.[10]

Space exploration will place more men on the moon for extended scientific research, improve weather forecasting, make it possible to view live telecasts from any place in the world, light entire cities from a mirror hung in space, and communicate messages quickly to any point on earth. Automation will make it possible for machines to perform the entire operation of bank clearinghouses with only a few workers keeping the machines in working order, will produce electronic devices for translating one language into another, and will enable libraries to swiftly tabulate and show on a screen information on any topic.

The new frontier will lie in the field of human relations. Our most eminent scientists tell us that the future of our civilization revolves around the ability of man to learn to live with his fellow men. This text has, therefore, emphasized the need for education for world understanding and for the lessening of intergroup tensions.

Reassurance from economic experts.   Despite the serious problems that beset our people, there are sound reasons to hope that they can be solved; economic experts point out that there is enough strength in the American economy to make solutions possible, providing our resources are used constructively. Long-range projections made by the United States Chamber of Commerce and the Joint Economic Committee of Congress point to greatly increased incomes for families and increased revenues for federal and local governments. They predict that (1) families currently earning $8,000 a year will be earning $25,000 a year by the year 2000, in terms of today's dollars; (2) by 1975 the Gross National Product will be $1.3 trillion; (3) by 1977 federal government revenues will have increased 122 percent over 1967; (4) revenues of local governments will increase even faster, so that money will be available for jobs, housing, education, and pollution control.[11] Although money alone cannot solve all our problems, it is reassuring to have evidence that the economy is basically strong.

SCHOOLS
FOR TOMORROW

Changes in American life during the next few decades will, no doubt, create a demand for many new kinds of educated talent which schools

[10]Ibid., 498–499.

[11]John Cunniff, "Economy Inherently Strong," *Norman* (Oklahoma) *Transcript,* December 18, 1968, 10.

and colleges will be expected to provide. Indeed, there seems to be general agreement that the future of our nation in an era of unprecedented change will depend largely on the scope and quality of our educational effort.

For several years, general magazines, newspapers, television, and radio have all been describing and picturing the "revolution in the schools"—the new programs and new teaching methods that have been evolved and are being used in some schools. Thus many citizens—not just those personally concerned with the schools—are now aware of the fact that the schools of tomorrow will differ in important respects from the schools of yesterday and from many of the schools of today. Although the innovations described by the mass media have so far been confined to a limited number of schools, they do provide glimpses of the shape of things to come in elementary and secondary schools. Leaders in the field of professional education have also become increasingly concerned with the changes in educational programs that the future will demand. Francis Keppel, for example, is one of these. He indicated the depth of his concern when he gave the title *The Necessary Revolution in American Education* to a book he wrote while he was U. S. Commissioner of Education.[12] He believes that the changes will be and must be made with both quality and equality as aims. As might be expected, his book includes analyses of many of the issues treated in this text.

New Directions for Teacher Education

The most serious handicap faced by school systems as they attempt both to implement the new curricula developed by projects at the national level and to adopt innovations in organization and instruction is the lack of teachers who are prepared for these new programs. No one who has been on the scene when the staff of a large school system has been struggling with these problems can fail to reach the conclusion that a new type of teacher education is the most needed reform in public education today.

Asking the wrong questions.   More than 1200 institutions of higher education prepare elementary and secondary teachers. At any one of them, when representatives of the various academic departments that participate in the preparation of teachers meet with representatives of the college of education to plan for improvements in the teacher education program, the dialogue seldom gets beyond the question of whether or not the quality of instruction in the schools could not be improved simply by requiring teachers to take more courses in the academic disciplines and fewer courses in education. On the other hand, when the members of the faculty of the college of education meet by themselves

[12]Francis Keppel, *The Necessary Revolution in American Education*, New York, Harper & Row, 1966.

to discuss their responsibilities in the preparation of teachers, their dialogue seldom gets beyond the point of how many courses in the various phases of professional education shall be required. Obviously, such discussions add very little to the solution of the critical problems confronting elementary and secondary schools.

Asking the right questions.   The careful selection of candidates for teacher education is perhaps as important as the courses the students take. If a student has a firm desire to teach, if he has a positive image of self, if he has a genuine interest in people, he is quite likely to become a successful teacher, as long as he has had thorough preparation. If he lacks these basic qualities, rarely will he become a successful teacher, no matter how thorough the curriculum to which he has been subjected.

Thus there is a basic question that must be faced by those who are responsible for formulating teacher education programs: How can an adequate proportion of the nation's most promising young people be attracted to teaching—and how can they be held in it? Committees that set up certification requirements frequently operate on the principle that a little of almost every discipline offered on the campus should be included; this results in ridiculous requirements that repel many capable young people who otherwise might enter teaching as a career. No doubt the next few decades will see drastic reforms in the certification process.

Teacher education programs in the future are likely to bring students into contact with children and classrooms much earlier in their college careers than now. The beginning teacher who has never seen a television program used in a classroom, who has never seen team-teaching in action, who has never seen the operation of a nongraded program, is poorly prepared for teaching.

Planning a teacher education program will in the future begin with an entirely different set of questions. It will begin with an effort to identify the truly professional tasks that teachers are expected to perform in school systems. It will then plan to provide students with experiences that will help them develop the competencies needed in the performance of these tasks. The old adage, "We teach as we were taught, not as we were taught to teach," should, and probably will, influence teaching on college campuses more in the future than it has in the past. There is no valid reason why college students should not be given opportunities in their college courses to experience *as students* team-teaching, learning by discovery, the use of a great variety of instructional media, and participation in the planning of class activities. These, after all, are some of the methods they will be expected to use when they join the staff of a public school system.

A More Humanistic Approach to Teaching

The mechanistic concept of learning dominated educational practice for many years. The industrial age that resulted from experimentation in the physical sciences had a great impact on man's thinking about the learning process. The human organism was regarded as merely a collection of specific parts operating like a machine in response to mechanical laws. The alphabet method of teaching reading and the drill method of teaching skills flowed naturally from this explanation of learning. Mechanical laws were formulated to govern the learning process; education served as the mechanical assembly belt to transmit the cultural heritage; the end product was the patterned mind.

Earlier chapters in this text have pointed out that improvement of teacher education involves more than merely reshuffling course content and adding courses to the requirements for certification. It involves nothing less than the development of a valid theory of instruction based on our changing social needs and on the new understanding of human behavior which has emerged from new research in the social sciences.

It is now widely accepted that the basic purpose of education is to help young people become fully *human*. The new humanistic approach has been explained as follows:

Within the past twenty years a whole series of new concepts about man and his behavior has appeared upon the scene. The social science breakthrough has resulted from the emergence in American psychology of a great new humanistic force, a new psychology deeply concerned with people, values, perceptions, and man's eternal search for being and becoming. The impact of these new ideas is powerful indeed. They promise new solutions to age-old human problems. Already they have profoundly influenced the work of several other professions. Little by little as they find their way into education, they promise similar revolutions for teaching and learning.[13]

The public school that is already emerging from this humanistic philosophy-psychology will increasingly become a place where basic concepts will emerge from searching, thinking, and experimenting. School will become a place where the excitement of discovery will cause children and youth to go out on their own in search of information; it will no longer be necessary for all the impetus to come from outside forces.

The Challenge of Broader Objectives

Most people will agree that the school is not a social club, not a hospital, not a church, and not a substitute for the home. It can be expected, however, that parents in the future will continue to look to the schools for assistance in the area of health, character development, personal finance, and appreciation for the fine arts; they are not likely to demand a return to the school of the three Rs or to the strictly academic high school. Leaders in American life will continue to expect the schools to provide education for intelligent citizenship, international understanding, intercultural harmony, and respect for legally-constituted authority. The schools of the future, with the aid of instructional media, will be expected not only to teach the fundamentals more thoroughly than they

[13]Arthur W. Combs, *The Professional Education of Teachers: A Perceptual View of Teacher Preparation*, Boston, Allyn & Bacon, 1965, p. vi.

now do but also to assist other educative agencies in producing adequate, fully functioning persons.

Increasing Emphasis on Concept Learning

If current trends are projected into the future, there can be little doubt that curriculum content will be organized around basic concepts or themes in the various curriculum areas. The rationale for this arrangement is not difficult to discover. One obvious reason is the explosion of knowledge in practically every field; it has been said that knowledge in the field of science doubles every ten years. Since imparting specific information in the various fields is no longer feasible, educators have adopted the scheme of having content specialists in the various disciplines list the basic concepts essential for an understanding of the discipline. For example, one publication lists fourteen themes around which the whole social studies program for Grades K–12 can be organized. The geographical, historical, political, economic, and social aspects of each theme are studied at every grade level. This practice provides the pupil with a scheme for organizing bits of specific information; it provides him with something resembling a drawer in a file cabinet into which he can place facts about a given topic; it helps him to see the interrelationships of information. Instead of teaching isolated facts, the schools of the future will increasingly assume the role of equipping each student with the intellectual tools and techniques of investigation that will enable him to investigate any field of knowledge on his own during a lifetime of learning.

The Challenge of Learning by Discovery

The discovery approach to teaching is essentially a procedure by which students discover for themselves a principle such as "metals expand when heated." It is the opposite of teaching by exposition. Learning by discovery has perhaps been best illustrated in the new programs in elementary school science. Using the discovery method requires a different conception of the role of facts in the educative process from that generally held by teachers. The facts of science are important, of course, but they are tools used in the solution of problems, rather than ends in themselves. Using the discovery method emphasizes (1) helping students find answers to their questions rather than giving them "ready-made" answers, (2) concern for the processes of science rather than the products, (3) providing many opportunities for students to investigate, and (4) developing the ability to think.

The Need for Specialized School Personnel

This text has emphasized the urgent need for the schools and colleges to make greater contributions to the strength of the nation during a period of revolutionary changes at home and abroad. It is obvious that improvements in the teaching-learning process itself are necessary, and this is one facet of educational reform that seems certain to gain momentum in coming years. It is widely recognized that one fundamental need is simply "time to teach," time for the teacher to do what he wants to do and is supposed to do—help children grow and learn. Many methods are being tried to gain this essential time: reducing the size of classes; providing clerical help; establishing central libraries with qualified librarians; employing special education teachers, school social workers, school psychologists, guidance workers, and playground and lunchroom supervisors. These improvements, however, have by no means materialized in all the schools. For instance, the United States Office of Education reported in 1965 that 69 percent of the nation's elementary schools still had no libraries and that spending for elementary school books averaged little more than $6 per pupil—an amount the OE said should be quadrupled.[14]

Along with these relatively familiar ways of dealing with the problem of improving the teaching-learning situation, some new and exciting developments are beginning to appear on the educational frontier. One of the most important of these is the addition of new types of workers to the school staff. These people who work with teachers are identified by many titles unknown to the pedagogical vocabulary of past years—teacher aides, volunteers, paraprofessionals, nonprofessionals, and auxiliary personnel. In other words, "New Branches Grow on the Educational Family Tree," as one article on the topic is titled. The writer describes the role of the "new branches" thus:

People, even if they are innocent of university degrees and consider education courses a retreat from reality, are able to take over 30 percent of what teachers now do—things that are done by people for children in homes and at parties or other places where children are found. These people are going to relieve teachers of direct and continuous involvement in such duties, and this will cause a great increase in the dignity and prestige of the teaching role. They will allow the teacher greater flexibility in using instructional resources and in responding to the whole range of each child's needs.[15]

The use of more specialized professional personnel and the use of nonprofessionals who can relieve the overburdened teacher seems likely to increase in a period of increasing abundance and leisure time.

Vertical Extension of Local School Programs
Recent research in the area of human growth and learning has highlighted the importance of the early years in a child's life in terms of subsequent achievement in school subjects and in terms of the develop-

---

[14]Sylvia Porter, "Book Shortage Blot on Nation," *Denver Post*, August 22, 1965, 9.
[15]Beatrice Boyles, "New Branches Grow on the Educational Family Tree," *National Elementary Principal* (May, 1967), 38.

ment of personality traits. Growth in both of these aspects takes place much more rapidly between the ages of 4 and 8 than it does during later years. The same research indicates that the environment plays an important role in growth and learning during these early years. As a result, it is now generally recognized that children should be admitted to the public schools at the age of 4 instead of 6. Indeed, the National Education Association recommended such a change several years ago. This practice would help materially in narrowing the gap between the educational opportunities of children from disadvantaged homes and children from more advantaged homes. It seems likely, therefore, that the schools of tomorrow will admit children at earlier ages than do schools of today.

The Educational Potential of Computers

Participants in a recent symposium on computer-assisted education sponsored by the National Academy of Science at the California Institute of Technology predicted that computers will have more of an impact on education than that of the development of printing. They pointed out that today's equipment makes it possible to teach 10,000 students through 700 computerized television consoles at a cost that would be only half that of using human teachers at a ratio of one for 15 students; that computers can monitor each student's progress minute by minute, correcting mistakes immediately; and that computers will soon be teaching the basic skills in reading and mathematics in one-tenth the time and at half the cost now required. They predicted that the egg-crate type of school building with each "slot" of the "crate" housing about 30 students and a teacher will disappear; that classrooms will be used many more hours a day; and that computer terminals will move into homes, where individuals of many ages will be learning together.[16]

These still rather startling predictions should not be taken to mean that the use of electronic equipment in teaching lies some distance in the future. Television teaching is not uncommon in today's schools; tape recorders and earphones enable teachers to program materials in harmony with levels of ability and rates of learning; and students in many schools know how to operate many types of electronic aids to learning with little assistance from teachers. Technology has already invaded the classroom.

The question always arises in connection with any discussion of the impact of technological aids on teaching: "Will machines replace teachers?" When textbooks began to appear in classrooms after the development of printing, some teachers viewed them with alarm. They have not, of course, replaced teachers. Hardware, no matter how modern, will never replace teachers. It will help the teacher get more work

---

[16]"Computers To Replace Teachers, Experts Say," *The Daily Oklahoman*, October 29, 1968, 5.

done and, when used properly, release the time of the teacher for the creative tasks that only a human being can perform.

Innovations in the Use of Space
The egg-crate type of school building is already being replaced in some school systems by a more functional arrangement. For example, the John F. Kennedy Elementary School in Norman, Oklahoma, has one large instructional area with approximately 16,000 square feet of floor space and no partitions. More than 400 pupils, 15 teachers, a resource director, and two teacher aides work in this area, which is carpeted and acoustically treated. Team-teaching and continuous progress are important features of the instructional program. Service areas include a materials center, an all-purpose room, a principal's office, a reception room, a conference room, a music room, a health room, a teachers' lounge, a supply room, and a study room used by pupils.

A visitor to this school may see one pupil reading quietly behind a screen or bookcase; a teacher working with a group of pupils in the reading, mathematics, science, or social studies center; a physical education class on the playground or in the all-purpose room; and a committee working on a special project around a table in a peripheral center. Space is allocated in terms of the function it is to serve rather than in terms of grade levels.

Glimpses of the future, coming to us from many sources, indicate that the rate of change in the future will be swifter than ever before. Human beings will need to learn faster than they have ever learned. Exciting new designs for teaching and learning are already emerging. The prospects for those who will be teaching America's children in the next few decades are indeed exhilarating.

SUMMARY
1. Trends that are easily observed in the life of today provide a basis for predicting what life is likely to be like in the foreseeable future.
2. Four of the principal threats to the future of mankind can be identified as power, population, prejudice, and pollution.
3. The release of the power stored in the atom has made it possible to produce enough food for a rapidly increasing population; there is no longer any valid reason for anyone in the world to be undernourished.
4. Automation offers the promise of a richer and fuller life for all mankind.
5. The educated man has become the central resource of today's society.
6. The problem of developing an industrialized economy and an educational system in the poor nations of the world poses a challenge to the people of these nations and to the human community as a whole.
7. The most serious aspects of prejudiced behavior relate to housing restrictions, discrimination in employment, and educational opportunities.

8. This text has presented evidence of the gap that exists between the life chances of the majority of Americans and those of members of minority groups; it has also presented estimates of the cost of a program to eliminate this gap.

9. The health hazards of water and air pollution continue to grow as industrial production increases, as more people move to the critics, and as more automobiles are used.

10. The consequences of the biological revolution offer hope for the virtual elimination of communicable disease, the transplanting of human organs, new cures for mental illness, the farming of the sea, and a great reduction in the use of domestic food animals.

11. The new frontier lies in the field of human relations; the future of our civilization depends on the ability of man to learn to live with his fellow men. The schools and colleges must, therefore, emphasize education for world understanding and intercultural education.

12. The next few decades will witness new directions in teacher education; a more humanistic approach to teaching; a broadening of educational objectives; increased emphasis on concept learning and learning by discovery; the use of more specialized professional personnel and more auxiliary personnel; and a vertical extension of local school programs.

SELECTED READINGS

Boyles, Beatrice, "New Branches Grow on the Educational Family Tree," *The National Elementary Principal*, May, 1967. An excellent article which deals with the use of nonprofessional personnel to work with teachers.

Combs, Arthur W., *The Professional Education of Teachers: A Perceptual View of Teacher Preparation*, Boston, Allyn & Bacon, 1965. Presents a forward-looking view of changes needed in teacher education programs.

Drucker, Peter F., *Landmarks of Tomorrow*, New York, Harper & Row, 1957. Chapter 2 presents a penetrating analysis of progress and innovation.

Foreign Policy Association, *Toward the Year 2018*, New York, Cowles Educational Corporation, 1968. A group of outstanding leaders in science and technology look 50 years into the future.

Hartford, Ellis Ford, *Education in These United States*, New York, Macmillan, 1964. Chapter 15, "The Promise of American Education," reviews recent trends and presents a forecast of schools of the future.

Keppel, Francis, *The Necessary Revolution in American Education*, New York, Harper & Row, 1966. Holds that the first revolution in American education was concerned with quantity, the second with quality, and that the third must be concerned with equality.

Kerber, August, and Wilfred Smith, *Educational Issues in a Changing Society*, Detroit, Wayne State University Press, 1964. Chapter 1 presents pertinent information on "Education and the Technological Revolution"; Chapter 20 presents a design for the future in education.

Morse, Arthur D., *Schools of Tomorrow—Today*, Garden City, New York, Doubleday, 1960. Presents specific examples of schools which have initiated innovations in team teaching, the use of television, nongradedness, and freeing the teacher to teach.

Nesbitt, Marion, *A Public School for Tomorrow* (rev.), New York, Dell, 1967. Chapter 11 is titled "We Look to the Future."

Raab, Earl, and Seymour M. Lipset, *Prejudice and Society*, New York, Anti-Defamation League of B'nai B'rith, 1963. Presents consequences of prejudiced behavior; cites examples of promising efforts to deal with the problem.

Ragan, William B., *Modern Elementary Curriculum* (3rd ed.), New York, Holt, 1966. Chapter 16 deals with the recent past and the foreseeable future.

APPENDIX
Selected Films

The following list is merely a suggestion of films that can be used to supplement chapters in this book. In addition to securing these films for rental, your nearest college or university library can provide you with other films. Addresses of the producers are given below for individuals who are interested in purchasing the films.

LIST OF
PRODUCERS

Agrafilm (AF)
  P.O. Box 967
  Athens, Ga.   30601
American Federation of Labor and Congress of Industrial Organizations (AFL-CIO)
  Department of Education
  815 16th Street, N.W.
  Washington, D.C.   20006
Anti-Defamation League (ADL)
  315 Lexington Ave.
  New York, N.Y.   10016
Bailey Films (Ba)
  6509 DeLongpre Ave.
  Los Angeles, Cal.   90028

Brandon Films (BF)
  200 West 57th Street
  New York, N.Y.   10019
Coronet Films (Cor)
  Coronet Building
  Chicago, Ill.   60601
Davidson Films (Da)
  1757 Union Street
  San Francisco, Cal.   94100
Encyclopaedia Britannica Films (EBF)
  1150 Wilmette Avenue
  Wilmette, Ill.   60091
Indiana University (IU)
  Audio-Visual Center
  Bloomington, Ind.   47401
McGraw-Hill Book Co. (McGH)
  Text-Film Dept.
  330 West 42nd Street
  New York, N.Y.   10036
National Association of Secondary-School Principals (NASSP)
  1201 Sixteenth Street, N.W.
  Washington, D.C.   20036
National Education Association (NEA)
  1201 Sixteenth Street, N.W.
  Washington, D.C.   20036
National Education Television (NET)
  12 Columbus Circle
  New York, N.Y.   10023
New York University (NYU)
  Film Library
  26 Washington Place
  New York, N.Y.   10003
Ohio State University (OSU)
  Teaching Aids Lab
  1988 N. College Rd.
  Columbus, Ohio   43210
Pennsylvania State University (PSU)
  Audio-Visual Service
  Pattee Library
  University Park, Pa.   16802
Special Purpose Films (SPF)
  26740 Latigo Shore Dr.
  Malibu, Cal.   90265
Teachers College, Columbia University (TCCU)
  525 West 120th Street
  New York, N.Y.   10027
United World Films (UWF)
  221 Park Ave. South
  New York, N.Y.   10003
University of California at Berkeley (UCB)
  Ext. Media Center, Film Distr.

2223 Fulton Street
Berkeley, Cal.   94720
University of Michigan (UM)
  Audio Visual Education Center
  Frieze Bldg., 720 E. Huron Street
  Ann Arbor, Mich.   48104
University of Texas (UT)
  Visual Instruction Bureau
  Austin, Tex.   78712
Wayne State University (WSU)
  Audio-Visual Department
  Detroit, Mich.   48202

DESCRIPTIVE LIST
OF 16MM FILMS

I.   Education in a Changing Society

All in a Lifetime (NEA, 30 min). Schools of the past are compared with those of the present. An American city (Mansfield, Ohio) is the place for the comparison.

Are Our Schools Up-to-Date? (NEA, 30 min). Presents the opinions of experienced educators on the following questions: Are the schools doing anything in research? What is guidance? What should be done when a teacher and a student clash? What is motivation? Are interscholastic sports overemphasized?

Assignment: Tomorrow (NEA, 32 min). Describes the vital role of the schoolteacher in American communities. Stresses the importance of teachers in school-community relations.

Introduction to Student Teaching (IU, 19 min). Compares the experiences of three beginning teachers. Suggests methods of getting acquainted with students, personnel, and instructional materials.

Not by Chance (NEA, 28 min). Shows teaching as a highly skilled profession that requires a very special kind of preparation.

Rafel: Developing Giftedness in the Educationally Disadvantaged (Ba, 20 min). Film about an educationally gifted child in an environmentally disadvantaged home. Explains some of the causes of educational disadvantages and ways of abating them in classrooms.

Schoolhouse in the Red (EBF, 42 min). A typical rural school board is confronted with the problem of improving their school.

Teachers (AFL-CIO, 20 min). The various aspects of the responsibilities in teaching are portrayed, including social and economic pressures that affect these responsibilities.

Teaching Machines and Programmed Learning (UWF, 28 min). B. F. Skinner, A. A. Lumsdaine, and Robert Glasen discuss the implications and importance of teaching machines and programmed instruction.

What Is a Teacher? (UT, 59 min). Defines the concept of a teacher by showing teacher-student situations in Grades 1–6.

II.   Forces Affecting American Education

America: The Edge of Abundance (NET, 59 min). Social and economic changes in America are viewed by British television. Traces America's growth from a rural to an urban economy.

America's Crisis: The Community (NET, 59 min). An evaluation of the cultural, educational, religious, and physical aspects of America's urban communities. Discusses the similarities and differences in communities.

America's Crisis: The Individual (NET, 59 min). Probes the problems of the individual in a complex, industrial society. The basic issues is man's search for identity.

America's Crisis: The Parents (NET, 59 min). A documentary report on the effects of rural-urban-suburban social change. Shows how today's parents are trying to find identity, purpose, and meaning in their lives.

Classical Realist View of Education (NET, 29 min). An interview with Harry S. Broudy, renowned classical realist philosopher, about human nature, knowledge, values, and the good society.

Development of Individual Differences (McGH, 13 min). Reviews current theories about the relative influence of heredity and environment on individuals.

Developmental Characteristics of Pre-Adolescents (McGH, 22 min). Shows how teachers with knowledge of pre-adolescent behavior patterns can provide better education for these students.

Discovering Individual Differences (McGH, 25 min). How teachers can get to know and understand each child through the use of interviews, observation, records, journals, and conversations with other teachers.

Each Child Is Different (McGH, 22 min). A vivid illustration of what elementary teachers must know about individual differences in order to meet the needs of each student.

Early Social Behavior (EBF, 10 min). An analysis of personality development of ten children (eight weeks to seven years of age), pointing out the importance of social settings, parent-child relationships, and sibling interactions.

Education: The Public Schools (NET, 29 min). Examines the forces that have shaped the form of our public schools. Among forces discussed are mobility of population, population explosion, new educational theories, increased government participation, building costs, and new trends in school architecture.

Education for Cultural Reconstruction (NET, 29 min). An interview with Theodore Brameld, leading spokesman for the educational philosophy of cultural reconstruction. Discussion of reconstructionist beliefs about values, knowledge, and the good society.

Education in America: 17th and 18th Centuries (Cor, 16 min). Colonial Schools are viewed as forming the foundations for our free public school system.

Education in America: The 19th Century (Cor, 16 min). Education trends that grew out of the Northwest Ordinance and the Westward Movement. Important developments include introduction of textbooks, secularization of learning, rise of the district school, and state control.

Education in America: 20th-Century Developments (Cor, 16 min). Effects of the industrial revolution, new concepts in childhood education, appearance of the junior high school, and World War II.

Experimentalist View of Education (NET, 29 min). An interview with H. Gordon Hullfish. The discussion centers on experimentalist views of values, human nature, knowledge, and the good society.

Focus on Behavior: Learning About Learning (NET, 30 min). In developing new theoretical concepts about man's ability to learn, this film explores the work of Howard Kendler, Tracy Kendler, Kenneth Spence, Harry Harlow, and B. F. Skinner.

Heredity and Environment (Cor, 10 min). Overview of cultural inheritances, genetics, and environmental influences and the interrelationships.

Philosophies of Education: Education for National Survival (NET, 29 min). Stresses the point that our national strength depends upon spending a larger proportion of our national income on education.

Piaget's Developmental Theory (Dav, 28 min). Piaget's developmental psychology is analyzed from his definition of children's mental growth and development, including environmental and physiological conditions affecting mental maturity.

Problem Children (OSU, 20 min). How the personalities of two children are affected by home and school environments.

Segregation in Schools (McGH, 20 min). Reactions of Southerners following the U.S. Supreme Court's 1954 Brown *v*. Board of Education decision.

Social Class in America (McGH, 16 min). Describes factors that determine whether an individual will be lower, middle, or upper class.

Social Development (McGH, 16 min). Analyzes social behavior at different age levels.

III.   Issues and Innovations in American Education

And No Bells Ring (NASSP, 56 min). A review of the "Trump Report" on reorganization of secondary school staff. Interviews are held with educators, including J. Lloyd Trump, who are involved in this experimental program.

Broader Concept of Method, Part I: Developing Pupil Interest (McGH, 20 min). Compares conventional teacher-dominated lesson-hearing type of learning situation with alternative techniques for more student initiative and involvement.

Broader Concept of Method, Part II: Teacher and Pupils Planning and Working Together (McGH, 22 min). Illustrates how students learn to plan and work together; present their findings in a team report.

Broader Concepts of Curriculum (McGH, 21 min). Surveys curriculum in secondary schools and suggest ways to improve them.

Challenge of the Gifted (McGH, 11 min). Shows how one community tried to devise a school program to meet the special problems and needs of the gifted child.

Characteristics of a Core Program (UCB, 20 min). Explains some outstanding characteristics of the core program: what it is, how it functions.

Fundamental Skills in a Unit of Work (Ba, 20 min). An elementary school teacher develops a unit of work as an integrated learning experience involving books, films, exhibits, etc.

Making Learning More Meaningful (McGH, 11 min). How a teacher used spontaneous interests of a class to develop arithmetic skills, and to relate this new information to the world around them.

Motivating the Class (McGH, 19 min). How a teacher translates the values of the subject into terms pupils can understand and want to master.

Personalized Education Series: Pt. I. Can Individualization Work in Your School System? (SPF, 41 min). Discusses the kinds of changes in school organization, curriculum, and methods that are needed to provide individualized instruction.

Personalized Education Series: Pt. II. How Can You Make Individualization Work in Your School System? (SPF, 35 min). Examples of how classroom factors such as course content, assignments, and teaching methods can be varied to provide individualized instruction.

Personalized Education Series: Pt. III. Why Are Team-Teaching and Non-Grading Important? (SPF, 49 min). Team-teaching and nongrading are explained as methods that can bridge the gap between the problems of school organization and individual learning differences.

Personalized Education Series: Pt. IV. How Can You Apply Team-Teaching and Non-Grading to Your School? (SPF, 35 min). This film considers the types of decisions that principals and teachers must make to apply team-teaching and nongrading to the classroom. Relevant factors include peer group composition, teaching style, and placement of students in instructional groups.

Personalized Education Series: Pt. V. How Can the Curriculum for Individualized Education Be Determined? (SPF, 35 min). Summarizes the major aspects of individualized education, i.e., academic content, teaching skills, school organization, and individual differences.

Problem of Pupil Adjustment: Part I. The Drop-Out (McGH, 20 min). The causes of dropouts are related to the lack of purposeful, concrete, interesting experiences.

Teacher as Observer and Guide (TCCU, 20 min). How teachers can guide pupils of various talents through problems which promote individual growth and character.

What Is Science? (Cor, 10 min). Defines the word science and the major steps of scientific method.

Will We Have School Year 'Round? (NEA, 30 min). Educators answer the following questions: Will we have year-round schools? Are we overemphasizing education for the gifted child at the expense of other children? What do physical fitness tests measure?

IV.   Education in the Inner Cities

And So They Live (NYU, 30 min). Rural, southern poverty is shown as a condition affecting family diet, housing, and education.

America's Crisis: The Hard Way (NET, 59 min). Discusses the problems of poverty in the most affluent nation in the world. Shows how today's poor are not like those of past generations.

Challenge to America: The Role of Education in Intergroup Relations (ADL, 25 min). Illustrates techniques of bringing about good human relations among people of various backgrounds.

The Coleman Report: Equality of Educational Opportunity (ADL, 55 min). Daniel P. Moynihan and Thomas Pettigrew lead discussions about the ramifications of the 1966 U.S. Office of Education report referred to as the "Coleman Report." The report indicates that quality education must of necessity be racially and socioeconomically integrated.

Down in the Street (PSU, 52 min). Neighborhood conditions in a Negro ghetto. Points out the psychologically dulling effect of slum environments.

Eleventh Street (PSU, 29 min). Problems of acculturation in Spanish Harlem.

For All My Students (ADL, 36 min). Students and teachers in a depressed area high school in Palo Alto, Cal., probe the reasons for successful and unsuccessful pupil-teacher interactions.

Mike Makes His Mark (NEA, 30 min). A boy who resents being forced to attend school commits an act of vandalism. The reactions of the teacher and the counselor illustrate ways to handle student alienation.

Overcoming Resistance to Change (RTP, 30 min). Focusing on industry, this film shows how administrators can prevent or overcome tendencies of their employees to oppose new ideas and procedures.

Portrait of a Disadvantaged Child: Tommy Knight (MCGH, 16 min). A day in the life of a slum child. Depicts some of the special problems, needs, and strengths of an inner-city child.

Portrait of the Inner City (McGH, 17 min). Shows home, school, and community aspects of an urban inner-city community. Also shows how an inner-city boy found a middle-class role model.

Portrait of the Inner City School: A Place to Learn (McGH, 19 min). Illustrates how teachers may unconsciously discriminate against culturally disadvantaged children; how textbooks discriminate through illustrations and materials that are unfamiliar to the inner-city child.

White Guilt: Black Shame (UM, 28 min). An analysis of how white guilt and black shame prevent community residents from overcoming barriers to integration.

Who Am I? (UM, 28 min). An examination of why the Negro child is constantly questioning and searching for his identity.

V.   The Promise of American Education

How Good Are Our Schools? Dr. Conant Reports (AF, 28 min). J. B. Conant reports on the deficiencies in American secondary schools and points out what he believes every secondary school should be prepared to do.

Report on Tomorrow (OSU, 26 min). Surveys the present educational situation and stresses the need for continuing growth and public support of the states' system of higher education.

Schools for Tomorrow (WSU, 22 min). Focuses on using citizens' advisory committees, school personnel, and architects to build better schools.

Worlds Apart (ADL, 16 min). Martin Deutsch, director of the Institute for Developmental Studies, designed the preschool curriculum shown in the film. It illustrates techniques for bridging the gap between the slum school and the white, middle-class-oriented curriculum.

Index

70 71 72 73   7 6 5 4 3 2 1